ELLET'S BRIGADE

Area of operations of the Ram Fleet

Reprinted, by permission, from John D. Milligan, *Gunboats down the Mississippi*
(Annapolis: Naval Institute Press, 1965)

ELLET'S BRIGADE

THE STRANGEST
OUTFIT OF ALL

CHESTER G. HEARN

LOUISIANA STATE UNIVERSITY PRESS

BATON ROUGE
MM

00   02   04   06   08   09   07   05   03   01
2   4   5   3   1

Designer: *Rebecca Lloyd Lemna*
Typeface: *Galliard*
Typesetter: *Crane Composition*
Printer and binder: *Thomson-Shore, Inc.*

LIBRARY OF CONGRESS CATALOGING-IN-PUBLICATION DATA:

Hearn, Chester G.
  Ellet's Brigade : the strangest outfit of all / Chester G. Hearn.
      p. cm.
Includes bibliographical references and index.
  ISBN 0-8071-2559-8 (alk. paper)
  1. Mississippi River Valley—History—Civil War, 1861–1865. 2. United States. Army.
Mississippi Marine Brigade. 3. United States—History—Civil War, 1861–1865—
Riverine operations. 4. United States—History—Civil War, 1861–1865—Regimental
histories. 5. Mississippi River Valley—History—Civil War, 1861–1865—Regimental
histories. 6. Ellet, Charles, 1810–1862. 7. Stanton, Edwin McMasters, 1814–1869.
I. Title.
  E470.8 .H43 2000
  973.7′462—dc21

                                                           99-050668

To Ann and Chet
and the beloved memory of Wendy

CONTENTS

CONTENTS

ILLUSTRATIONS

ILLUSTRATIONS

Colonel Ellet sends *Lioness* with his son on board
to demand the surrender of Memphis

Medical Cadet Charles Rivers Ellet hoisting the Stars and Stripes
over the post office at Memphis

following page 192

CSS *Arkansas*

USS *Essex*

Queen of the West attacks the transport *City of Vicksburg*

The capture of *Queen of the West*

The ironclad gunboat USS *Indianola*

Rear Admiral David Dixon Porter

Lieutenant Colonel John A. Ellet

Captain Warren D. Crandall

Lieutenant Edward C. Ellet

Lieutenant Richard S. Ellet

Captain Isaac D. Newell

Lieutenant Colonel George E. Currie

Rear Admiral David Glasgow Farragut

ACKNOWLEDGMENTS

Every book begins long before the first word is entered on a keyboard, and the inducement to write about a subject usually begins when writing about something else. Interest in the Ram Fleet and the Mississippi Marine Brigade began for me while writing the biographies of two Civil War admirals, David Dixon Porter and David Glasgow Farragut. I did not fully understand the character or relationship of the Ram Fleet and the Marine Brigade, how they were organized, or how the Ellet family fit into their history. I suspect that others may have had the same problem.

Both Porter and Farragut utilized portions of the Ram Fleet in their operations on the Mississippi River, and Porter encouraged the formation of the Mississippi Marine Brigade as long as it was financed by the War Department but reported to him. These unusual arrangements led to many disputes and disruptions on the western rivers that began the day Secretary of War Edwin M. Stanton engaged Colonel Charles Ellet, Jr., to build the Ram Fleet and Brigadier General Alfred W. Ellet to organize the Marine Brigade. The Ellets did not want to be encumbered by reporting to either the army or the navy, and Stanton, after financing the two fleets engaged in the enterprise, wanted to keep his private navy under his immediate control. Such an anomalous unit operating so far from communication with Washington invited friction among the Union commanders responsible for winning the war in the west. As a consequence, the Ellets often did exactly as they pleased—sometimes helping the war effort and sometimes disrupting it.

Little has been written on this subject, mainly because most of the Marine Brigade's war documents had been lost or omitted from the army's *Official Records*. Many readers who have attempted to follow the war on the western waters became confused between the Ram Fleet and the Mississippi Marine Brigade, never realizing that the two units were formed at different times under two different Ellets. Not until late 1862 did Alfred Ellet physically consolidate both units under his command.

Reconstructing the history of the Ram Fleet and the Mississippi Marine Brigade required far more than the casual research involved in recasting the same works over and over again. Because of the scarcity of official correspondence and battle reports, a national documents search began, and for this I am indebted to dozens of people.

With help from Rebecca Livingston at the National Archives, I found numerous letters in Record Groups 45 and 107 which do not exist in print anywhere else. E. Cheryl Schnirring, the curator at the Illinois State Historical Library in Springfield, aided greatly in extracting from eleven boxes of documents in the Warren D. Crandall Collection those letters, diaries, and journals that bore on the wartime activities of the Marine Brigade. Another large collection is contained in the Missouri Historical Society in St. Louis, and with help from Dennis Northcott, we were able to add diaries and memoirs written by many of the brigade's survivors. Ervin L. Jordan, Jr., curator of the Alderman Library, University of Virginia, provided a number of documents in the Cabell-Ellet Collection, which contained considerable correspondence between Charles Ellet, Jr., and his daughter. Evelyn Leasher of the Clarke Historical Library, Central Michigan University, located the diary of the *Diana* and the Clarke Historical Collection, which contains all the letters of George E. Currie of the Marine Brigade. James Fox, special collections curator at the University of Michigan, holds a huge collection of Charles Ellet, Jr.'s, family papers. These documents trace the founder of the Ram Fleet from early life as a civil engineer to his death on the river after the action off Memphis. This collection is also on microfilm at the University of Illinois Library. Janie C. Morris, curator at Duke University Library, provided a large collection of Alfred Ellet's letters and documents which helped to fill many of the voids in the history of the Marine Brigade.

Many others provided willing and valuable assistance with this project. Susan Brandau and Mary Harrison of the public library in Milton, Pennsylvania, Evelyn Burns of the Brown Library in Williamsport, Pennsylvania, and Evelyn Wesman of the Erie County Library in Erie, Pennsylvania, gathered much primary-source material through the interlibrary loan service. Hugh D. Gurney of the Historical Society of Michigan in Ann Arbor led me to other important sources, as did Elizabeth H. Joyner, museum curator, at the Vicksburg National

Military Park. Charles R. Haberlein of the Naval Historical Center and Randy Hackenberg and John Slonaker of the U.S. Army Military History Institute in Carlisle, Pennsylvania, provided much assistance with maps and photographs. Thanks also go to Judy Bolton of the Special Collections Library at Louisiana State University and to many others who have helped on this project and brought it to a successful conclusion.

The Ram Fleet and the Mississippi Marine Brigade rank among the most unorthodox and controversial fighting units organized during the Civil War. In a state of desperation, Stanton formed the Ram Fleet. In a state of pique, he formed the Mississippi Marine Brigade. He gave the units up and then got them back. The Ringling Brothers could not have created a more tumultuous three-ring circus.

ABBREVIATIONS

B&L	Robert U. Johnson and Clarence C. Buel, eds. *Battles and Leaders of the Civil War.* 4 vols. New York, 1884–87
CMU	Central Michigan University, Mount Pleasant
DUL	Duke University Special Collections Library, Durham, North Carolina
ISHL	Illinois State Historical Library, Springfield
LC	Library of Congress, Washington, D.C.
MHS	Missouri Historical Society, St. Louis
NA	National Archives, Washington, D.C.
ORA	*War of the Rebellion: A Compilation of the Official Records of the Union and Confederate Armies.* 130 vols. Washington, D.C., 1880–1901.
ORN	*Official Records of the Union and Confederate Navies in the War of the Rebellion.* 30 vols. Washington, D.C., 1894–1922.
UM	University of Michigan, Special Collections Library, Ann Arbor.
USNAM	U.S. Naval Academy Museum, Annapolis, Maryland
UV	University of Virginia, Alderman Library, Charlottesville

ELLET'S BRIGADE

INTRODUCTION

The Mississippi Ram Fleet, organized and commanded by Charles Ellet, Jr., contained all the elements of a family affair. Though a staunch supporter of the Union, Ellet entered the war to test a theory the Navy Department rejected—a theory dating back to the sixteenth-century Battle of Lepanto, where ramming with oar-driven galleys had become a popular naval tactic for wrecking enemy vessels. Approaching the subject using 1860 steam technology, Ellet believed that fast, un-armed rams could win battles against conventional gunboats. To prove his point he engaged his brother, Captain Alfred W. Ellet of the 59th Illinois Infantry, and twelve other members of the family, including sons, nephews, cousins, and in-laws, in the enterprise. Confident of suc-cess, he arranged a promotion to lieutenant colonel for Alfred, and later two of his sons obtained commissions. One son, nineteen-year-old Charles Rivers Ellet, a medical cadet, became a colonel in the Ram Fleet and perhaps the youngest full colonel in the Union army. When Alfred Ellet formed the Mississippi Marine Brigade, Charles Rivers Ellet—known as Charlie—became the brigade commander, John A. Ellet took command of the Ram Fleet, and Richard C. Ellet became a lieutenant in a cavalry battalion of the Mississippi Marine Brigade. Edward C. Ellet, Alfred's son, acted as a lieutenant on his father's staff. While the two elder brothers of the family—Charles, Jr., and Alfred—might be accused of nepotism, it would be difficult to find a more daring group of men than the Ellet clan.[1]

Of all the units engaged in the Civil War, few were as bewildering as the two commands led by the Ellets. Nor was there ever a unit that

---

1. Edward C. Ellet, "Military Career of Alfred W. Ellet," Alfred Washington Ellet Papers, DUL; Warren D. Crandall and Isaac D. Newell, *History of the Ram Fleet and the Mississippi Marine Brigade* (St. Louis, 1907), 5. For the complete study of Charles Ellet's background, see Gene D. Lewis, *Charles Ellet, Jr.: The Engineer as Individualist, 1810–1862* (Urbana, Ill., 1968).

confounded district military and naval commanders with such consistency. Later, when transferred to the command of David Dixon Porter and eventually to Ulysses S. Grant, the Ellets still preferred to send their reports to the secretary of war. The two commands were neither a conventional squadron of naval vessels nor by any military standard a typical brigade. The original Ram Fleet contained mostly civilian boatmen with a small sprinkling of infantry to act as boat guards. The men of the Mississippi Marine Brigade, though rank-and-file infantry, cavalry, and artillery, were mostly convalescents who came from sixteen different states.

Months of command confusion can be traced to Secretary of the Army Edwin M. Stanton, who empowered Charles Ellet, Jr., to organize the Ram Fleet. Stanton gave its officers army rankings, but rather than place the flotilla under the army or the navy, he retained it as his own. He chose to do this because the navy had no interest in Ellet's rams and no army commander wanted to be burdened with a small fleet of unarmed riverboats the secretary would not permit him to use as transports. Eventually, President Abraham Lincoln ordered that the rams be placed under a professional commander.[2]

Born on January 1, 1810, on the family farm at Penn's Manor, Pennsylvania, Charles Ellet, Jr., was of Quaker descent and became one of America's outstanding engineers. Self-educated and with a brilliant aptitude for mathematics, he worked as an engineer on canals and developed methods for suspending bridges across broad waterways. After building the first suspension bridge in America over the Schuylkill River, he became president of the Schuylkill Navigation Company and went on to design and erect the first bridge to cross the Niagara River, three miles below the great chasm.

In 1849 Ellet completed the longest suspension bridge in the world—a span of 1,010 feet over the Ohio River at Wheeling. The city of Pittsburgh objected to the structure and brought suit, claiming the bridge restricted river traffic. The Supreme Court agreed and banned its use, but Ellet adroitly obtained an amendment to a Post Office appropriation bill that declared the bridge a postal route, thereby overturning the injunction of the Supreme Court. The opposing counsel in

2. Purdy to Crandall, August 20, 1889, James H. Purdy Letters, Civil War Collection, MHS; Benjamin P. Thomas and Harold M. Hyman, *Stanton: The Life and Times of Lincoln's Secretary of War* (New York, 1962), 181.

the bridge dispute was Edwin M. Stanton, who many years later would form a special alliance with his onetime foe.[3]

Ellet's work on waterways increased his awareness of the ravages of floods, and he devised novel methods for flood control and for improving navigation on the Mississippi and Ohio Rivers. Few of his ideas gained political support, mainly because Congress had turned its attention to expanding the country's network of railroads. Even the rapidly growing city of St. Louis, content with its ferries, rejected Ellet's proposal to bridge the Mississippi. Frustrated by a lack of interest in his ideas, Ellet traveled to Europe and during the Crimean War visited the besieged city of Sebastopol. On the voyage across the Atlantic he learned that the huge Collins liner *Arctic* had been sunk at sea after being struck by a small steamer. The accident convinced him that by deploying speedy steamers equipped with iron prows the naval siege could be broken at Sebastopol. He offered to build and command the vessels. The Russians showed interest, but the proposal died after the assassination of the czar. Ellet then tried to interest the British, also without success. When he returned to the United States in 1855 he presented the concept of the ram to the Navy Department, but Secretary James C. Dobbin, who had recently raised money for six new steam frigates and sought additional funds to build five screw-propelled sloops of war, wanted nothing to do with rams—an idea he attributed to an uninformed "landsman."[4]

In early 1861, as murmurs of war pervaded the divided country, Ellet renewed his efforts to interest the navy in a squadron of rams. Because of his quarrelsome nature, he had fallen out of favor as a civil engineer and needed work to support his family. Wars created employment, and after failing to interest the government in a plan to relieve Fort Sumter, he offered to paralyze communications in Virginia. With a few volunteers, he would seize a train at Alexandria and burn all the bridges and train stations as he and his raiders chugged down the rails of the South on a suicide mission.

3. Crandall and Newell, *Ram Fleet*, 9–10; G. D. Lewis, *Charles Ellet, Jr.*, 1–30; Patricia L. Faust, ed., *Historical Times Illustrated: Encyclopedia of the Civil War* (New York, 1986), 238–39 [hereinafter cited as Faust, *HTI*].

4. Ellet to Grand Duke Constantine, January 16, Palmerston to Ellet, February 21, Ellet to Lord Derby, March 7, 1855, Charles Ellet, Jr., Papers, UM; Charles Ellet, Jr., *Coast and Harbour Defenses, or the Substitution of Steam Battering Rams for Ships of War* (Philadelphia, 1855), 14–15; Paolo E. Coletta, ed., *American Secretaries of the Navy* (2 vols.; Annapolis, 1980), I, 286–87.

With every passing day, Ellet hatched new schemes to punish the enemy and end the war. He frequently made the rounds, pestering bureaucrats and military officers for support. After all efforts failed, he once again badgered the Navy Department, warning that the South had already adopted his idea and was fitting iron plates to fast steamers. Nobody listened.

Soon after the Virginia militia captured the Gosport Navy Yard across from Norfolk on April 20, 1861, word leaked that the Confederacy had started work to salvage the USS *Merrimack* and convert it into an ironclad ram. Then came rumors that four more ironclads were being built, two at Mobile and two at New Orleans. Ellet feared that the South would have rams before he could persuade the politicians running the northern war machine that his scheme had merit.[5] To make public his frustration, he published in early 1862 a pamphlet titled "Military Incapacity" and circulated it through government channels, criticizing the Navy Department and warning:

> We have not yet a single vessel at sea, nor, so far as I know, in course of construction, able to cope at all with a well-built ram. If the *Merrimack* is permitted to escape from the Elizabeth River, she will be almost certain to commit great depredations on our armed and unarmed vessels in Hampton Roads, and may even be expected to pass out under the guns of Fortress Monroe and prey upon our commerce in Chesapeake Bay. Indeed, if the alterations have been skillfully made, and she succeeds in getting to sea, she will not only be a terrible scourge to our commerce, but may prove also to be a most dangerous visitor to our blockading squadrons off the harbors of the Southern coasts. I have attempted to call the attention of the Navy Department and the country so often to this subject during the last seven years that I almost hesitate to allude to it again.[6]

5. Anonymous, "Colonel Ellet and His Rams," newsclips in Warren Daniel Crandall Collection, ISHL; G. D. Lewis, *Charles Ellet, Jr.,* 170–81. Between July 26 and September 21, 1861, the Ellet Papers in the Special Collections Library of the University of Michigan show numerous letters written to Lincoln, Secretary of War Simon Cameron, Secretary of the Treasury Salmon P. Chase, Major General George B. McClellan, General Winfield Scott, Secretary of the Navy Gideon Welles, and others. See also Herbert P. Gambrell, "Rams versus Gunboats . . . A Landsman's Naval Exploits," *Southwest Review,* XXIII (October 1937), 51.

6. Charles Ellet, Jr., *Military Incapacity and What It Costs the Country* (Philadelphia, 1862), 11–12.

Ellet published another pamphlet, titled "The Army of the Potomac and Its Mismanagement." In it he condemned Major General George B. McClellan for failing to engage General Joseph E. Johnston's Confederate army at Manassas, where southern forces remained weak. The national presses rebuked Ellet for denouncing the Federal commander, on whose military skills the country depended. By January 6, 1862, however, Ellet began receiving letters like one sent by the editor of the *Chicago Tribune,* who said, "We are very reluctantly coming around to your opinion."[7]

Secretary of the Navy Gideon Welles still dismissed Ellet's schemes, referring to the bridge builder as "full of zeal to overflowing [but] not, however, a naval man." He had already put his faith in a new type of vessel, naval engineer John Ericsson's *Monitor,* but Stanton voiced doubts about the craft and called Ellet to Washington to get another opinion.[8]

To most acquaintances, the fifty-two-year-old engineer presented a rather queer appearance, being a slender, thin-faced man with long, grayish hair. He "looked like a character out of a fairy story," wrote one observer, "one who would have fitted nicely into elf's clothes." Most of Washington's bureaucrats simply viewed Ellet as a crank. Stanton, however, had great faith in the "elf's" talents, though the two had been enemies for twelve years. They still did not like each other, but they hated the rebellion even more. Ellet studied the design of *Monitor* and warned that it could not be relied upon. He also condemned Welles for being too "weak-minded" to see the advantage of fitting out rams. Stanton agreed, but by then it was too late to alter the course chosen by the navy.[9]

Monitor's raftlike structure, heavily encased in iron, supported a rotating turret containing two 11-inch guns and presented a vast departure from Ellet's concept of a fast unarmed steamer cladded with an iron bow. *Monitor* fit Ellet's definition of a gunship, not a ram.

---

7. *Chicago Tribune,* January 6, 1862.

8. Gideon Welles, *The Diary of Gideon Welles, Secretary of the Navy Under Lincoln and Johnson* (3 vols.; Boston and New York, 1909–11), I, 180; Ellet to Edward Ellet, March 11, 1862, Ellet Papers, UM.

9. Virgil Carrington Jones, *The Civil War at Sea* (3 vols.; New York and Chicago, 1960–62), I, 395; Ellet to Mrs. Ellet, March 11, 1862, Ellet Papers, UM; Thomas and Hyman, *Stanton,* 181; Gambrell, "Rams versus Gunboats," 48–50, 54–55.

The term *ram* began to assume many variations. When Confederates converted *Merrimack* and renamed it *Virginia,* they made the vessel into a heavily casemated ironclad, armed with ten heavy guns and fitted with an iron prow. Shipbuilders at New Orleans created another variety by converting the steamer *Enoch Train* into the ironclad ram CSS *Manassas.* This vessel more closely resembled a ram than a gunship because it carried only a small 32-pounder carronade. Neither vessel met Ellet's concept of a battering ram. He believed that because they carried so much plating, ironclad rams would not be able to generate enough speed to overtake and sink steam-powered vessels. His concept relied upon the formula $F = MV^2$ (force equals mass times the square of velocity). This required fast wooden steamers, reinforced from stem to stern, with a covering of iron only on the bow. He did not particularly care whether the vessels carried guns because he wanted speed, maneuverability, and expendability—not superfluous weight.[10]

Ellet was still awaiting word from Stanton when on March 8, 1862, CSS *Virginia* made her debut in Hampton Roads, Virginia, punched a hole in the sloop *Cumberland,* set the frigate *Congress* ablaze, and retired for the night after sinking both vessels. *Monitor* made a timely appearance the following morning, and for three hours the clumsy ironclads battled to a standoff. Once again *Virginia* withdrew, but in Washington a continued state of emergency compelled Stanton to summon Ellet for another conference. The interview took place on March 14 and lasted about four hours. Stanton and Ellet developed an action plan empowering the latter to purchase several strong steamers and fit them as battering rams. Armed with letters of authority, Ellet departed for Hampton Roads, but upon arrival at Fort Monroe he obtained no cooperation from either Captain John Marston or Major General John E. Wool. Marston said he needed no help and sent Ellet back to Washington. Finding it impossible to execute the plan, Ellet abandoned the project and explained the reasons to Stanton.[11]

---

10. Faust, *HTI,* 787; *Official Records of the Union and Confederate Navies in the War of the Rebellion* (30 vols.; Washington, D.C., 1894–1922), Statistical Data, Ser. 2, I, 148, 259, 270–71 [hereinafter cited as *ORN,* with all references to Series 1 unless otherwise noted]. See also Alfred W. Ellet, "Charles Ellet, Jr., and His Steam Rams," Ellet Papers, DUL.

11. Ellet to Stanton, March 12, 14, 15, Ellet Papers, UM; Thomas to Ellet, March 14, Stanton to Halleck, March 25, 1862, *ORN,* XXII, 665, 672; Alfred Ellet, "Charles Ellet, Jr., and His Steam Rams," Ellet Papers, DUL; Faust, *HTI,* 335.

Charles Ellet's participation in the Civil War might have come to an end on March 25 had not Major General Henry W. Halleck mentioned to Stanton that "the rebels are building one or more river boats at [New Orleans], clad in railroad iron, like the *Merrimack*." Halleck's comment, though not quite accurate, raised the level of concern in the War Department. Fearing that such vessels might ascend the river and destroy Flag Officer Andrew Hull Foote's Mississippi flotilla—which operated out of Cairo, Illinois—Halleck suggested that Stanton confer with Welles and urge the navy to build river monitors. Having Ellet fresh on his mind, Stanton replied that "the universal opinion among naval and military engineers in the East" was to sink an ironclad vessel by running it down. "Charles Ellet, a distinguished engineer, has given the subject much attention," Stanton added. "I will send him tomorrow to see and consult you, and with authority to act as you deem best. He is a man of courage and energy, and willing to risk his own life."[12]

Before Halleck could give thought to whether he wanted to consult with anybody, Stanton conferred once more with Ellet, who convinced him that "the Rebels had already resorted to the same mode of [battering ram] warfare and were most likely to sweep our flimsy naval craft from the Mississippi waters."[13]

Ellet may have learned through his own sources that gunboat rams were being outfitted at New Orleans, or it might have been a good guess on his part. In January, Confederate secretary of war Judah P. Benjamin had obtained an appropriation of $1 million to fit up fourteen riverboats as gunboat rams, man them with steamboat captains and steamboat crews, and organize them under the command of Major General Mansfield Lovell for the defense of New Orleans. When Lovell began running out of money, Benjamin raised another $300,000 to ensure that each vessel received an iron prow and two or three 32-pounders. Lovell divided the so-called River Defense Fleet

12. Halleck to Stanton, Stanton to Halleck, March 25, 1862, *War of the Rebellion: A Compilation of the Official Records of the Union and Confederate Armies* (130 vols.; Washington, D.C., 1880–1901), VIII, 642–43 [hereinafter cited as *ORA*, with all references to Series 1 unless otherwise noted]. See also Alfred Ellet, "Charles Ellet, Jr., and His Steam Rams," Ellet Papers, DUL. The two ironclads being built at New Orleans were the CSS *Mississippi* and *Louisiana*. Both bore a likeness to the CSS *Virginia*.

13. Warren D. Crandall, "The Battle Before Memphis: The True Story of the Surrender and the Hoisting of the Flag," Civil War Collection, MHS.

into two commands and gave one of them to James E. Montgomery and the other to J. H. Townsend.[14]

Ellet's report to Stanton must have been compelling, because on March 27, acting on his own authority, the secretary dispatched Ellet to Pittsburgh with instructions to "provide steam rams for defense against ironclad vessels on the Western waters." He ordered the Quartermaster's Department to purchase vessels selected by Ellet and to pay for their conversion. Ellet reached Pittsburgh the following day and opened communications with Halleck, offering his help but making it clear that his instructions came from the secretary of war. He planned to work down the river from Pittsburgh, stopping at Cincinnati and New Albany, Indiana, to purchase additional steamers and fit them for service as rams. Stanton stressed urgency, but because Halleck did not take the project seriously, the secretary became entirely reliant on Ellet.[15]

On March 29, Ellet, though still a civilian, informed Stanton that as soon as the boats were ready *he* intended to go down to Island No. 10, "or any other stronghold of the rebels . . . and run down before the batteries and drive our rams at full headway into the rebel boats." Stanton, who had asked for daily reports, discovered that Ellet worked, planned, and executed at lightning speed and was already sifting about the riverfront looking for a crew. "The men must take service with a full knowledge of the dangerous nature of the duty," Ellet warned. "I would like to be authorized to assure them that their names will be reported to the Secretary of War, who will recommend them if they do well to the President and Congress." Stanton offered to have "two or three good naval officers detailed, if you desire, to take command of your squadron when it is ready." But Ellet already had thoughts on who should command his rams and replied, "I prefer daring and skillful river men, if they can be got, to handle the boats; but will apply for naval officers if there is any difficulty in procuring the proper men . . . which I do not expect."[16]

14. Benjamin to Lovell, January 14, 1862, Investigation of the Navy Department, *ORN,* Ser. 2, I, 662, 736–38; Lovell to Benjamin, January 18, Benjamin to Lovell, January 19, 1862, *ORN,* VI, 809–11.

15. Stanton to Ellet, March 27, Ellet to Halleck, March 28, 1862, *ORN,* XXII, 680, 681; Crandall to Taussig, January 28, 1889, Mississippi Ram Fleet and Marine Brigade Papers, NA; George C. Gorham, *Life and Public Services of Edwin M. Stanton* (2 vols.; New York, 1899), II, 292–94.

16. Ellet to Stanton, March 29, 31, Stanton to Ellet, March 31, 1862, *ORN,* XXII, 682–84.

Ellet's intellect and energy astounded Stanton, and the secretary confided to his staff: "He has more ingenuity, more personal courage, and more enterprise than anybody else I have ever seen . . . he is a clear, forcible, controversial writer. He can beat anybody at figures. He would cipher anybody to death. If I had a proposition that I desired to work out to some definite result, I do not know of anyone to whom I could entrust it so soon as Ellet. His fancy and will are predominant points, and once having taken a notion, he will not allow it to be questioned."[17]

Stanton seemed content, at least for the moment, to let Ellet run his own show. On March 31 the secretary wrote, "The crew is of great importance. I will give honorable reward and, also, prize money, for successful courage, in large and liberal measure." In 1866, keeping this promise resulted in much difficulty because the War Department disposed of many of the command's wartime records.[18]

The enticements were generous, but if Ellet expected to retain control of his experiment, he realized that he must continue to impress Stanton with performance. On March 31, 1862, he was still Mr. Ellet, a civilian acting as Stanton's agent, and a commander for the Ram Fleet had not yet been chosen.

Charles Ellet never told his wife, Elvira—whom he called Ellie—of his plans, only that he was fitting out vessels for the War Department. Nor did she know that he and their son Charles Rivers Ellet—who at the time was only eighteen—had plans to accompany the rams into battle. In a letter to her husband written on May 2, 1862, Ellie begged him to answer the question, "Tell me distinctly, so I can understand, what are these boats going to do?" There is no evidence that Ellet ever gave her an answer.[19]

In the late 1880s, when the Office of Naval War Records began to prepare for the publication of the *Official Records of the Union and Confederate Navies*, Warren D. Crandall became concerned that the compilers would leave the brigade "out in the cold" because of its "anomalous character." Crandall had served as the brigade's assistant adjutant general, and for many years after the war he acted as recorder and historian of the unit's Society of Survivors. In February 1889,

17. Quoted in Gambrell, "Rams versus Gunboats," 56–57.
18. Stanton to Ellet, March 31, 1862, *ORN*, XXII, 685.
19. Elvira Ellet to Charles Ellet, May 2, 1862, Ellet Papers, UM.

Professor James R. Soley, one of the compilers, decided that though the Ram Fleet had been organized under the secretary of war, it was "largely nautical in nature, if not chiefly so . . . and constitute[d] some of the most important and brilliant episodes in the history of the war on the Mississippi River." Soley admitted that if the navy did not publish the official papers of the Ram Fleet, its history during the Civil War would be lost, and if Crandall had not assiduously collected and protected copies of those papers, they most certainly would have been omitted from the *Records*.[20]

For this obscure unit, Crandall accumulated hundreds of documents, both official and unofficial, including logbooks, journals, diaries, newspaper accounts, personal reminiscences, biographies, and stacks of miscellaneous papers far in excess of those that eventually found a home in the *Official Records* of the armies and the navies. Were it not for Professor Soley and his assistants, the history of Ellet's Ram Fleet and the Mississippi Marine Brigade may have remained buried in the archives of the Illinois State Historical Society and the Missouri Historical Society—a poor tribute to the men who fought and died in what was truly "the strangest outfit of all."[21]

20. Crandall to Taussig, January 28, Soley to Crandall, February 2, March 15, Crandall to Soley, March 9, 1889, Mississippi Ram Fleet and Marine Brigade Papers, NA.

21. Crandall to Soley, March 18, 1889, June 19, 1891, Crandall to Rush, November 15, 1894, *ibid.;* H. Allen Gosnell, *Guns on the Western Waters: The Story of River Gunboats in the Civil War* (Baton Rouge, 1949), 20.

CHAPTER 1

MR. STANTON'S NAVY

On March 28, 1862, Charles Ellet, Jr., checked into the Mononga-hela House at Pittsburgh and discovered that Stanton had already telegraphed the city magistrates—as far down the Ohio River as New Albany, Indiana—soliciting their cooperation. The secretary acted with urgency because the war in the west had reached a critical stage. "Spare nothing to accomplish your object at the earliest moment," he de-manded, "for time is precious."[1]

Major General Ulysses S. Grant had captured Fort Henry on February 6 and Fort Donelson on February 16, and Brigadier General Don Carlos Buell had taken Nashville on February 23. Having secured Kentucky and western Tennessee, Grant and Buell now prepared their armies for a campaign into Mississippi. Stanton expected trouble be-cause Grant and Buell would be pitting their forces against two highly regarded Confederate generals, Albert Sydney Johnston and Pierre G. T. Beauregard.

---

1. Halleck to Burnett, March 27, 1862, *ORA*, Ser. 3, I, 952–53, 955; Ellet to Halleck, March 28, 1862, *ORN*, XXII, 681; Stanton to Ellet, March 29, 1862, Ellet Papers, UM.

On the western waterways, Flag Officer Foote's naval flotilla had been spread thin. While part of his squadron cooperated with Grant and Buell on the Cumberland and Tennessee Rivers, his gunboats on the Mississippi had been stopped about sixty river miles below Columbus, Kentucky, at Island No. 10. Though Flag Officer David G. Farragut intended to bring his West Gulf Blockading Squadron into the lower Mississippi for an attack on New Orleans, he had not yet done so, and Confederate secretary of the navy Stephen R. Mallory, oblivious to the danger from Farragut, moved Commodore George Hollins's mosquito fleet upriver to block Foote's descent. Stanton viewed the experimental battering rams as the fastest way to meet the threat, provided they proved to be as potent as Ellet claimed.[2]

As the armies of Grant and Buell moved south, Stanton worried about keeping them supplied. One solution would be for the navy to get by Island No. 10 and capture Memphis. On March 31 this did not look promising, so Stanton urged Ellet to "adopt whatever mode . . . you deem proper" to expedite the creation of the Ram Fleet. "It must be done in twenty days," Stanton declared. Ellet promised "to go down to Island No. 10, or any other stronghold of the rebels" as soon as he could purchase and refit the boats. The commitment came from a civil engineer having neither a commission nor a crew. As Ellet began to purchase steamers, he found all the dry docks and yards jammed with navy work, so he appealed to Stanton, asking for authority to have his modifications made "at any place on the river I may select." Stanton promptly agreed, and Ellet hurried some of his boats down the river to New Albany, where Mayor Alexander S. Burnett promised to have "two or three" of them fitted and armored within thirty days.[3]

Stanton advised Joseph C. Butler, president of the Board of Trade at Cincinnati, that he did not expect to be charged speculative prices for purchasing Ellet's steamers, and if confronted by unreasonable terms, he would seize the boats and leave the owner the task of seeking remuneration from Congress. The warning worked wonders, and on April 10, three days after reaching Cincinnati, Ellet wired the War

2. Investigation of the Navy Department, *ORN*, Ser. 2, I, 464; Faust, *HTI*, 272–73, 274, 388.

3. Stanton to Jeffrey, April 1, Stanton to Ellet, April 3, Ellet to Stanton, Stanton to Ellet, and Burnett to Stanton, April 7, 1862, *ORA*, Ser. 3, II, 1, 4, 11, 12, 13; Ellet to Stanton, March 29, 1862, *ORN*, XXII, 682. See also Alfred Ellet, "Charles Ellet, Jr., and His Steam Rams," Ellet Papers, DUL.

Department and asked the secretary to authorize Butler to buy two large steamers, *Queen of the West* for $16,000 and (at Madison, Indiana) *Switzerland* for $13,000, both fast side-wheelers. Stanton approved the funds, and after that Ellet wasted no time. He purchased *Monarch,* another large side-wheeler, for $14,000 and sent it to New Albany for fitting. Finding no more large steamers to his liking, he bought *Lancaster,* a smaller but sturdy side-wheeler, and kept it at Cincinnati to be fitted.[4]

Ellet returned to Pittsburgh, where he had induced shippers to sell three stern-wheelers, *Lioness, Sampson,* and *Mingo,* all hefty Ohio River towboats, and threatened to seize the vessels if the owners held out for exorbitant prices. At a cost of $20,000 he added to his flotilla two small, swift stern-wheelers, *Dick Fulton* and *T. D. Horner,* vessels intended to be used as tenders and dispatch boats. The five steamers purchased at Pittsburgh proved too large for the locks on the Ohio River, and Ellet had to hurry modifications so they could be floated over the falls before the river fell. Many of vessels did not have their bows armored until they reached New Albany or Mound City, but by the end of April Ellet reported all nine vessels ready for service.[5]

During Ellet's buying spree, two events occurred that might have given Stanton reason to change his mind about activating the rams. On April 6 Grant barely escaped disaster at Shiloh, but on the following day, after sustaining 13,047 casualties, he and Buell drove Beauregard back to Corinth. In early April, Flag Officer Foote succeeded in sending two ironclads past Island No. 10, enabling Major General John Pope, on April 7, to land on the lightly defended eastern shore of the island and force the enemy's surrender. This opened the Mississippi all the way to Fort Pillow, an earthwork fortifying the east bank of the river about forty miles above Memphis.[6]

Foote had been wounded during the attack on Fort Donelson, but he refused to let his injuries interfere with his efforts to capture

4. Stanton to Butler, April 2, Ellet to Stanton, April 10, Stanton to Butler, April 11, Ellet to Stanton, April 14, 1862, *ORA,* Ser. 3, II, 1–2, 14, 15, 16; Ellet to Nimick, April 6, 1862, Ellet Papers, UM.

5. Ellet to brother, March 30, 1862, Ellet Papers, UM; Ellet to Stanton, April 14, 24, Nimick to Stanton, April 19, 1862, *ORA,* Ser. 3, II, 16, 123; Ellet to Stanton, Stanton to Halleck, April 28, 1862, *ORN,* XXIII, 80; Wyble to Crandall, November 1, 1904, William F. Wyble Letters, Civil War Collection, MHS. William F. Wyble was second master on *Lioness* and present during the vessel's modifications.

6. Faust, *HTI,* 277, 386, 684–85.

Island No. 10. On April 15 three surgeons warned him that if he did not go home and rest, the inflammation would worsen. Foote wrote Welles, suggesting that he be relieved by Captain Charles H. Davis. During this period he learned that "someone" was converting steamers "into gunboats or rams" without his knowledge. Thinking they were intended for his squadron, he sent Lieutenant Wilson McGunnegle to investigate, expedite their completion, and advise "when they may be expected to leave for this service." With Grant's and Buell's armies perfectly safe in western Tennessee, and Island No. 10 removed as another obstacle on the Mississippi, Stanton no longer had reason to retain Ellet's rams under the auspices of the War Department, but he did, even after learning that Farragut had closed the door to the lower Mississippi by capturing New Orleans.[7]

On April 26 McGunnegle found Ellet at Pittsburgh working for the secretary of war and not modifying boats for the navy. They were not the type of craft envisioned by Foote, merely old riverboats carrying no guns. The Pittsburgh stern-wheelers, *Lioness, Sampson,* and *Mingo,* were each about 170 feet long and 30 feet abeam, with holds about 5 feet deep. The four side-wheelers, *Queen of the West, Switzerland, Monarch,* and *Lancaster,* were all about 180 feet long and 37 feet abeam, with holds of 8 feet. Of the four, *Lancaster* was the smallest. The two tenders, *T. D. Horner* and *Dick Fulton,* were stern-wheeled towboats not intended for fighting.

To protect the boilers and machinery from hostile fire, Ellet had the rams fitted with heavy bulwarks consisting of three layers of 12- to 16-inch square timber. Securely bolted to the hull, the beams extended from stem to stern down the main deck with one heavy beam fitted to the keelson. He cut down the upperworks and reinforced the prows by filling them with heavy timbers that reached back about midway into the boat. Iron stays strapped the machinery and boilers into position from all directions to prevent them from shifting during impact. Each ram received a coat of shiny black paint, and hose connections were fitted to the boilers so scalding water could be used for fighting at close quarters. Ellet could have sheathed the boilers with iron, but he did not want the extra weight. He depended upon surprise, speed, and

---

7. Foote to Welles, and Ludlow, McNeeley, and Jones to Foote, April 15, Foote to McGunnegle, April 17, Stanton to Ellet, April 27, 1862, *ORN,* XXIII, 62, 63, 64, 78.

strength, vowing that his rams would "either control the Mississippi or be sunk in the attempt."[8]

Foote left no record of his reaction to the news that nine vessels had been commissioned by the War Department for service against Confederate gunboats, but he must have thought it peculiar, if not inappropriate. Inspectors for the Union navy watched as ordinary house carpenters modified the rams. Two of the boats leaked badly enough to keep men working the pumps day and night until the vessels could be patched. If Stanton ever entertained second thoughts about mobilizing his own flotilla, he never admitted it, and by the end of April he had made too many commitments to Ellet to change course. Besides, Welles had previously expressed no interest in the rams, and Stanton did not want the embarrassment of offering the boats to the navy and having them refused. From Cairo, Fleet Captain Alexander M. Pennock growled, "I am glad the Navy is not responsible." An agent, however, began lobbying for one of the rams, and for a while Ellet feared that the "meddlesome, pretentious government officer sent here to help aid me, has altered plans which I fear will deprive me of my best boat."[9]

Ellet extended Stanton's commitment to the Ram Fleet on April 19 when he asked for authority to recruit crews, suggesting that since the men would be civilian volunteers they be paid Mississippi River wages with extra allowances for hazardous duty. It may have been some relief to Stanton when Ellet declared that "what we do with these rams will probably be accomplished within a month after starting the first boat." Ellet did not look beyond Memphis, nor did Stanton. Ellet asked for a total of 350 men and suggested that each boat be commanded by a senior officer. He also asked for a military guard of twelve to twenty men, commanded by a lieutenant, to be assigned to each boat. He then proposed an elaborate scheme for determining bonus money—an extra month's pay for every fortified position passed, and

8. Ellet to McGunnegle, April 27, 1862, *ibid.*, 78–79; George E. Currie, "Battle of Memphis," Civil War Collection, MHS; Ellet to Stanton, March 29, 1862, Ellet Papers, UM; Herbert Quick and Edward Quick, *Mississippi Steamboatin': A History of Steamboating on the Mississippi and Its Tributaries* (New York, 1926), 268.

9. James M. Merrill, *Battle Flags South: The Story of the Civil War Navies on Western Waters* (Rutherford, N.J., 1970), 178; Pennock to Davis, May 16, 1862, Loose Papers, Mississippi River, NA; Charles Ellet to Alfred Ellet, May 2, 1862, Ellet Papers, UM.

prize money for destroying "the enemy's floating war property." After adding a surgeon and a clerk to his manning requirements, Ellet asked permission to pick the officers who would command the guard.[10]

Six days passed before Stanton replied, suggesting that the secretary may have reflected on his creation before giving it his final endorsement. By then news of the enterprise had leaked to the press. Critics condemned the venture, calling the boats "brown paper rams" because of their outward flimsiness. The press ridiculed Ellet for hatching the idea and scoffed at the secretary for investing public money in the scheme. Stanton, however, approved all of Ellet's proposals except the bonus for passing fortified positions, declaring it beyond his ability to define. Because he viewed the unit as a regiment rather than a brigade, and because no one understood its character better than its originator, he made Ellet a colonel—the highest grade Stanton had the authority to grant—"so long as may be necessary for the complete execution of the enterprise." Stanton attached Ellet to the staff of Major General John C. Frémont but made him subject only to the orders of himself. He then authorized Ellet to apply to Frémont for men to serve as guards and wisely directed him to confer with the "Naval Commander on the Mississippi River" before taking any precipitous action, "for there must be no conflicting authorities in the prosecution of the war." For a person who warned against conflicting authorities, Stanton could not have created a more tangled confusion of command than by forming his own flotilla.[11]

Ellet immediately reacted to Stanton's reply, stating that he would prefer not to hold a military rank, but if the secretary insisted, he would prefer that it be higher. He also did not want to muddle through the military chain of command to find soldiers, and suggested that his brother, Captain Alfred W. Ellet, be transferred from the 59th Illinois Infantry as second-in-command and bring with him a "limited number of reliable men of his own selection." He mildly objected to coordinating his activities with the navy because he did not feel that Foote had confidence in "my mode of warfare." Ellet already had volunteer captains and river boatmen engaged as crews, and he privately wanted the Ram Fleet to remain under civilian control to go where he wished and do what he wanted—much like privateers operating under letters of

10. Ellet to Stanton, April 19, 1862, *ORA*, X, Pt. 2, pp. 112–12.

11. Stanton to Ellet, April 25, 28, 1862, Ellet Papers, UM; Anonymous, "Colonel Ellet and His Rams," newsclips in Crandall Collection, ISHL.

marque. Civilians hired by Ellet were not sworn into the service but signed instead a "Military Obligation" for six months.[12]

The tone of Ellet's reply provided Stanton one more chance to transfer the rams to either the army or the navy, but the secretary ignored the opportunity. Instead, he implied that while a higher grade might be appropriate, he could not grant one without the Senate's approval, and this would cause delays. He offered an acceptable compromise, however, by promoting Alfred Ellet to lieutenant colonel and transferring him to the Ram Fleet with men from Company I, 59th Illinois. He also promised to notify the navy that it was not to attempt to control the movements of the rams "unless they shall manifestly expose the general operations on the Mississippi to some unfavorable influence." Ellet accepted the terms and thanked the secretary for placing his brother at his side. As a final favor, he asked Stanton to issue orders for Alfred Ellet to meet him at New Albany with six lieutenants and fifty privates. Knowing that the 59th Illinois served under Brigadier General John M. Schofield, on April 27 Ellet issued the orders himself.[13]

On April 27 Stanton learned that Farragut had captured New Orleans. Thinking the remainder of the Mississippi River would fall in a few weeks, he urged Ellet to put his rams in motion and get down to Memphis as quickly as possible. Not wanting to miss any of the action—or the prize money—Ellet began his departure from Pittsburgh two days later with *Mingo, Lioness,* and *Sampson,* followed soon afterwards by the fleet's two tenders. Before casting off he sent a final request to Stanton asking for three hundred rifle muskets, ammunition, three hundred cutlasses, and nine cases of hand grenades to be delivered at Cincinnati. None of the boats was completely ready for service, but the bows had been plated and only deck work remained. On the trip downriver *Lioness* punctured its coal barge when going over the falls at Louisville, adding a little anxiety to the colonel's rush to get into the war.[14]

12. Ellet to Stanton, April 25, 1862, *ORA,* X, Pt. 2, pp. 127–28; Wyble to Crandall, November 1, 1904, Wyble Letters, Civil War Collection, MHS; John D. Milligan, *Gunboats down the Mississippi* (Annapolis, 1965), 71.

13. Stanton to Ellet, Ellet to Stanton, April 26, 28, 1862, *ORA,* X, Pt. 2, pp. 130–31; Ellet to Schofield, April 27, Ellet to Stanton, April 28, 1862, *ORN,* XXIII, 78, 80.

14. Stanton to Ellet, April 27, 1862, *ORA,* LII, 243; Ellet to Stanton, April 28, 30, 1862, *ibid.,* Ser. 3, II, 28; Wyble to Crandall, November 1, 1904, Wyble Letters, Civil War Collection, MHS.

Forty-one-year-old Alfred Ellet was not surprised when he received orders to meet his brother at New Albany—they had been in contact with each other for several weeks. Ten years younger than Charles, and the youngest of six brothers, Alfred had settled at Bunker Hill, Illinois, and engaged in farming. He developed a gigantic physique, being six feet, two and one-half inches tall, with strength proportionate to his size. On August 20, 1861, he had joined the 9th Missouri Infantry—which later became the 59th Illinois—as captain of Company I. He gained a little experience in warfare during the Battle of Pea Ridge, but not the type his brother had in mind.[15]

When Alfred Ellet received his transfer to the Ram Fleet, the orders stipulated that he take from the 59th Illinois not six but three first lieutenants—John H. Johnson of Company B, George E. Currie of Company C, and Warren D. Crandall of Company D—along with "one hundred picked men to be Volunteers for extra hazardous service." Crandall, who later wrote a history of the unit, said, "All supposed the service to be a temporary one, and expected if they survived its perils, to return to the [regiment] they were now parting from in the near future." Alfred Ellet reached New Albany on the night of May 2 with fifty-three volunteers and two more Ellets—Edward and John, his son and nephew. He found the colonel still dressed in civilian clothes and engaged in superintending the loading of supplies.[16]

Charles Ellet had not bothered to buy a uniform. Various maladies during the past three years had made him frail, and the sudden exertion, poor food, and unbearable heat placed a steady strain on his constitution. He had decided to not waste precious time casting about for a uniform until brother Alfred insisted that he must. The colonel finally complied, but Charles did not wear it until the end of May. He then discovered that an "eagle on the shoulder, and a military hat, are better passports than brains or character."[17]

In the meantime, Stanton issued a strange message to General Halleck, who had shifted his headquarters from St. Louis to Pittsburg

15. Alfred Ellet Biography, Ellet Papers, NA; Faust, *HTI,* 238.

16. Special Orders No. 159, April 29, 1862, quoted in Crandall and Newell, *Ram Fleet,* 37, 38, 245–47; Edward Ellet, "Military Career of Alfred W. Ellet," Ellet Papers, DUL. See also Norman E. Clarke, Jr., ed., *Warfare along the Mississippi: The Letters of Lieutenant Colonel George E. Currie* (Mount Pleasant, Mich., 1961), x, who states that all the lieutenants came from Company C.

17. Ellet to wife, May 29, 1862, Ellet Papers, UM; Gambrell, "Rams versus Gunboats," 59, 60.

Landing, Tennessee, and superseded Grant as field commander. He informed Halleck that though Ellet held an army commission, the colonel would be subject to the orders of Flag Officer Foote. This occurred two days after Stanton assured Ellet that he would not be under Foote's "direct control." The secretary did not want Halleck tinkering with the Ram Fleet, and the best way to prevent it was to deceive him by saying that Ellet reported to the navy. There is no record that Foote or the Navy Department ever received a communication from Stanton explaining Ellet's role or range of operations. On May 9, Foote, because of his injury, turned the Mississippi flotilla over to Captain Charles H. Davis, leaving no instructions regarding the Ram Fleet because he had none to give.[18]

Fifty-five-year-old Charles Henry Davis had grown up in Boston, attended Harvard, joined the navy as midshipman at the age of seventeen, and after only three years of service qualified for lieutenant. Known for having a brilliant, scientific mind, Davis might have found much in common with Ellet, but their personalities were virtual opposites. Davis, who wore a long handlebar mustache and silvery whiskers below his chin, faced his duties each day as a scholar pondering some new incomprehensible problem, while the tireless, energetic Ellet made decisions quickly and acted on them.[19]

A cautious man though an acceptable administrator, Davis did not think strategically. He had served as fleet captain under Flag Officer Samuel F. Du Pont during the expedition that captured Port Royal, South Carolina, but he lacked Foote's aggressiveness and would not risk his vessels on brazen missions. He took care not to exceed his perception of authority, and because he complained less often and less loudly than Foote, he received less attention from the Navy Department. This was partly the fault of Welles, who intended to restore the command to the ailing Foote. When Davis took command of the Mississippi flotilla, nobody told him how the Ram Fleet fit into the naval equation on western waters. A few days later he would learn the hard way.[20]

<hr />

18. Halleck to Grant, April 9, Stanton to Ellet, April 26, 1862, *ORA*, X, Pt. 2, pp. 99, 130–31; Stanton to Halleck, April 28, Foote to Welles, May 9, 1862, *ORN*, XXIII, 80.

19. Faust, *HTI*, 206, 254.

20. Foote to Welles, May 10, 1862, *ORN*, XXIII, 86; Charles H. Davis, *Life of Charles Henry Davis, Rear Admiral, 1807–1877* (Boston and New York, 1899), 222, 231. See also Reuben Elmore Stivers, *Privateers and Volunteers: The Men and Women of Our Reserve Naval Force* (Annapolis, 1975), 273.

Davis, having many old friends in the service, received quick sympathy over the intrusion of Ellet's command. Du Pont expressed the opinion of many naval officers when he somewhat contemptuously confided to his wife, "We do not understand the 'Ram Fleet' under a colonel, who of course overshadows Davis."[21]

On May 10 Ellet was still at New Albany attempting to find four more lieutenants and seventy-five more men. He succeeded in obtaining Lieutenant David M. Dryden—on sick leave from the 1st Kentucky due to wounds—from the local military post, but recruitment went slowly and delayed his descent to the Mississippi.

When Ellet could not charm civilians into the service, he stole them from the army. On one occasion a steamboatman who had enlisted in the army learned of rams being fitted in his hometown and decided he preferred service afloat to carrying a rifle and facing long marches. He deserted his outfit and signed with the Ram Fleet. When he was missed at roll call, the company commander sent an officer to the shipyard to "take him back and shoot him." The skipper of the ram admitted that the deserter had come on board but did not agree the man should be shot. "He's a good steamboatman, and we need him," said the skipper, "what do you want to shoot him for?" Puzzled, the infantry officer replied, "You say he signed on? What do you mean by that?" Standing firm on his point, the skipper answered, "Why he signed up with us; took service on the ram we're building to lick the Rebs with. What more do you want?" The provost guard thought for a moment and said, "Oh, you mean he enlisted with you. Well, I'm willing," he said thoughtfully, "he was a damn poor infantryman, anyway."[22]

Under pressure from the War Department to get under way, Ellet called his officers together and issued instructions for the movement of each boat. He discussed methods for cooperating during an engagement, a system for exchanging signals, and a procedure for repelling boarders. The rams were capable of steaming at speeds up to twenty miles per hour when traveling with the current, and Ellet did not believe an enemy gunboat or shore battery capable of hitting a speeding ram. He flatly told his captains that the purpose of the ram was to cut down enemy gunboats, and since a ram was an expendable weapon, he

21. Du Pont to wife, June 16, 1862, John D. Hayes, ed., *Samuel Francis Du Pont: A Selection from His Civil War Letters* (3 vols.; Ithaca, N.Y., 1969), II, 114.

22. Ellet to Nelson, May 10, 1862, *ORN,* XXIII, 87; Quick and Quick, *Mississippi Steamboatin',* 269–70.

expected them to lose it in battle. To make certain his orders were understood, he repeated them daily and charged his officers with the duty of making his wishes clear to the soldiers. He then designated *Switzerland* as his flagship and began the descent to Cairo, where he had sent his brother to fill out the crew.[23]

On May 16 Alfred Ellet reached Cairo with five of the rams. According to Lieutenant Crandall, they created quite a stir as they passed down the Ohio, being received by "loyal greetings at all landings, and points where groups of people gathered to witness the novel sight the rams presented, with their barricaded boiler decks, and cleared-away upper decks, and iron-cased pilot houses." Alfred Ellet found a message waiting for him from Stanton, authorizing him to pick up three hundred navy revolvers and an equal number of carbines from naval stores at Cairo. The secretary also authorized him to engage Dr. James Robarts of Carbondale, Illinois, as fleet surgeon. Two weeks had passed since Colonel Ellet had requested arms, and had he not reminded the War Department by telegraph on May 15, the rams might have entered hostile waters without the most elementary means of defense.[24]

Alfred Ellet waited for a sixth boat before departing from Cairo for Fort Pillow, where he expected to communicate with Foote. Instead, he found Davis in charge of the naval squadron. The Ellets missed the naval action on May 10 when Captain James E. Montgomery, commanding the Confederate River Defense Fleet's eight gunboat-rams, attacked seven Union vessels at Plum Point Bend. Davis misinformed Welles by claiming he had sunk three enemy vessels, and because the Rebels withdrew, he claimed an easy victory, but Alfred Ellet missed a perfect opportunity to test his brother's rams on an advancing enemy column. Instead, Montgomery tried his rams on two of Davis's ironclads—*Cincinnati* and *Mound City*—and inflicted enough damage to force both vessels aground in the shallows to keep from sinking. After thirty minutes of fighting, Montgomery returned to Fort Pillow with all of his boats and only two killed and one wounded. Davis, however, had just taken command of the Mississippi flotilla, and the sudden disaster induced him to fear the formidable-

---

23. Ellet's Report, June 4, Watson to Ellet, May 12, Ellet to Watson, May 15, 1862, *ORN*, XXIII, 43, 93, 95.

24. Ellet to Watson, Stanton to Alfred Ellet, May 15, 1862, *ibid.*, 95, 96.

looking River Defense Fleet more than its actual strength warranted. On the heels of this embarrassing setback, Alfred Ellet arrived with most of the uninvited Ram Fleet and passed down through Davis's flotilla.[25]

At Plum Point Bend the men of the Ram Fleet observed some of the finest vessels in the western waters, the most impressive being the ironclads *Carondelet, St. Louis* (later *Baron de Kalb*), *Pittsburg, Cairo,* and *Benton,* all built by James B. Eads of St. Louis. Two others, *Cincinnati* and *Mound City,* had been badly damaged by Montgomery's rams because Davis failed to post a picketboat. The news of the engagement induced Colonel Ellet to hurry down from New Albany in a tender and join his squadron before it missed another fight.[26]

The colonel arrived at Plum Point on May 25, and wanting action, he immediately sought an interview with the flag officer. Davis greeted him cordially but manifested so much caution that Ellet departed in disgust, advising Stanton, "The Commodore intimates unwillingness to assume any risk at this time. . . . To me, the risk is greater to lie here with my small squad and within an hour's march of a strong encampment of the enemy, than to run by the battery and to make the attack." Ellet antagonized Davis two days later when he proposed "a joint movement to destroy the enemy's fleet and command the Mississippi below Fort Pillow." Davis promised to reply but never did, and Ellet impatiently fumed, warning Stanton that "delay will be fatal to the usefulness of this fleet." Davis's refusal to work with the Ram Fleet marked the beginning of an adversarial relationship between the Ellets and professional naval officers that continued as long as the unit remained an independent command. Ellet reached the pinnacle of exasperation with Davis on June 2 and advised Stanton that the Ram Fleet would move against the enemy with or without the support of the navy. He also wrote his wife, grumbling that "this confounded . . . Commodore won't move, or give me any satisfaction!"[27]

Delay was not fatal, but there would be no more surprise attacks by Montgomery's River Defense Fleet. General Halleck had consolidated the armies of Grant, Pope, and Buell into a huge force of 120,000 men

25. Davis to Welles, May 10, 11, 12, 17, Montgomery's Report, May 12, 1862, *ibid.,* 13, 14, 55–57.

26. Davis to Welles, May 11, 12, 1862, *ibid.,* 14, 17.

27. Ellet to Stanton, May 26, 30, 1862, *ORA,* X, Pt. 2, pp. 215, 231; Ellet to Davis, June 2, 1862, *ORN,* XXIII, 39; Ellet to wife, June 2, 1862, Ellet Papers, UM.

and in late April crossed into Mississippi to attack Corinth. After several days, and with only 66,000 men, Beauregard slowed Halleck's progress to inching the Union army forward before finally withdrawing the Confederates on the night of May 29–30 to Tupelo. Beauregard began to pull troops from Memphis, but he kept Montgomery's rams there to watch Davis's flotilla and to serve in an emergency. If Ellet wanted action, he would have to initiate it himself, and that was exactly what he intended to do.[28]

Sensing that the colonel was contemplating some kind of suicide mission, Thomas Littell, one of *Monarch's* pilots, demanded his pay and said he quit. When asked why, the pilot replied that when coming on board he had not expected to be placed in danger, exposed to shot, or harmed in any way, and he would not remain on *Monarch* "if she is really to be exposed to the casualties of war." On June 1 Ellet released the man, but he wondered if there would be others. If so, he could lose no more time.[29]

Ellet sought action, and when he observed an enemy gunboat on picket along the east bank above Fort Pillow, he advised Davis that he planned to draw it out and attack it. Using the tender *Dick Fulton* to decoy the enemy upriver, Ellet intended to hide *Queen of the West, Lancaster, Lioness,* and *Horner* around a bend in the river and turn them loose as soon as the Rebel vessel came in sight. Giving the matter further thought, he decided to take all his rams, run by the fort, and get below. Being unarmed, he asked Davis to supply "at least one gunboat," and if not, then a few "brave men of your command" to serve as marines.[30]

The crew of *Queen of the West* unexpectedly altered Ellet's plans when the captain, two of the three pilots, the first mate, and all the engineers refused to join the attack and departed on a barge with their baggage. Ellet hastily formed a group of volunteers, including two privates from the 63rd Illinois who claimed to be engineers, and personally took command of *Queen.* In company with *Monarch,* he made a run at the enemy gunboat and pursued the vessel to Fort Pillow. Though they were forced to give up the chase, the exercise provided a useful reconnaissance. From the fort, seven or eight guns had fired on the rams without effect, but Ellet had penetrated the defensive screen.

28. Mark M. Boatner III, *The Civil War Dictionary* (New York, 1959), 176.
29. Ellet to Littell, June 1, 1862, Ellet Papers, UM.
30. Ellet to Davis, June 1, Ellet's Orders, June 1, 1862, *ORN,* XXIII, 37, 38.

He counted eight vessels of the River Defense Fleet below the fort and learned of four more boats at Fort Randolph, twelve miles downriver. When reporting the engagement to Stanton, Ellet complained, "Davis will not join me in a movement against [the enemy], nor contribute a gun-boat to my expedition, nor allow any of his men to volunteer, so as to stimulate the pride and emulation of my own [men]. I shall therefore first weed out some bad material, and then go without him."[31]

Ellet and Davis continued to quarrel. "I would thank you to inform me how far you consider yourself under my authority," Davis snarled, "and I shall esteem it a favor to receive from you a copy of the orders under which you are acting." As a response, Ellet pieced together Stanton's letters and dispatched them to Davis, adding, "While regretting sincerely your disposition [not] to cooperate in a movement against the enemy's fleet, lying within easy reach, I take great pleasure in giving you all the information you ask for. I do not consider myself under your authority." Though Stanton had promised to inform "the naval commander" of Ellet's "peculiar" service, he had not done so.[32]

When Ellet first appeared on the Mississippi he wore no uniform, and Davis envisioned the colonel as a freelance civilian adventurer acting under no military authority, doing "exactly according to his own fancy, receiving orders from no one." Learning that Ellet worked for Stanton, Davis suffered a mild shock when he discovered that the colonel had direct access to the War Department. It would not play well for him, as flag officer, to behave like an obstructionist, but he was also aware that the rams carried no guns and believed that Ellet would not initiate action without the help of gunboats. His attitude toward Ellet suddenly mellowed, and he agreed to work with the colonel on future operations. Plans were afoot for a movement on Fort Pillow, Davis confided, and he promised to make Ellet "acquainted with all the details" and invite his cooperation.[33]

By then Stanton had digested all of Ellet's complaints and formed a low opinion of Davis's qualifications as a naval commander. Rather than expose his little operation by sharing his concerns with Welles, he

31. Ellet to Stanton, June 4, 1862, *ORA*, X, Pt. 1, p. 900, Pt. 2, pp. 257–58; Ellet to Mary Ellet, June 4, 1862, Ellet Papers, UM; Alfred Ellet's Report, June 4, 1862, *ORN*, XXIII, 44. The volunteer engineers from the 63rd Illinois were Privates R. L. Groomes and W. Jackson.

32. Davis to Ellet, June 2, Ellet to Davis, June 2, 3, 1862, *ORN*, XXIII, 39, 40, 41.

33. Davis to Ellet, June 3, 1862, *ibid.*, 42–43; C. H. Davis, *Life of Davis*, 231.

wrote Halleck, condemning Davis for refusing to lend Ellet a single gunboat for protection or allow him "to attack on his own hook." What Stanton expected the slow-moving Halleck to do from his distant headquarters at Corinth is unclear. Lincoln had already refused to burden Halleck by tying the Ram Fleet to the general's command.[34]

Stanton now had a dilemma. He had financed and officered an independent naval force responsible only to himself. From his isolated ministry in Washington he seemed to be stuck, if not mildly embarrassed, with his peculiar creation. He could turn neither to Welles nor to Lincoln for advice without feeling foolish, and he had no authority to issue orders to Flag Officer Davis. Manifestations of doubt pervaded his thoughts. He forced himself to hope for the best, placing his ebbing confidence in Ellet, the persuasive engineer who got him into the mess.

34. Stanton to Halleck, June 5, 1862, *ORN,* XXIII, 48.

CHAPTER 2

THE RAMS AT MEMPHIS

When General Pope departed with his army to join Halleck's invasion of Mississippi, he detached two regiments under Colonel Graham N. Fitch and on April 16 left them with Flag Officer Foote. Pope's withdrawal annoyed Foote because he wanted to capture Fort Pillow and open the way to Memphis. When Davis arrived to replace Foote, both officers agreed that Fitch's force was too small to attack Fort Pillow. Then the annoying Ellets arrived and on a daily basis began to press Davis to take action. After Fitch returned from a three-day reconnaissance of the fort, he and Davis agreed that a combined assault by the infantry, preceded by a naval bombardment, might do some good. They set the attack for the morning of June 4, but Alfred Ellet's unexpected attempt to destroy an enemy picketboat aborted it. Seeing his plans upset, Davis blamed Ellet's "foolish movement" for delaying the attack and rescheduled it for 7 A.M. on June 5, but once again neglected to inform Ellet.[1]

During the early-morning hours of June 5, Colonel Ellet observed

1. Pope to Foote, Butler to Fitch, April 16, Foote to Welles, April 17, 19, Fitch to Pope, and Davis Diary, June 5, 1862, *ORN*, XXIII, 7, 8, 9, 45–46, 53.

Davis's flotilla coming downriver, and as the ironclads rounded Craighead Point he hailed them. Learning that Davis intended to attack Fort Pillow, Ellet put his rams under a full head of steam and quickly passed the lumbering ironclads. As the rams approached the fort, Ellet heard gunfire and observed smoke blackening the sky above the earthworks. Alfred Ellet took a handful of men from *Monarch* and rushed ashore to investigate. Smoke poured from the abandoned fort, ammunition exploded, every gun lay disabled, and the River Defense Fleet had withdrawn to Memphis. Alfred Ellet planted the Stars and Stripes and signaled his brother to bring up the rest of the rams.[2]

Before Davis and Fitch could launch their joint attack, the Ellet brothers secured possession of the hurriedly evacuated fortifications. In his report to Welles, Davis mentioned nothing about the Ellets or the Ram Fleet, writing, "We [meaning Fitch and himself] are now in possession of the works." Lieutenant S. Ledyard Phelps of *Benton* wandered through the fort later that day and reported the battlements in good condition and the guns indifferently spiked. More importantly, he observed that Davis had wasted a whole month. The Union ironclads could have safely passed the fort by clinging to the bank because the guns emplaced on the bluffs could not be depressed to bear along shore.[3]

Davis brought his squadron down to Fort Pillow and anchored it across the channel, but Ellet took three rams and with his brother steamed downriver searching for enemy vessels. Stopping at Fort Randolph, twelve miles below Fort Pillow, Alfred Ellet went ashore under a flag of truce. He found guns dismounted and hundreds of bales of cotton used to strengthen the earthwork still smoldering. Met only by civilians, he demanded the town's surrender, ran up the national emblem, and extracted from the small crowd a promise to respect the Union colors. Finding no shipping to molest, Colonel Ellet returned upriver to bring down the remainder of his rams, leaving his brother in possession of Fort Randolph. On his return to Fort Pillow, Ellet passed Davis's squadron moving downriver. Davis did not com-

2. Alfred Ellet, "Charles Ellet, Jr., and His Steam Rams," Ellet Papers, DUL; Ellet's Report, June 5, 1862, *ORN,* XXIII, 48–49.

3. Davis's Report, and Phelps to Davis, June 5, 1862, *ORN,* XXIII, 47–48, 50–51; Henry Walke, *Naval Scenes and Reminiscences of the Civil War in the United States* (New York, 1877), 271–72.

municate with Ellet, neither to ask of conditions below nor to disclose his plans, but steamed down to Island No. 45. He put the squadron in attack formation and anchored it about two miles above Memphis.[4]

At Fort Pillow, Ellet detached a courier with a message to Stanton, which read, "I presume there will be no further obstacles unless we encounter one at Memphis." Then, before he lost the advantage of daylight, he took the lead in *Queen of the West* and steamed back down the river, followed in order and at half-mile intervals by *Monarch, Lancaster, Switzerland, Dick Fulton, T. D. Horner, Mingo,* and *Lioness.* Darkness intervened and the rams anchored about sixteen river miles above Davis's squadron.[5]

Just before 5 A.M. on June 6, Ellet heard the firing of heavy guns in the vicinity of Wolf's Island, about a mile above Memphis. He hailed *Monarch, Switzerland,* and *Lancaster,* and taking the lead in *Queen of the West,* steamed toward the sound of battle. Davis had been looking for the rams, but he had mentioned nothing to Ellet about needing them. The colonel had intended to communicate with Davis at daylight, but the sound of gunfire induced him to forego the conference and push directly into the action. He had received no indication that a fight was expected, and no signals existed for communication between the two fleets. From the bend in the river a mile above Memphis, Ellet could see enemy gunboats roving in plain sight off the city and seized the opportunity to attack. From the hurricane deck of *Queen* he hollered to his brother on *Monarch,* "Round out and follow me! Now is our chance!" Carrying a full press of steam, the two rams passed swiftly downriver.[6]

Ellet never explained why he rushed into battle to engage the entire Confederate flotilla with only two of his rams. His crews had been timorous, and perhaps somebody had to set the example, so who better than himself? *Lioness, Mingo,* and *Horner,* towing coal barges, could

4. Davis to Welles, June 6, 1862, *ORN,* XXIII, 49, 118; Alfred Ellet, "Charles Ellet, Jr., and His Steam Rams," Ellet Papers, DUL; Walke, *Scenes and Reminiscences,* 275.

5. Ellet to Stanton, June 5, 1862, *ORN,* XXIII, 48; Alfred Ellet, "Charles Ellet, Jr., and His Steam Rams," Ellet Papers, DUL.

6. Ellet's Order, June 5, Ellet's Report, June 6, 1862, *ORN,* XXIII, 125; Ellet to Stanton, June 8, 1862, *ORA,* X, Pt. 1, p. 909; Alfred W. Ellet, "Ellet and His Steam-Rams at Memphis," *B&L,* I, 456–57; W. F. Warren, "The Ellet Ram Fleet," Civil War Collection, MHS.

not move until securing them to shore, but Ellet expected *Switzerland* and *Lancaster* to follow him into the fight.[7]

Commodore James E. Montgomery's River Defense Fleet had arrived at Memphis about noon on June 5, short of coal but anxious to smash up Davis's flimsy ironclads. He seized the coal carried by five commercial steamers languishing at the wharf and sent details scouring the town for more. Memphis, having no fortifications, put its fate entirely in the hands of Montgomery, who vowed to sink the invaders.[8]

The Confederate navy had beaten the Federal government in commissioning rams, but six vessels of the River Defense Fleet had been destroyed in April when Farragut's squadron passed Forts Jackson and St. Philip. The balance of the flotilla, composed of *General Beauregard, General Lovell, General Price, General Bragg, General Jeff. Thompson, General Van Dorn, Sumter,* and Commodore Montgomery's flagship, *Little Rebel,* now ranged off Memphis. Unlike Ellet's unarmed rams, Montgomery's boats carried from three to five light guns. Montgomery's squadron should have been no match for the Union's heavily armed ironclads, but Davis remained unduly cautious. The Confederate vessels were commanded by riverboat captains—"a breed of men," Major General Mansfield Lovell once complained, that would "never agree on anything once they get underway."[9]

Montgomery's rams had been modified with the assumption that they would never have to retreat. Their bows were cladded and thought to be shot-proof, and Montgomery believed that as long as his boats faced the enemy, they could not be seriously damaged. The boilers on the Confederate vessels, unlike those on Ellet's rams, had been lowered into the hold for protection. This left the sides of the rams very lightly protected, and their sterns not at all. Montgomery's squadron represented the last assemblage of Confederate warships still worthy of the name "fleet," and after whipping Davis's ironclads at Plum Point Bend, he had great confidence in them.[10]

7. Warren, "The Ellet Ram Fleet," L. B. Sanford, "Recollections of the Ram Fleet," and Currie, "Battle of Memphis," all in the Civil War Collection, MHS.

8. Thompson to Beauregard, June 7, 1862, *ORN,* XXIII, 139; Charles C. Coffin, *Four Years of Fighting* (Boston, 1866), 103.

9. Samuel Carter III, *The Final Fortress: The Campaign for Vicksburg, 1862–1863* (New York, 1980), 49.

10. Thompson to Beauregard, June 7, 1862, *ORN,* XXIII, 139; Currie, "Battle of Memphis," Civil War Collection, MHS; Milligan, *Gunboats down the Mississippi,* 73.

General Beauregard, operating from his headquarters at Baldwyn, Mississippi, did not share Montgomery's optimism. After learning of the hasty evacuation of Fort Pillow, he sent a telegram to Brigadier General M. Jeff. Thompson, who commanded the Missouri State Guard, and instructed him to cooperate with Montgomery in the defense of the city. When the message arrived, Thompson was at the train station with his command awaiting transportation to Grenada. That evening, June 5, he and Montgomery met in the Gayoso House, where the commodore invited the citizens of Memphis to "come down at sunrise and see him sink the Yankee fleet." He promised to accomplish the feat in one hour. "I have no intention of retreating any farther," he told the assembled crowd. "I have come here, that you may see Lincoln's gunboats sent to the bottom by the fleet which you built and manned." Montgomery had not learned of Ellet's rams, and the surprise would be fatal.[11]

Montgomery's little surprise began shortly after dawn when Colonel Ellet took the lead and, coming abeam *Monarch,* shouted across the water to his brother, "it is hardly possible that [our] rams will survive the action, but they are sufficiently strong to take with them when they go down any enemy vessels of greater strength." *Queen of the West,* followed closely by *Monarch,* closed on a trio of approaching enemy gunboat-rams. Ellet expected *Lancaster* and *Switzerland* to follow behind *Monarch,* but the two rams played no part in the early-morning action. William F. Warren, one of the sharpshooters on *Monarch,* later claimed that *Switzerland* had been held back "by some derangement of her machinery," and *Lancaster* developed trouble when it accidentally ran ashore and broke its rudder. The other rams, "true to the letter of their orders, remained behind [*Switzerland*] and took no part in the battle."[12]

Davis's squadron also remained in the background. The flag officer had ordered most of his command a short distance upriver to enjoy a hearty breakfast of coffee, bread, and beef before going into battle. Montgomery observed the movement and believed Davis was

11. Thompson to Beauregard, June 7, 1862, *ORA,* X, Pt. 1, p. 913; Crandall and Newell, *Ram Fleet,* 61; Charles C. Coffin, *My Days and Nights on the Battlefield* (Boston, 1887), 200.

12. Ellet's Report, June 8, 11. 1862, *ORN,* XXIII, 128–29; Cabell to Mahan, April 14, 1883, Loose Papers, Mississippi River, NA; Warren, "The Ellet Ram Fleet," and Sanford, "Recollections of the Ram Fleet," Civil War Collection, MHS.

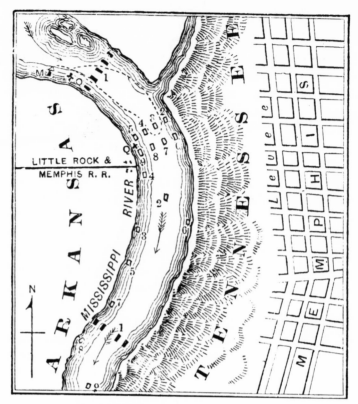

Naval engagement at Memphis, June 6, 1862
Reprinted from Charles Carlton Coffin, *Drum-Beat of the Nation*
(New York: Harper and Brothers, 1888)

KEY TO MAP

1   Position of Flag Officer Davis's ironclads at the opening of the
battle; left to right, *Benton, Carondelet, Louisville, St. Louis,* and *Cairo*

    2–9   Lineup of Confederate rams:

      2   *General Beauregard*

      3   *Little Rebel*

      4   *General Price*

      5   *Sumter*

      6   *General Lovell*

      7   *General Jeff. Thompson*

      8   *General Bragg*

      9   *General Van Dorn*

Q (upper)   Position of *Queen of the West* at start of engagement

M   Position of *Monarch* at start of engagement

- - - - -   Attack of *Queen of the West* and *Monarch*

Q (lower)   Position of *Queen of the West* when disabled

All points below the Little Rock and Memphis Railroad show the
scattering and locations of destruction of the Confederate Ram Fleet
and the advance of Flag Officer Davis's flotilla.

withdrawing. Davis misread Montgomery's intent, thinking the commodore intended to present a flag of truce on behalf of the city. To Davis's surprise, Montgomery opened with his rifled guns, and the sharp, distinct echo was what drew Ellet into the fray.[13]

Memphis occupied the east bank of the Mississippi and stood on ground sloping toward the river, terminating on a bluff about fifty feet high. Though the morning was perfectly clear, mist and smoke covered the water, and shots fired from Montgomery's rams whizzed harmlessly over Davis's ironclad flagship, *Benton*. A large crowd of spectators thronged the city's waterfront, watching as Ellet's two swift rams wound through the Union squadron and closed on the River Defense Fleet. Because a cloud of smoke lay thick over the river, observers ashore could only see two sets of pipes proceeding at great speed downriver, and tension built as they waited for the vessels to come into open sight.[14]

As *Queen of the West* and *Monarch* sped through the Union squadron, Davis's sailors waved their caps and cheered, perhaps wondering why their flag officer had left all the perilous work to Stanton's unarmed rams. Ellet stood between two pilots, urging speed, and sharpshooters waited at their posts, staring grimly at three Confederate gunboats—*Little Rebel, General Lovell,* and *General Price*—waiting to greet them head-to-head. A few shells from two Union ironclads whizzed overhead and dropped in the water near the enemy boats, but as *Queen of the West* and *Monarch* emerged from the wall of smoke blanketing the river, Davis stopped firing.[15]

General Lovell and *General Price* held way, side by side, with the other boats close behind, but as *Queen* bore swiftly head-on, Montgomery's vessels began to back, breaking formation off Beale Street. Ellet closed, unable to decide which boat to strike first, but the captain of *Lovell*, a vessel of equal size, made a fatal error when he attempted to turn and run. He underestimated *Queen*'s speed and exposed his

13. Sutherland's Report, June 6, 1862, *ORN*, XXIII, 133; *New York Tribune*, June 11, 1862; Walke, *Scenes and Reminiscences*, 276; Coffin, *Days and Nights on the Battlefield*, 295–96.

14. Warren, "The Ellet Ram Fleet," Civil War Collection, MHS; A. W. Ellet, "Ellet and His Steam-Rams," *B&L*, I, 456; Log of *Benton*, June 6, 1862, *ORN*, XXIII, 671; Charles B. Boynton, *The History of the Navy During the Rebellion* (2 vols.; New York, 1867), I, 573–74.

15. Ellet's Report, June 11, 1862, *ORN*, XXIII, 133.

vulnerable beam. Ellet capitalized on the mistake. Using his hat to signal *Monarch* to attack *Price,* he took advantage of a five-mile-per-hour current and drove *Queen of the West* into *Lovell's* forward quarter just ahead of the wheelhouse, snapping timbers and nearly slicing the vessel in two. "The crash was terrific," Ellet declared, and with "everything loose about the *Queen,* tables, pantryware, and a half-eaten breakfast were overthrown and broken by the shock. The hull of the rebel steamer was crushed in, [and] her chimneys surged over" across *Queen's* bow. Had the two rams met head-on, they would probably have destroyed each other.

Lovell began to sink. Her crew leapt overboard, losing all but eighteen of eighty-six. But Ellet had his own problems. *Queen's* iron bow remained embedded in *Lovell,* and he could not extract the vessel by backing engines. While Ellet tried to free *Queen,* the ram *General Beauregard* appeared off the port beam, slammed into the wheelhouse, and knocked the ram loose. "This blow broke [*Queen's*] tiller rope," Ellet recalled, "crushed in her wheel and a portion of her hull, and left her nearly helpless." The crew had barely recovered from the impact when *Sumter* appeared off the other beam, but its captain observed *Monarch* approaching dead ahead. He came about to avoid contact, and skedaddled downriver.[16]

Ellet emerged from the pilothouse to assess the damage, but as he reached deck a pistol shot from *Beauregard* struck him just above the knee. Though disabled, he refused to go below. With *Queen* crippled, he made for the Arkansas shore opposite Memphis. After grounding near the bank, he remained on deck to follow the engagement of his brother's ram, *Monarch.*[17]

Moments after *Queen* rammed *Lovell, Monarch* struck *General Price* a glancing blow that sheared off the enemy's starboard wheel and disabled the vessel. In sinking condition, *Price* used its port wheel to

---

16. Ellet's Report, June 6, 11, Ellet's Incidents, June 10, 1862, *ibid.,* 125, 133–34, 135; A. W. Ellet, "Ellet and His Steam-Rams," *B&L,* I, 456–57; *St. Louis Daily Democrat,* June 18, 1862.

17. A. W. Ellet, "Ellet and His Steam-Rams," *B&L,* I, 457. W. F. Warren, who served on *Monarch,* later wrote that Colonel Ellet received his wound during a pistol *duel* with the captain of *General Lovell,* but this cannot be corroborated. See Warren, "The Ellet Ram Fleet," MHS.

paddle to the Arkansas shore and errantly collided with *Queen*. Ellet ordered his squad of marines to board *Price* and demand its surrender, from which he collected eighty-one prisoners.[18]

After recovering from the shock of striking *General Price*, Captain David Dryden righted *Monarch,* gathered headway, and steamed after *Beauregard,* which had just disengaged from *Queen* and was endeavoring to escape. *Beauregard* exposed its beam while righting itself, and *Monarch* rammed it with full force. The gunboat's side buckled, planks snapped and splintered, and piles of furniture catapulted from the deck of *Beauregard* onto *Monarch*. Sailors on *Beauregard* began climbing to the deck waving anything white, but a shot from a Union gunboat struck the ram's boiler and engulfed the vessel in steam. With its engines disabled, *Beauregard* surrendered to *Monarch*.[19]

Alfred Ellet let *Beauregard* drift and went after *Little Rebel,* Montgomery's flagship. Having been struck by fire from Davis's gunboats, *Little Rebel* could not make headway when Ellet sighted it limping toward the Arkansas shore. *Monarch* reached the ram just as it touched the shallows off Hopewell and pushed it hard and fast aground. With no guns to force the surrender of *Little Rebel*'s crew, Ellet solemnly watched as Commodore Montgomery and most of his crew waded ashore and vanished into the woods. Later, the capture of the Confederate ram became a contentious issue. Davis forcibly removed Ellet's marines, declared it a prize of the Union navy, and refused to return it to the Ram Fleet.[20]

The remnants of the River Defense Fleet dispersed, so Alfred Ellet took *Beauregard* in tow and tried to save it. On a nearby bar the Confederate ram sank to her boiler deck, and Ellet began removing prisoners. All about him lay the wreckage of Montgomery's fleet when a dispatch boat came abeam with an order from the wounded colonel: "Continue the pursuit as long as there is any hope of overtaking the

---

18. A. W. Ellet, "Ellet and His Steam-Rams," *B&L,* I, 457; Ellet's Incidents, June 10, 1862, *ORN,* XXIII, 135.

19. Ellet's Report, June 6, 11, 1862, *ORN,* XXIII, 125, 134; A. W. Ellet, "Ellet and His Steam-Rams," *B&L,* I, 457.

20. Ellet to Davis, June 10, Davis's Report, June 6, 1862, Log of *Carondelet, ORN,* XXIII, 120, 147, 684; Crandall and Newell, *Ram Fleet,* 68–69.

enemy." Alfred Ellet left the last survivors of *Beauregard* calling for help as they clung to the vessel's texas, which was still above water.[21]

Davis started to bring his squadron downriver a few minutes after *Queen of the West* sank *General Lovell*. His vessels depended upon fire-power, not speed, and though they came down with the current, the ironclads traveled no faster than ten miles per hour. When the Union flotilla entered the melee, the River Defense Fleet had begun to scatter. Shells from Davis's gunboats struck *General Jeff. Thompson,* forcing the ram ashore. The crew escaped, but the vessel burned to water's edge. Once fire reached the magazine, the boat blew to pieces. Davis captured *Sumter* and *General Bragg,* and *Monarch* chased *General Van Dorn* thirty-five miles downriver, but Alfred Ellet's concern for his wounded brother induced him to give up the pursuit and return to Memphis.[22]

What action Davis would have taken had Ellet not led the attack with his rams will never be known, but the Union squadron was fully capable of destroying the River Defense Fleet. Men like Commander Henry Walke of the USS *Carondelet* and Lieutenant Phelps of the flagship *Benton* had already been battle-tested and manifested no fear of the enemy. Commodore Montgomery, after inviting the people of Memphis to watch his gunboat-rams destroy the Union navy, never issued a battle report. Caught by surprise by Ellet's rams, Montgomery had not antici-pated losing two of his largest vessels—*General Lovell* and *General Price*—in the first few minutes of fighting. General Thompson, who witnessed the battle from shore, wrote, "I saw a large portion of the engagement . . . and am sorry to say that in my opinion many of our boats were han-dled badly or the plan of battle was very faulty." In attempting to describe the battle from his station ashore, Thompson believed that *Beauregard* and *Price* had collided with each other while attempting to run down *Monarch,* which slipped between them. What Thompson probably saw was *Monarch* striking *Price,* and *Beauregard* striking *Queen,* as five vessels converged on the same area of the river at the same time.[23]

Davis's battle report contained several inconsistencies, and some

21. A. W. Ellet, "Ellet and His Steam-Rams," *B&L,* I, 457–58; Memorandum, June 6, 1862, *ORN,* XXIII, 123; *Memphis Argus,* June 6, 1862; Walke, *Scenes and Reminiscences,* 287.

22. Davis's Report and Memorandum, June 6, 1862, *ORN,* XXIII, 119–21, 123; Warren, "The Ellet Ram Fleet," MHS; *St. Louis Daily Democrat,* June 10, 1862.

23. Thompson to Beauregard, June 7, 1862, *ORA,* X, Pt. 1, p. 913. Montgomery eventually submitted a garbled and inaccurate report, but it was not included in the *Official Records.* See Crandall and Newell, *Ram Fleet,* 78–79.

were not his fault. When *Queen of the West* and *Monarch* picked their targets and attacked, smoke and mist still partially obscured the vision of Davis and his captains, and once the rams made contact with the enemy it became difficult for anyone a mile away to see what was happening after the vessels became entangled. Phelps's report, though interesting, was inaccurate because he attempted to describe a battle he could not see. Walke simply reported what he saw, giving no details but writing, "*Queen of the West* and *Monarch* steamed boldly down the river past us, and ran into the enemy's rams and gunboats, several of which they sunk and disabled during the fight." Davis praised Ellet's "conspicuous gallantry" but used words implying that the whole affair had been a cooperative effort when in reality there had been no communication between himself and Ellet. One of the pilots of *Carondelet,* writing immediately after the fight ended, observed that by the time Davis got his squadron in motion, Ellet's much maligned "rotten and worthless steamboat rams . . . left us far behind," sinking two of the enemy rams and throwing the others into such confusion that by the time the gunboats entered the fray, "the rebels started off on a grand skedaddle."[24]

Davis eventually salvaged four of the Confederate rams, *General Price, General Bragg, Sumter,* and *Little Rebel.* He discovered they were much better boats than expected and added them to his flotilla, but he offered none of them to Ellet.[25]

When Davis passed downriver with his squadron to collect the prizes, he left some unfinished business behind, an oversight quickly corrected by Colonel Ellet when a member of *Queen*'s crew pointed to white flags flying at Memphis. On June 1 the colonel's son, Medical Cadet Charles Rivers Ellet, had arrived on the day of his nineteenth birthday and surprised his father. He came on board *Queen* and asked to join the Ram Fleet. At the time, the colonel had remonstrated with his wife, writing, "I have already a very large stake in this fleet and was unwilling to increase it so much, but [Charlie] is here now, and in fact there will be plenty for him to do." Since the colonel's wound prevented him from attending to the surrender personally, he sent his son. Ellet expressed urgency because he could hear locomotives whistling

24. Davis's Report and Walke's Report, June 6, Phelps's Report, June 9, 1862, and Log of *Carondelet, ORN,* XXIII, 118–19, 122–23, 135–36, 684; Crandall and Newell, *Ram Fleet,* 79.

25. Walke, *Scenes and Reminiscences,* 290.

behind the city and knew the Confederates were making every effort to save their rolling stock and escape with their military supplies.[26]

Lieutenant Crandall arrived with *Lioness* and conveyed the colonel's son and two marines from the 59th Illinois—Sergeant William McDonald and Private Cyrus Lathrop—to Memphis. The four men landed in a rowboat at the levee, and young Ellet delivered his father's order to Mayor John Park. The colonel knew he could not hold the city and merely demanded that his son be permitted to raise the Stars and Stripes over the customhouse and the post office "as emblems of the return of your city to the care and protection of the Constitution." Park argued that Confederate troops had abandoned the city and as civil magistrate he had no authority to surrender, but he admitted having no power to prevent the occupation of the town or the raising of flags. He advised the four men to return to their boat, as he could not guarantee their safety. Medical Cadet Ellet replied that his orders required that he raise the Stars and Stripes and he fully intended to do it. Park protested, declaring that "to do this before troops were landed . . . would be very unwise," and he pleaded with the envoys to not endanger themselves and "the whole city by attempting it." Finding his appeals useless, the mayor, who weighed about three hundred pounds, agreed to conduct them to the post office. Surrounded by an excited mob, one of the marines lost a flag when someone in the crowd snatched it away and tore it to shreds. With their one remaining flag, the foursome proceeded to the post office.[27]

Several civilians led Crandall and Charlie Ellet up four stories to an unfinished floor where a stanchion, with slats nailed to it, led to a hatchway on the roof. McDonald and Lathrop remained on a lower level to keep unauthorized personnel off the floor during the flag-raising effort. On reaching the roof, Crandall found no flagstaff and returned to the third floor. There he found a flat board about six feet long and carried it back to the roof. He and Charlie Ellet split the plank, and using bandages carried in the pocket of the latter, spliced the two sections together and tied the flag to the makeshift staff. They carried the assembly

---

26. W. D. Crandall, "The Battle Before Memphis," and Wyble to Crandall, November 1, 1904, Wyble Letters, both in Civil War Collection, MHS; Ellet to wife, June 2, 1862, Ellet Papers, UM; Ellet to daughter, June 6, 1862, Cabell-Ellet Papers, UV.

27. Ellet's Report, June 7, Park to Ellet, June 6, 1862, *ORN*, XXIII, 126–27; A. W. Ellet, "Ellet and His Steam-Rams," *B&L*, I, 458; Sanford, "Recollections of the Ram Fleet," and W. D. Crandall, "The Battle Before Memphis," Civil War Collection, MHS.

across the roof to the front of the building and jammed it into a flue so the flag dangled over the street. While Ellet and Crandall paused to admire their work, a local prankster closed the trapdoor and locked it, stranding the pair on the roof. The Union colors quickly caught the attention of stone-throwing spectators. "We were greeted with wild yells from the street below," Crandall recalled, "and several shots were fired at us from the opposite side, but we were untouched."[28]

When the hefty mayor observed the trouble on the post office roof, he feared the city would be bombarded. Battering his way through the crowd, he lumbered down to the levee and hollered out to *Lioness* for help. Captain Shrodes came ashore and threatened to fire on the city "if those men are not released in ten minutes." He then suggested that the mayor would be wise to get his police and disperse the crowd. Mayor Park had no police and the ram had no guns, but Shrodes sent the full complement of *Lioness*'s marines ashore armed with carbines and hand grenades. Thousands of people who had watched the morning battle jeered and hollered as they followed the marines to the post office, but below town a warehouse suddenly exploded, sending shock waves through the city, and most of the crowd dispersed to investigate the new disturbance. Shrodes placed four men outside the entrance to the post office and sent others up the stairway to rescue their comrades. Freed at last, Crandall and Ellet led the marines to the city square and removed Confederate flags from all buildings. At 3 P.M. they formed ranks and marched to the landing just as the steamer *Henry Von Phul,* carrying the first of Colonel Fitch's infantry, appeared off the levee.[29]

One Confederate flag—a large banner nailed to the top of a tall pole situated on the bluff in front of the city—remained untouched. Fitch sent a detail ashore with orders to form a hollow square and chop down the pole. As *Lioness* pulled away from the levee, the pole fell with a crash. Moments later, Davis's squadron appeared below, making its way back to Memphis to join in the surrender.[30]

28. Ellet to daughter, June 6, 1862, Cabell-Ellet Papers, UV; Sanford, "Recollections of the Ram Fleet," and W. D. Crandall, "The Battle Before Memphis," Civil War Collection, MHS. Crandall omitted being locked on the roof, probably from embarrassment.

29. Sanford, "Recollections of the Ram Fleet," Civil War Collection, MHS; Fitch to Pope, June 6, 7, 1862, *ORA,* X, Pt. 1, pp. 906, 911; Crandall and Newell, *Ram Fleet,* 60.

30. W. D. Crandall, "The Battle Before Memphis," MHS; Clarke, ed., *Warfare along the Mississippi,* 51–52.

Colonel Ellet detailed a boat to advise Davis that four men from the Ram Fleet had taken possession of Memphis and would need military assistance. Davis steamed up to the levee and dispatched a note to the mayor demanding the city's surrender—a formality already performed by Ellet, but Davis naturally wanted his name associated with the victory. The mayor may have thought it odd to be badgered by two officers of the same naval force and simply replied that the civil authorities had "no resources of defense" and were "in your power." In his report to Welles, Davis failed to mention that the Ellets had gotten to Memphis first, though few Union triumphs were ever more decisive or one-sided than the Battle of Memphis.[31]

Colonel Ellet proved the viability of his unarmed battering rams, but he paid for it with his life. At first his wound did not seem dangerous, and though he suffered much, he had the best surgical attention available. He continued to send dispatches and issue orders from his bed on *Switzerland,* where he had been moved to recover. On June 8 he advised Stanton that he had temporarily transferred the command to his brother and planned to send the rams downriver, adding that he was much surprised to have received an offer from Davis "to send a gunboat along." His relations with Davis, however, remained circumspect. He had been unable to recover the prize *Little Rebel,* and suspected Davis of providing a gunboat merely to gobble up any prizes taken by the Ram Fleet. Because of exhaustion he never finished a report started on June 10, and in a brief, also unfinished, letter he acknowledged that "ram fighting and prizes are scarcely compatible" because the object of the ram was not to capture but to destroy. He seemed to make a pitch for adding guns to his vessels, but he put the report aside to finish at a later time.[32]

Charles Rivers Ellet watched as infection spread rapidly around his father's wound. In a letter to his sister, Mary, he wrote, "There was not the least necessity for it but [Father] never thought at all of taking care of himself. His wound is two to three inches above the knee." Alfred also wrote Mary, declaring that "Brother Charles need not have been hurt; but forgetful of everything save the demonstration of his principle of warfare, he exposed himself to witness the effect of his blows."[33]

31. Davis to Park, Park to Davis, June 6, Fitch to Pope, June 7, 1862, *ORA,* X, Pt. 1, pp. 910–11; Davis to Welles, June 6, 1862, *ORN,* XXIII, 121.

32. Ellet to Stanton, June 8, 10, Ellet's Incidents, June 10, 1862, *ORA,* X, Pt. 1, pp. 908, 924–27.

33. C. R. Ellet to Mary, June 9, A. W. Ellet to Mary, June 7, 1862, Ellet Papers, UM.

On the morning of June 10, Ellet's surgeon, Dr. Robarts, removed the ball from the colonel's leg. Two hours later Ellet dispatched a brief letter to his wife, writing, "My anxiety is now for you, and Mary and our dear little ones. Join me here my dear wife and let us study out the future and talk over the past. But let me meet you in good health."[34]

While resting, Ellet received a telegram from Stanton, which read, "The news of your glorious achievement at Memphis reached here last evening [June 8], and our joy was only dampened by your personal injury." The secretary felt vindicated. His investment had been proven valid after all, and he tried to keep the colonel in good spirits by promising to send Mrs. Ellet and daughter Mary to Memphis. Before the colonel's heartbroken wife arrived, the infection worsened. In his last letter to Stanton, he wrote, "I can do nothing here but lie in my bed and suffer." He sensed death, and added, "The conspicuous part acted by the Lieutenant Colonel [Alfred Ellet] at Memphis will make it easier for him to command than anybody else," but he left that decision to Stanton, writing, "I do not propose to leave Lieut. Col. Ellet any instructions."[35]

Mary Ellet Cabell, the colonel's daughter, had two small children, and she believed that her father's frail health would hinder his recovery. On June 9, before leaving Washington, she sent Secretary Stanton a telegram, begging him to relieve her brother Charlie of active service and send him home. No record exists of Stanton's answer. When Mary reached Memphis, she and her mother appealed to Charlie directly, but he would not listen. His appetite for war had merely been whetted.[36]

On the night of June 18 the colonel, his wife, and his daughter departed for home, but as the vessel approached Cairo, blood poisoning took the life of Charles Ellet, Jr. On reaching Philadelphia, he received a full military funeral at Independence Hall, complete with infantry, artillery, marines, and the Pennsylvania militia. His grief-stricken wife survived him by only a few days, and both were buried on June 25 at Laurel Hill Cemetery in the City of Brotherly Love. The colonel, who never wanted the bother of wearing a uniform, lapsed into history as the "brilliant genius" who captured Memphis with his unarmed rams.[37]

34. Ellet to wife, June 10, 1862, Cabell-Ellet Papers, UV.

35. Stanton to Ellet, June 9, 1862, *ORN*, XXIII, 129–30; Stanton to Mrs. Ellet, June 8, 9, 1862, RG 107, NA; Ellet to Stanton, June 16, 1862, *ORA*, LII, Pt. 1, p. 257.

36. Mary Ellet to Stanton, June 9, 1862, Cabell-Ellet Papers, UV.

37. Brooks to Stanton, June 21, 1862, *ORA*, LII, Pt. 1, 258; A. W. Ellet, "Ellet and His Steam-Rams," *B&L*, I, 458; Ellet Obituary, newsclips in Crandall Collection, ISHL.

The poor relations between the flag officer and the colonel spilled over into Davis's biography, published by his son in 1899. Davis must have commented many times about his antagonistic relationship with the colonel, otherwise his son would not have written that Ellet's "wound was not considered serious at first, and he probably would have recovered had he regarded the surgeon's advice; but he really died from incessant writing to newspapers." This was not an opinion of a doctor, but of a son who loved and respected his father enough to follow him into the navy.[38]

In the end, Stanton credited Ellet with the capture of Memphis, and Secretary Welles gave the credit to Flag Officer Davis, mainly because the latter claimed it. Ellet and Davis both deserved a share of credit, because without each other the battle could have provoked a different outcome.[39] Several years later Admiral David Dixon Porter studied the battle and wrote:

> Rear-Admiral Davis had no military authority over the ram fleet. He could only request co-operation, which the Commander, Col. Ellet, was eager to give. The latter fought well, but unfortunately his vessels did not keep together and therefore did not accomplish as much as they would have done by combined attack. Three of the rams did not get into action until after the *Queen of the West* and *Monarch* had made their charge upon the enemy. Had they made a rush at the same time, it is probable that five of the enemy's vessels would have been sunk, and not even the *Van Dorn* would have escaped. However, as matters turned out, it was a brilliant victory, and the Union commander had every reason to be satisfied with it.[40]

Though Charles Ellet, Jr., died on June 21, 1862, there were other Ellets to carry on the work of the Ram Fleet—but nothing would ever quite be the same.

38. C. H. Davis, *Life of Davis*, 231.

39. Welles to Davis, June 18, 1862, *ORN*, XXIII, 137. This letter, though written by Welles, may have been composed prematurely and never mailed, as it did not appear in the *Annual Report of the Secretary of the Navy* (Washington, D.C., 1862).

40. David Dixon Porter, *The Naval History of the Civil War* (New York and San Francisco, 1886), 171.

CHAPTER 3

CAMPAIGNING WITH DAVIS

Following the capture of Memphis, Secretary of War Stanton once again had the option of offering the Ram Fleet to the navy, but he chose to keep it. On June 24 he placed Lieutenant Colonel Alfred W. Ellet in charge of the rams, but at the insistence of the president he instructed the new commander to take his orders from Flag Officer Davis. Having commanded Company I, 59th Illinois, at Pea Ridge, Alfred Ellet had more experience at warfare than his deceased brother, and his bold attack off the city of Memphis demonstrated that he enjoyed fighting. His own relations with Davis had been no better than his brother's, however, and whether the president's directive would make any difference remained to be seen.[1]

Many days passed before Stanton's instructions reached Alfred Ellet. On June 19 his orders still came from his dying brother, and after a brief bedside conference he departed with *Monarch, Lancaster, Lioness, Mingo,* and *Fulton* to the mouth of the St. Francis River, where

---

1. Stanton to Ellet, June 24, 1862, *ORA*, XV, 497; Stanton to Halleck, June 27, 1862, *ibid.*, XVII, Pt. 2, p. 40; Stanton to Ellet, June 30, 1862, Ellet Papers, UM; Faust, *HTI*, 238.

he stopped at nightfall. In the morning he sent two boats upstream in search of prizes. Finding nothing but cotton smoldering on abandoned barges, he ventured down the Mississippi to Helena. Being short-handed, he recruited several Union refugees fleeing Arkansas conscription and engaged a number of blacks to assist the crew.

Three miles below Helena, Ellet captured a ferryboat used to transport troops across the river. After questioning the crew, he learned that *General Van Dorn* had "hurried down the river so fast she made no stop at Helena but threw out a bottle with the news of the fight at Memphis." Observers reported that the ram flew a white flag of truce for forty miles downriver before the captain felt secure enough to haul it down. Ellet burned the ferryboat and steamed down to Friar's Point, Mississippi, where he learned that *Van Dorn* had fled up the Yazoo River after warning away all shipping.

At White River, Ellet hailed a detachment from Davis's squadron, but they claimed to be occupied and showed no interest in communicating their plans. Without waiting, Ellet gathered up his rams and continued the descent toward Vicksburg.

On the evening of June 22 the rams reached Greenville, Mississippi, where smoke lay heavy on the river from bales of burning cotton and the white residents of the town seemed to have vanished. At Paw Paw Island the boats paused while the crew of *Fulton* repaired a burned boiler. When the boat became operable again, Ellet left *Lioness* and *Mingo* behind to guard the coal barges and headed downriver with *Monarch, Lancaster,* and *Fulton.*

On June 24 the rams arrived at the mouth of the Yazoo River—twelve miles above Vicksburg—and picked up from a skiff a German who claimed to be a Union man. He confirmed that every boat on the river had gone up to Yazoo City, including the ironclad *Arkansas.* It had been aground about fifty miles up the Yazoo, but *Van Dorn* pulled it off. More importantly, Ellet learned that Flag Officer Farragut had come up from New Orleans with a portion of his squadron and anchored it a few miles below Vicksburg. Farragut intended to attack the city as soon as all of the steam sloops, mortar schooners, corvettes, gunboats, and Brigadier General Thomas Williams's infantry brigade arrived. Keeping the German on board, Ellet continued downriver to confer with Farragut and tied up off Young's Point.[2]

2. Log of *Lancaster, ORN,* XXIII, 241–42; Crandall and Newell, *Ram Fleet,* 86–88.

Farragut did not want to remain up the falling river in his heavy sloops of war, and on the morning of June 25, as he came to anchor below Vicksburg, he had hoped to meet Davis's squadron and together force the city's surrender. Ellet's informant explained that communications could be opened with Farragut by crossing De Soto Point, a peninsula formed by a huge horseshoe bend opposite Vicksburg. The German agreed to guide anyone willing to hike through two miles of marshes and sloughs to make contact with the lower fleet. Charlie Ellet volunteered to carry a message to Farragut. With him went Sergeant E. W. Bartlett, Edward C. Ellet, and William F. Warren, all dressed in civilian clothes. Touching shore at the neck of the peninsula, the German led the way through woods snarled with underbrush and infested with mosquitoes.[3]

Though he had sought a career as a doctor, young Charlie Ellet left his father's bedside on June 19 to continue his adventures with the Ram Fleet. At the age of eighteen he had worked at the Union hospital at Georgetown, where he attended to soldiers wounded during the Battle of First Manassas. During the spring of 1862 he learned that his father had gone to war and, without his mother's knowledge, sought to join him. Because of the unusual character of the outfit, he could not enlist through normal channels, so one morning at daybreak he walked to Stanton's home and camped on the doorstep until the secretary appeared. At first Stanton hesitated to accept the lad, but as he drove him in his carriage to the War Department he agreed to provide young Ellet with the necessary orders and passports. Mrs. Ellet, who worried constantly about her husband, could not dissuade her son from leaving home, and on his nineteenth birthday, June 1, 1862, Charles Rivers Ellet reached Cairo and joined his father on the day before the battle off Memphis.[4]

Armed only with navy revolvers, Charlie Ellet's detail slogged across the peninsula, hailed a boat, and was rowed to *Hartford*, Farragut's flagship. No one believed that a flotilla of unarmed rams had run the river from Memphis, so the men were taken for spies with forged credentials. For three hours, while waiting for Farragut to return from an inspection of his squadron, naval officers questioned the odd party who came out of the swamps dressed in civilian clothes.

---

3. Ellet to Stanton, June 25, 1862, *ORA*, XV, 498; Log of *Hartford*, *ORN*, XVIII, 727.
4. *Washington, D.C., Evening Star*, March 12, 1892.

Delighted to see an emissary from the upper fleet, Farragut asked Medical Cadet Ellet if he would take a communication back to Davis, as he intended to run the batteries and needed coal. He also asked that Davis bring down his ironclads so the two squadrons, working together, could batter Vicksburg into submission. Ellet dutifully recrossed the peninsula and on the morning of June 26 delivered the message to his uncle, who promptly dispatched *Fulton* with a communication for Davis.[5]

Brigadier General Thomas Williams had accompanied Farragut with 3,300 troops, ostensibly to garrison Vicksburg after it fell, but finding the city's defenses too strong, he refused to land his troops on the east bank. Instead, he landed them on the western shore, and on earlier advice from Major General Benjamin F. Butler, began employing thousands of blacks to dig a canal across the peninsula close to the point where Ellet crossed. While the laborers dug, *Lioness* backed into the cut on the western side of the peninsula and attempted to divert the current into the canal by churning its paddle wheel to gouge out an opening, but the effort failed.[6]

At Farragut's suggestion, Alfred Ellet detached *Monarch* and *Lancaster* for a reconnaissance up the Yazoo River, which, of course, Davis knew nothing about. Giving Medical Cadet Ellet command of *Lancaster*, Alfred Ellet led the two rams sixty-five miles up the river to Liverpool Landing, a point twenty-five miles below Yazoo City, before reaching an obstruction supported by a four-gun battery. Just below the battery lay three gunboats—*General Van Dorn, Polk,* and *Livingston*—refugees from the Memphis disaster. As the Ellets approached the raft obstructing the river, the enemy set fire to the two boats, which swung into *Van Dorn* and set it on fire. Fearing everything would be blown to pieces by explosives carried in the boats, crews cut the lines and set the burning vessels adrift. *Monarch* and *Lancaster* backed and took refuge behind a point just as *Van Dorn* exploded. "I was obliged to leave the river to escape the conflagration," Alfred Ellet reported, no doubt amazed that the enemy would torch vessels supported by shore batteries when confronted by two unarmed rams. At Yazoo City,

5. Farragut to Ellet, Ellet to Stanton, Ellet to Davis, June 25, 1862, *ORN*, XVIII, 584, 585; Log of *Lancaster, ibid.,* XXIII, 242.

6. Thomas Williams, "Letters of General Thomas Williams, 1862," *American Historical Review*, XIV (January 1909), 322–23; Wyble to Crandall, November 1, 1904, Wyble Letters, Civil War Collection, MHS.

twenty-five miles above the raft, lay the unfinished *Arkansas,* but Ellet knew he could not reach it.[7]

Believing that Farragut's message had been carried to Davis by *Fulton,* the two Ellets returned to the peninsula to rejoin the rams. Much to their surprise, Farragut had passed the Vicksburg batteries on the morning of June 28 with eight vessels and anxiously waited for the arrival of Davis. Puzzled by the upper squadron's absence, Alfred Ellet communicated with Farragut and agreed to carry another message to Davis. By then Farragut realized that Vicksburg could not be carried without reinforcements from Halleck, and having explained his situation by letter to the general, he hoped that fresh regiments arriving at Memphis would be diverted to Vicksburg.[8]

This time Ellet assigned his nephew to the important mission of locating Davis, delivering Farragut's message by way of *Lancaster,* and then proceeding up to Memphis—which had become a new staging area for Halleck's army—to await the expected infantry reinforcements and guide them to Vicksburg.[9]

On the morning of June 29, *Lancster* loaded coal and started for Memphis. The following afternoon, Medical Cadet Ellet found Davis's squadron idling at Island No. 75, near Ozark, Arkansas, and delivered Farragut's meassage. Though Davis had already received Farragut's first message, he said nothing to Ellet. Instead, he handed Ellet a bundle of correspondence and told him to carry it to Memphis. Thinking that a large number of transports might be awaiting his arrival, Charlie Ellet hurried up to the city. Arriving very late on July 1, he waited until morning before going ashore, only to discover a large force disembarking with orders to join Halleck, not Farragut. Unwilling to lose time away from the action, Ellet refueled and started back downriver, accompanied by *Switzerland* and the repaired *Queen of the West.*[10]

On the morning of July 1, Davis's fleet approached Young's Point, led by *Benton, Carondelet, Cincinnati,* and *Louisville* and followed by four river steamers, three tugs, four mortar boats, and two hospital

---

7. Ellet to Stanton, June 28, 1862, *ORA,* XV, 515; Log of *Lancaster, ORN,* XXIII, 243; Montgomery's Report, July 1, 1862, in Crandall Papers, Crandall Collection, ISHL.

8. Farragut to Davis, Ellet to Stanton, June 28, 1862, *ORN,* XVIII, 589, 591.

9. Log of *Lancaster, ibid.,* XXIII, 243; Farragut to Halleck, June 28, 1862, *ibid.,* XVIII, 590.

10. Log of *Lancaster, ibid.,* XXIII, 243; Davis to Welles, June 28, Davis to Grant, June 30, 1862, *ibid.,* XVIII, 592, 593.

boats. Farragut took one look at Davis's squat, ugly ironclads and likened them to giant "turtles"—an abomination when compared to his graceful steam sloops. He knew Davis personally and wanted little time lost formulating a plan of action. Below Vicksburg, Commander David Dixon Porter's mortar schooners had been shelling the city's batteries since June 27 with little effect. Davis agreed to place his mortar scows above Vicksburg, and on July 2 the two commands joined in a bombardment that continued for several days. Both flag officers waited to hear from Halleck, who on July 3 messaged Farragut that the "scattered and weakened condition" of his enormous army rendered it "impossible . . . to detatch any troops to cooperate with you at Vicksburg." Halleck had done virtually nothing since occupying Corinth, and his reply was more incredible than either Farragut or Davis realized.[11]

Stanton understood the importance of capturing Vicksburg and urged Halleck to send a force to support the navy. The general refused but promised to give the matter his full attention. Instead, he detached troops and sent them to Alabama, Tennessee, and Kentucky. By then President Lincoln had decided that Halleck would make a better administrator than a field commander and recalled him to Washington as general in chief. Stanton, much relieved, reinstalled Grant as commander of the Army of the Tennessee and the Army of the Mississippi.

While convolutions in Washington occupied the first seventeen days of July, Farragut and Davis waited at Vicksburg for developments. Major General William T. Sherman arrived at Memphis with no orders concerning the situation at Vicksburg. Halleck's aversion to advancing deeper into Mississippi had bought precious time for the Confederates. By the time Grant resumed command of the Army of the Tennessee, General Braxton Bragg had replaced Beauregard and was concentrating a large force at Chattanooga, Major General Earl Van Dorn had reinforced Vicksburg, and Union major general Samuel R. Curtis's advance west of the Mississippi had been checked in central Arkansas.[12]

The Ram Fleet bided its time by running dispatches to Memphis

11. Farragut to Mrs. Farragut, July 2, 1862, Farragut Papers, USNAM; Loyall Farragut, *The Life of David Glasgow Farragut, First Admiral of the U.S. Navy* (New York, 1879), 282–83; Davis to Welles, July 2, Halleck to Farragut, July 3, 1862, Log of *Hartford,* and Alden's Journal, *ORN,* XVIII, 593, 593, 728, 751–52; *Grenada (Miss.) Appeal,* June 27, 1862.

12. Stanton to Halleck, June 23, July 14, Halleck to Stanton, June 28, July 15, 1862, *ORA,* XV, 494, 515, 518–19; General Orders No. 56 and 62, July 17, 21, 1862, *ibid.,* XVII, Pt. 2, pp. 102, 110–11.

and making reconnaissances up the Yazoo to watch for the ironclad ram *Arkansas*. Roving enemy cavalry and bands of guerrillas infested the banks of the river, and for the protection of his boats, Alfred Ellet obtained ten brass 12-pounders from Captain James C. Brooks, the fleet's quartermaster. Most of the crew had never fired a weapon larger than a musket, so Ellet asked for seventy-five men from the 7th Illinois Infantry. A few days later, while Ellet reconnoitered the Yazoo, a well-hidden band of guerrillas opened on the rams with muskets. Much to the enemy's surprise, Ellet scattered them with a few rounds of canister.[13]

Ellet preferred working with Farragut, who seemed more determined than Davis to fight the enemy. When invited to *Hartford* for a conference, he appreciated being included and eagerly complied. Informants warned Farragut to watch out for *Arkansas,* stating it would soon come down the Yazoo to attack the Union fleet, but the most recent reconnaissance placed the ironclad above the raft at Liverpool, twenty-five miles below Yazoo City. With Davis's concurrence, Farragut wanted regular patrols established of one ram, one ironclad, and one gunboat, the latter to carry a detachment of General Williams's infantry to chase away guerrillas infesting the Yazoo's heavily forested banks.[14]

Ellet agreed to detail *Queen of the West,* his fastest ram, and directed Lieutenant James M. Hunter to follow the gunboat *Tyler,* commanded by Lieutenant William Gwin, "as far as the officer of that boat deems it necessary to proceed for the purposes he has in view." Ellet did not clearly explain the "purpose in view" but told the lieutenant to keep his men under cover and the guns loaded. "If the *Tyler* should be attacked by the [*Arkansas*]," Ellet added, "dash [*Queen*] to her rescue . . . sinking the enemy's boat by running full speed right head on into her." Hunter, an infantry officer from the 63rd Illinois Infantry, had commanded the *Queen's* marines during the Battle of Memphis. After taking the vessel to Cairo for repairs, he brought it down to the mouth of the Yazoo and remained in command. The mission, from Hunter's perspective, had all the trappings of another harmless reconnaissance.[15]

At 4:30 A.M. on July 15, *Tyler* stopped alongside *Lancaster* to bor-

13. Sketch of Ram Fleet History, James C. Brooks Papers, Crandall Collection, ISHL; Ellet to Stanton, July 13, 1862, *ORA,* XV, 521–22.

14. Farragut to Ellet, July 14, 1862, *ORN,* XVIII, 636; Farragut to Welles, July 17, Davis to Welles, July 16, 1862, *ibid.,* XIX, 4, 6.

15. Ellet's Report, June 9, 1862, *ibid.,* XXIII, 131; Ellet to Hunter, July 14, 1862, Crandall Papers, Crandall Collection, ISHL.

row Richard Smith, a pilot familiar with the Yazoo's bars. Minutes later, Commander Walke's *Carondelet* fell into line about a mile behind *Tyler,* and *Queen of the West* took a position about a quarter of a mile behind *Carondelet.* Together, the trio departed for the Yazoo.

A morning mist lay on the river, limiting visibility, but it promised to be a clear day. As the two gunboats and the ram passed through the fleet, few of Farragut's or Davis's vessels showed any smoke. Responding to a shortage of coal, they had banked their fires, and some had shut down to clean their boilers. Despite reports that *Arkansas* had started down the Yazoo, neither Farragut nor Davis expected trouble from the ironclad.[16]

For several weeks, Lieutenant Isaac Newton Brown, commanding *Arkansas,* had been rushing its completion with full knowledge that the Union fleet dallied above Vicksburg with its fires down. By most standards, *Arkansas* ranked among the Confederacy's smaller ironclad rams— being 165 feet in length, 35 feet abeam, 11 ½ feet deep, and cladded with 4 ½ inches of railroad iron. The ram carried a crew of two hundred men and ten guns—two 8-inch columbiads forward, two 6-inch guns astern, and a 9-inch, 6-inch, and 32-pounder in each broadside.[17]

On the morning of July 15, Lieutenant Brown brought the ram down to the mouth of Old River and through the early-morning mist spotted the smoke of three steamers making their way upstream. Seeing they were headed toward him, he opened fire on *Tyler* with his two forward columbiads and ordered steam. A shot from *Tyler* shattered *Arkansas'* pilothouse, mortally wounding the pilot and injuring both Brown and a second pilot. *Arkansas* replied, tearing *Tyler's* deck to pieces. After losing thirteen killed, thirty-four wounded, and ten missing, Gwin backed down, firing as he retreated. *Queen of the West* abruptly came about and skeddadled downriver, leaving *Carondelet* to face the enemy alone. Walke exchanged shots until *Arkansas* approached at close quarters. Having fired seventy-three rounds and seeing his projectiles carom harmlessly off the ironclad's shield, he swung about after having his steerage disabled and drifted against the bank, losing four killed, eighteen wounded, and eight missing or drowned.[18]

16. Log of *Lancaster, ORN,* XXIII, 244; Crandall and Newell, *Ram Fleet,* 98.
17. Wilson Papers, *ORN,* XIX, 132.
18. *Ibid.;* Walke's Report, July 15, Gwin's Report, July 15, 16, 1862, *ibid.,* IX, 37–39, 41–42; Williams's Report, July 17, 1862, *ibid.,* XV, 31–32. See also Isaac N. Brown, "The Confederate Gun-Boat *Arkansas,*" *B&L,* III, 572–75.

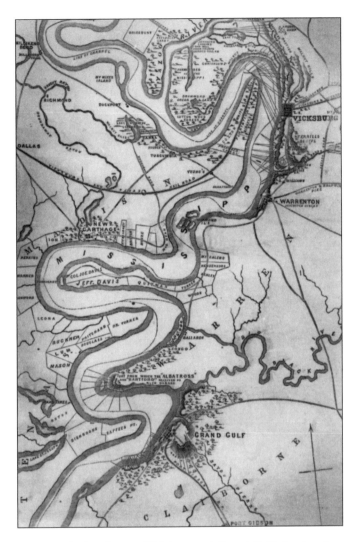

*The Mississippi River between Vicksburg and Grand Gulf, showing the area
and range of river covered by Confederate guns*

Reprinted from *Harper's Weekly*, May 23, 1863.
Courtesy of Louisiana State University Libraries

Lieutenant Gwin, who had no business fighting an ironclad with
his flimsy wooden gunboat, nonetheless attempted to delay the descent of *Arkansas,* well aware that Davis and Farragut were not prepared for battle. When *Queen of the West* fled, Gwin hoped the ram

would get to the fleets and spread the alarm, but he was miffed at Hunter, who "behaved in the most cowardly and dastardly manner, basely deserting us without making an attempt to bring his vessel into action." Without ever having to explain why, Hunter acted contrary to Ellet's order by not "running full speed right head on into her." Instead, he hurried down to *Hartford* to communicate with Farragut but created more confusion by rounding to off the flagship's stern, fouling the anchor chains, and swinging helplessly alongside.[19]

When Farragut first heard the heavy gunfire, he thought it came from Davis's two gunboats engaging enemy artillery hidden in the woods along the river. Not until *Queen* came abeam and the sound drew nearer did he discover the true cause, but by then it was too late. Men went to quarters, but the vessels lay anchored on both sides of the river and few could maneuver. *Arkansas* steered right down the middle of the fleet, firing each gun as it passed. USS *Richmond* managed to get off a full broadside as the ironclad passed, as did most every vessel. By the time *Arkansas* rounded De Soto Point, its engine output had dropped to about one mile an hour.[20]

All of Ellet's rams lay anchored above the fleet, and when *Arkansas* hove in sight, Medical Cadet Ellet cut *Lancaster*'s cable, rounded to, and nosed upstream to give the ironclad "a little of our kind of warfare." After he got the ram under way, a 64-pound ball struck its bulwarks, plowed through eight feet of coal, nipped three feet off the steam drum, scalded the engine crew, and instantly crippled the vessel. The pilot, Sylvester Doss, stuck to the wheel until he dropped from a wound, but by then eight balls had shattered the wheelhouse. The Union fleet, attempting to fire into *Arkansas,* overshot, buried three balls in *Lancaster*'s port timbers, and sprayed the vessel with several hundred pounds of grape and canister. Neither Ellet nor Captain Thomas O'Reilly bothered to count the casualties, but of forty-three blacks serving on the ram, only six survived the fight. After *Arkansas* passed through the fleet and made its way to Vicksburg, *Queen of the West* came out from under *Hartford* and towed *Lancaster* back to its mooring.[21]

19. Gwin's Report, July 16, 1862, Log of *Tyler, ORN,* XIX, 39, 41; Ellet to Hunter, July 14, 1862, Crandall Papers, Crandall Collection, ISHL.

20. Farragut to Welles, July 17, 1862, Log of *Hartford,* Alden's Journal, *ORN,* XIX, 4, 705, 747–48; I. N. Brown, "The Confederate Gun-Boat *Arkansas,*" *B&L,* III, 575–76.

21. Sylvester Doss to Crandall, October 8, 1894, Sylvester Doss Letters, Civil War Collection, MHS; Log of *Lancaster, ORN,* XXIII, 244.

Two months and three weeks had passed since Farragut won the great distinction of having captured New Orleans, and now he experienced the pain of writing Welles: "It is with deep mortification that I announce to the Department that, notwithstanding my prediction to the contrary, the ironclad ram *Arkansas* has at length made her appearance and took us all by surprise." Having observed the ram's injuries as it passed through the fleet, Farragut wanted to attack it immediately, using Davis's ironclads to occupy Vicksburg's batteries. Davis argued that the rusty, unpainted *Arkansas* would be difficult to find in the dark, and declared a daylight attack too risky. He tried to calm Farragut's fears by proclaiming *Arkansas* "comparatively harmless, where she was," but Farragut knew better and finally coaxed Davis into supporting a night attack. Three ships of Farragut's squadron and all his mortars still lay below the city, and he could not allow *Arkansas* to make repairs and go on another rampage. He considered the vessels of his squadron posted below Vicksburg—as well as every other vessel all the way down to the Gulf—in imminent danger. Like it or not, he had to sink the ironclad, with or without Davis's help.[22]

That evening Farragut led all eight of his vessels and the former Confederate ram *Sumter* downriver, letting the flimsier gunboats hug the far shore while using his heavy sloops to probe for *Arkansas* under the brow of the city. Davis sent three ironclads down to De Soto Point to engage Vicksburg's batteries during Farragut's descent, but he started late. "We got down very well," Farragut reported, "but . . . it was so late when we got off the town that there was nothing to be seen of the ram." *Hartford* had literally hugged the shore looking for it, but, Farragut added, "We could see nothing but the flash of the enemy's guns to fire at."

In the morning Farragut communicated with Davis, this time suggesting that Commander William D. "Dirty Bill" Porter take a crack at *Arkansas* with the ironclad *Essex*. "He could do it, I think, without risk," Farragut declared. Aware that Davis had nothing to lose by leaving the worry of *Arkansas* to himself, Farragut grumbled, "While this is on my mind I can not rest."[23]

When Welles received word of *Arkansas'* attack, he wrote Farragut: "I need not say to you that the escape of this vessel and the attending

22. Farragut's Report, July 17, Farragut to Davis, July 15, Davis to Farragut, July 17, 1862, Bell's Diary, *ORN,* XIX, 4, 7–8, 9–10, 713.
23. Farragut's Order, July 15, Farragut to Davis, July 16, 1862, *ibid.,* 8–9.

circumstances have been the cause of serious mortification to the Department and the country. It is an absolute necessity that the neglect or apparent neglect of the squadron on that occasion . . . be wiped out by the capture or destruction of the *Arkansas,* which I trust will have been effected before this reaches you."[24]

For Farragut, the whole matter had reached the stage of personal exasperation. Davis controlled the ironclads but would promise nothing, and Farragut's wooden vessels were no match against the Confederate ram. His daily dispatches to the upper fleet urging action were all deflected because Davis preferred to wait for *Arkansas* to come out from under the protective batteries of Vicksburg. Farragut knew if that happened, his wooden gunboats would bear the attack while Davis's squadron remained safely above Vicksburg and out of the action. Because of existing navy protocol, Farragut could not issue orders to Davis—he could only plead. Had he known that on July 16 Congress passed an act creating the grade of rear admiral—he being at the top of a list of four and Davis not on it at all—he might have exercised the leverage he needed to goad his fellow flag officer into action. Instead, he glumly promised Welles, "Be assured, sir . . . that I shall leave no stone unturned to destroy her."[25]

The Ram Fleet had been injured by *Arkansas,* and Alfred Ellet "chafed" under the failure of his boats to meet the emergency. With his personal prestige wounded by *Queen*'s dismal performance, he sought vindication and called upon Davis with a plan to attack *Arkansas* where she lay at the Vicksburg wharf. If Davis would order his gunboats to engage the batteries, Ellet would volunteer to personally take one of his best rams, "strike the rebel, and if possible, destroy her." Davis did not reply, but when Farragut learned of Ellet's proposal he walked across the peninsula for a conference. Farragut would not have Ellet engage in an act of suicide without the support of both fleets, but he used Ellet's proposal as a catalyst for inducing Davis to participate. After a long conference on *Benton,* Davis finally agreed to a joint attack at 3 A.M. on July 22. He concurred with Farragut that Commander Porter should lead the attack in the ironclad *Essex,* but he also condescended to let Ellet—since the lieutenant colonel insisted—send along a ram, though he doubted it would do much good. Farragut's part in

24. Welles to Farragut, August 2, 1862, *ibid.,* 5.

25. Farragut to Welles, July 17, Farragut to Davis, July 16, Davis to Farragut, July 17, 1862, Faxon to Farragut, March 13, 1863, *ibid.,* 4, 8, 9, 661; *Navy Register,* 1862, NA.

the attack would be small, mainly because his squadron would have to work upriver. He would open with mortars the moment *Essex* rounded the upper bend, bring forward his heavy sloops of war to engage the lower batteries, and send the captured ram *Sumter* upriver to aid the attack on *Arkansas.*[26]

Like most of Davis's operations, it started late. *Benton, Cincinnati,* and *Louisville* did not reach the bend at De Soto Point until dawn, and "Dirty Bill" Porter, though he tried to ram *Arkansas,* merely grazed the vessel and accidentally drove *Essex* ashore. For ten minutes the ironclad drew heavy enemy fire while Porter scrambled to back off the mud. *Sumter*'s captain, Lieutenant Henry Erben, changed his mind about joining the attack and inexplicably withdrew.[27]

Only Alfred Ellet's unarmored ram remained in the action. For the hazardous enterprise he had chosen *Queen of the West,* a vessel ten to twelve years old but the best in his command. For his crew he accepted only twenty-eight handpicked volunteers. Some of *Queen*'s engineers had been placed under arrest for insubordination, and those who volunteered came from *Switzerland* and *Mingo.* His second-in-command, Lieutenant Hunter, had fled from *Arkansas* during its attack on the Union fleet, and now Hunter wanted redemption. Four privates from the 63rd Illinois volunteered as sharpshooters, and a pilot transferred from *Switzerland.* The rest of the crew came from *Queen.*[28]

Taking a position behind *Essex,* Ellet waited in the dim glow of early dawn for Porter to lead the attack. As *Essex* started the descent, *Queen* followed, but as Ellet approached *Benton* he saw Davis on deck waving his arms and shouting "Good luck! Good luck!" Ellet could not hear over the swish of the paddle wheels and thought Davis said, "Go back! Go back!" so he ordered the engines reversed and paused to speak with Davis. The time lost placed *Queen* too far astern of *Essex* for a united attack.[29]

Under way again, Ellet hugged the west shore, giving himself

26. Farragut to Bell, July 21, Ellet to Davis, July 20, 1862, Bell's Diary, *ORN,* XIX, 16, 44, 714.

27. Porter to Davis, July 22, August 1, Farragut to Welles, September 11, 1862, *ibid.,* 50, 60, 61, 62–63.

28. David S. Taylor to Crandall, April 10, 1895, David S. Taylor Letters, Civil War Collection, MHS; Hunter's Roster of Officers, Crew and Volunteers, [July 22, 1862], Crandall Papers, Crandall Collection, ISHL.

29. Alfred Ellet, "Ram Fleet," MS in Ellet Papers, UM; newsclip in Crandall Papers, Crandall Collection, ISHL.

enough room to build momentum with the current. When *Essex* struck *Arkansas*, Ellet was still far back but coming fast. With the huge paddles of the side-wheeler fiercely slapping the water, *Queen* closed rapidly. Swinging into midstream, Ellet came hard aport and sliced diagonally across the river to where *Arkansas* lay. Then he noticed *Essex* aground near the ram and wondered why.

Arkansas had been moored with her stern ashore and her bow presented to the river—a position well chosen to protect her vulnerable beam from a ram attack. To get a better angle on *Arkansas'* beam, Ellet maneuvered in midstream. He lost headway and then struck an eddy, causing him to veer at a much sharper angle and lose more momentum. *Arkansas* opened with a broadside, jarring *Queen* seconds before impact. Ellet delivered a hard but glancing blow that sheared several lengths of plating off the ironclad's sides. *Queen* bounded sharply away, the momentum carrying her ashore. Ellet struggled to reverse the engines and paddle back into the current. By the time he got the vessel under way, *Essex* had dropped downriver and joined Farragut, and Davis's gunboats had withdrawn around the point.

"I had the undivided attention of all the enemy's batteries and sharpshooters," Ellet reported, and "the consequences were that the *Queen* was completely riddled with balls and very much damaged." Because of the small crew, he lost not a man, and by the grace of good fortune, the boilers and engines continued to deliver full power. Ellet had to make a choice—to follow *Essex* to the safety of Farragut's fleet, or risk being slowed by the current and sunk attempting to return upriver. Not wanting to be separated from his command, he chose the latter, but he also wanted to confront Davis, who had withdrawn the gunboats after covering the retreat of *Essex*. It seemed to Ellet that Davis counted the rams as nothing, and he wasted no time expressing his irritation to Stanton.[30]

Porter, rather than Ellet, missed an opportunity to capture the ironclad by withdrawing. That morning, only six of *Arkansas'* officers and twenty-eight of the crew were on board to serve the guns—too few to fight more than two guns at one time. Instead of coming head-on, Porter swerved, and at the moment of collision the guns of both vessels were muzzle to muzzle. Each fired broadsides, but Porter's first shot drove plates through the forward starboard port, and the second

30. A. Ellet, "Ram Fleet," Ellet Papers, UM; Ellet to Stanton, July 23, 1862, *ORN*, XIX, 45–47; Sketch of Ram Fleet History, Brooks Papers, Crandall Collection, ISHL.

shot entered the vessel and passed diagonally through the gun deck, killing eight and wounding six. "Had Porter . . . thrown fifty men on our upper deck," Lieutenant Brown admitted, "he might have made fast to us with a hawser, and with little additional loss might have taken the *Arkansas* and her twenty men and officers."

The time lapse between the attacks of *Essex* and *Queen* gave *Arkansas'* diminished crew time to reload, and at fifty feet they fired all three broadside guns into the ram. Brown claimed that *Queen* butted *Arkansas* "so gently that we hardly felt the shock" and caromed off the beam, running ashore under the muzzles of the ironclad's loaded stern guns. Had Brown been on board at the time, he might not have described the "bump" as "gentle," as the engine's connecting rods absorbed the shock. Projectiles from *Arkansas* struck *Queen*'s immense mound of baled hay, and Brown doubted if the charges did much damage. After Ellet disengaged and started upriver, *Arkansas* fired a port broadside, and as *Queen* crossed the enemy's bow the two forward guns opened, sending solid shot through the ram's upperworks. Once again *Arkansas* got the better of the fight, and though Ellet tried his level best to end the ironclad's career, its construction was such that no amount of "butting" would have sunk her. General Van Dorn, viewing the action from Vicksburg, wired Jefferson Davis, "An attempt was made this morning by two ironclad rams to sink the *Arkansas*. The failure so complete that it was almost ridiculous." The statement made good rhetoric, but for *Arkansas* the morning attack by Porter and Ellet marked the beginning of the end for the Confederate ironclad.[31]

Ridiculous or not, Ellet's effort came in a modified riverboat carrying two small fieldpieces while dozens of gunboats armed and fitted for war stood by and watched. To a navy man trained in the profession of war, Ellet's attack on *Arkansas* could be classed as either an irrational act of foolishness or a gallant act of heroism. Flag Officer Davis, whose aloof attitude toward the Ram Fleet had been endemic, admitted that Ellet "struck the *Arkansas* with sufficient force to do her some injury . . . [and] behaved on this, as on previous occasions, with great gallantry." Without physical evidence, neither Davis nor Van Dorn could judge whether or not *Arkansas* had been injured. Nor could Stanton,

---

31. I. N. Brown, "The Confederate Gun-Boat *Arkansas*," *B&L*, III, 577–78; Van Dorn to Davis, July 22, 1862, *ORN*, XIX, 74; A. Ellet, "Ram Fleet," Ellet Papers, UM.

who after reading battle reports praised Ellet for "great gallantry" and recommended that he be raised to the rank of brigadier general.[32]

The feeble effort to sink *Arkansas* ultimately became an embarrassment for Davis. "Dirty Bill" Porter released a grossly distorted battle report to the newspapers in which he condemned Davis and Farragut for failing to support him and claimed to have been under fire "for upward of an hour." Not once did Porter mention the role of *Queen of the West* or his own failure to support the ram. Enormously annoyed by Porter's news release, Davis charged him with misstating the facts and "calumniating his commander in chief." In an effort to better understand the sequence of events, Welles asked Farragut—in whom he placed great trust—to submit his version of the fight. The admiral corroborated Davis's account, but added a new twist, writing, "Commander Porter desired the whole credit, and said [*Arkansas*] was his special prize, and he would therefore take or destroy her." Porter wanted all the glory, Farragut explained, and waved off every gunboat attempting to come to his assistance.[33]

During Welles's fact-finding exercise, Porter read Ellet's battle report and attempted to refute it by sending Stanton an "inexcusable letter, abusive of the military." By then "there was much censure for the apparent want of co-operation and the seeming willingness to let Ellet fall a victim of his own bravery." Embarrassed by the whole episode—and not entirely happy with Davis's role—Welles reproved "Dirty Bill" Porter and sent him before the Retiring Board. "Like all the Porters," Welles confided to his diary, "he is a courageous, daring, troublesome, reckless officer."[34]

Davis may not have been thorough in his communications with Porter prior to the July 22 attack, and this would not be inconsistent with his usual indifference toward the Ram Fleet. Whether Porter can be believed is questionable, but some months later he wrote Ellet, "I was unaware, at the time of the *Essex* running the Vicksburg batteries and attacking the *Arkansas* . . . that it had been contemplated for any of your rams to butt her. It was not mentioned in the programme arranged on the *Benton* between the flag officers and myself on the 21st, or rely on it, you should have had all the support I or the *Essex*

32. Stanton to Ellet, July 31, Davis's Report, July 23, 1862, *ORN,* XIX, 47–48, 49.

33. Davis to Welles, September 12, Porter's Report, August 1, Farragut to Welles, September 11, 1862, *ibid.,* 59–60, 60–62, 62–63.

34. Crandall and Newell, *Ram Fleet,* 109; Welles, *Diary,* I, 145.

could have given." Porter closed by adding that if he had known *Queen of the West* was to have followed him, he would have "waited for you until the *Arkansas* had sunk my ship, or I had destroyed her."[35]

After the attack, Farragut received orders from Welles to withdraw from the falling river and return the squadron to New Orleans. On reaching the Crescent City he prepared a final report on the *Arkansas* affair. "This was a daring act on the part of [Lieutenant] Colonel Ellet," he wrote, "and one from which both Flag-Officer Davis and myself tried to deter him."[36]

Though Ellet considered *Queen*'s attack a failure, something happened that morning that radically altered the career of *Arkansas*. The beginning of the end came when Major General John C. Breckinridge's two divisions departed from Camp Moore, Louisiana, on July 30 to recapture Baton Rouge. *Essex* and two of Farragut's gunboats lay off the city, so General Van Dorn ordered Lieutenant Henry K. Stevens to take *Arkansas* below and support Breckinridge's attack, scheduled for August 5. *Arkansas* departed from Vicksburg on the morning of August 3 and "steamed leisurely down the river." Fifteen miles above Baton Rouge a connecting rod on the starboard engine cracked and failed. The crew repaired the damage as well as possible and at 8 P.M. on August 4 declared the engine ready. At 4 A.M. Breckinridge advanced. Stevens heard the firing and steamed down to a point about five miles above Baton Rouge, where he cleared for action. The rod broke again, forcing Stevens to ease alongshore and lose another day repairing the engine. Breckinridge attacked, killed General Williams, and drove the Union troops from their camp near Magnolia Cemetery. Harassed by fire from Farragut's gunboats, Breckinridge pulled back and spent the afternoon waiting for *Arkansas*. Farragut's gunboats sighted the ram off Free Negro Point, and at 9 A.M. on August 6, *Essex* steamed upriver and prepared to open fire. Stevens ordered steam and cleared for action. After running about three hundred yards the port engine failed, forcing Stevens to run the vessel ashore. He ordered charges set and escaped with his men. An hour later the dreaded *Arkansas* blew up.[37]

35. Quoted from Crandall and Newell, *Ram Fleet,* 110.

36. Farragut to Welles, July 29, 1862, *ORN,* XIX, 96.

37. Breckinridge's Report, September 30, 1862, *ORA,* XV, 76–77; Van Dorn to Seddon, August 7, 1862, John A. Wilson Papers and Charles Read's Statement, *ORN,* XIX, 130, 131, 135.

Had one connecting rod broken, the failure could have been attributed to misalignment, but since both failed, a case can be made that disarrangement of the engine occurred when, on the morning of July 22, *Queen of the West* "butted" the ironclad. But for Ellet and the crew of *Queen,* there would be no prize money for destroying the ram. Commander Porter took the credit, writing deceitfully, "I steamed up the river and at 10 A.M. attacked the rebel ram *Arkansas* and blew her up. There is not now a fragment of her left." Months passed before the circumstances of the ram's destruction surfaced. Years later a member of *Arkansas'* crew admitted to Charles D. Falconer, who served on *Queen,* that the "butt" had sealed the ram's fate by disarranging the alignment of the vessel's engines.[38]

For Flag Officer Davis, all hopes of capturing Vicksburg during the summer of 1862 came to an end, and on August 1 he retired to Helena. By doing so, he reopened to the enemy a four-hundred-mile stretch of river from below Helena to Port Hudson. He erroneously believed his withdrawal would "not involve any loss of control over the river" because there was no high ground between Vicksburg and Memphis on which the enemy could build batteries. To his diary he complained, "There is no knowing what crazy project the Department may have in view or how this move of mine may be taken. But it seems to me that the only course now to be pursued is to yield to the climate and postpone any further action at Vicksburg till the fever season is over." He got his answer from the department in the next mail when Welles appointed him chief of the Bureau of Navigation, but Davis remained in command of the Mississippi Squadron until Welles could decide upon a replacement.[39]

Ellet had his own problems, and to solve them, something had to be done about the organization of the Ram Fleet—and for help, he had no choice but to confer with Stanton.

38. Porter to Farragut, August 6, 1862, *ORN,* XIX, 117; Ellet to Stanton, September 28, 1862, *ORA,* XVII, Pt. 2, pp. 241–42; Falconer to Crandall, June 18, 1909, Charles D. Falconer Letters, Crandall Collection, ISHL.

39. Davis to Welles, July 16, 1862, Mississippi Squadron Letters, NA; Davis's Diary, and Welles to Davis, August 1, 1862, *ORN,* XXIII, 271–72, 278.

*Colonel Charles Ellet, Jr., who organized the Ram Fleet
but never wished to own a uniform*
Reprinted from *Battles and Leaders of the Civil War*

*Charles Ellet, Jr., going from one department of the government to another
in an effort to promote his ram scheme*

Reprinted from *Harper's Weekly,* December 28, 1861.
Courtesy of Louisiana State University Libraries

Secretary of War Edwin M. Stanton, who authorized the Ram Fleet and later financed the Mississippi Marine Brigade

Courtesy of the U.S. Army Military History Institute

Brigadier General Alfred W. Ellet, who succeeded his brother as commander of the Ram Fleet and organized the Mississippi Marine Brigade

Courtesy of the U.S. Army Military History Institute

Colonel Charles Rivers Ellet, the reckless and courageous nineteen-year-old son of Charles Ellet, Jr.

Courtesy of the U.S. Naval Historical Center, Washington, D.C.

Flag Officer Charles H. Davis, who disliked the presence of the Ram Fleet and maintained a contentious relationship with the Ellets

Courtesy U.S. Naval Historical Center, Washington, D.C.

The Ram Fleet, with Monarch *in foreground, followed by*
Queen of the West, Lioness, *and* Switzerland

Reprinted from *Harper's Weekly,* July 5, 1862. Courtesy
of Louisiana State University Libraries

Action off Memphis—Queen of the West *(left) in disabled condition;*
Monarch *(center) running down* Beauregard; *Confederate rams*
General Price *and* Little Rebel *in background*

Reprinted from *Harper's Weekly,* June 28, 1862.
Courtesy of Louisiana State University Libraries

Action off Memphis—view in foreground shows the capture of the Confederate ram Sumter *and* Beauregard *sinking. View in background shows the Union fleet chasing the ram* Van Dorn *while Jeff. Thompson (right) blows up.*

Reprinted from *Harper's Weekly,* June 28, 1862.
Courtesy of Louisiana State University Libraries

Colonel Ellet sends Lioness with his son on board to demand the surrender of Memphis.

Reprinted from *Harper's Weekly,* June 28, 1862.
Courtesy of Louisiana State University Libraries

Medical Cadet Charles Rivers Ellet hoisting the Stars and Stripes
over the post office at Memphis

Reprinted from *Harper's Weekly*, July 5, 1862.
Courtesy of Louisiana State University Libraries

CHAPTER 4

ADMIRAL PORTER TAKES COMMAND

Alfred Ellet had no alternative but to accompany the withdrawal from Vicksburg and bring his problems with him. In the attack on *Arkansas, Queen of the West* had been so badly riddled with shot that Ellet had to send it to Cairo for repairs. Other rams reported their crews debilitated by malarial fevers. To keep the boats in service, Ellet replaced the sick with black freedmen, but he needed experienced hands. His situation worsened when Lieutenant Currie, the reliable officer of the ram *Mingo*, received promotion to captain in the 59th Illinois and rejoined his regiment in the field—not because he wanted to leave the Ram Fleet, but because Charles Ellet had not been authorized by Stanton to borrow officers above the rank of lieutenant. Losing veteran officers like Currie distressed Alfred Ellet because so many others—mainly civilian volunteers—had deserted their posts or disobeyed orders. "I have the parties under arrest," Ellet advised Stanton. "Where shall I send them?" The irregular nature of the Ram Fleet prevented Ellet from bringing anyone to trial through the judicial systems of the army or the navy. Halleck, answering for Stanton, advised Ellet to send the prisoners to Memphis for trial, and when the rams no longer needed the blacks, to turn them over to General Sherman.[1]

Ellet had other pressing concerns, and he dispatched Captain James C. Brooks, his quartermaster, to discuss them with the secretary. He wanted authorization to build and add a swift, well-armed ironclad to his fleet—a vessel that would put his squadron on par with the navy's. He then suggested reducing the number of rams in his fleet in exchange for stronger vessels. He also wanted Stanton's commitment on the distribution of prize money, a pledge Charles Ellet had made to the crews as an inducement to enlist. Stanton remembered the promise. "It is a new one in the War Department," he replied, promising "to look into it." He admitted that the Ram Fleet was entitled to "a large portion of the prizes at Memphis" but supposed that "the Navy will claim it all."

Frustrated by numerous desertions, Ellet urgently needed to replace about half his force, and to attract volunteers he wanted to establish new rates of pay. Because of the irregular nature of his command, he wanted to offer wages slightly higher than standard military pay. He hoped to recruit new crews from commercial riverboats, where wartime wages had escalated well above soldiers' pay. On August 16 Captain Brooks promised to send "Mr. Stanton's decision before I leave here," but months passed before Ellet received an answer. After Major General George B. McClellan's disaster on the Virginia peninsula and General Pope's defeat at Second Manassas, Stanton gave little thought to Ellet's problems.[2]

The withdrawal of Farragut and Davis from Vicksburg reopened the Mississippi to Confederate commerce from Helena, Arkansas, to Port Hudson, Louisiana. Transports bearing troops and riverboats laden with arms, ammunition, and supplies once more ventured down the Red and Yazoo Rivers and tied to landings at Vicksburg, Grand Gulf, and Port Hudson. In mid-August Ellet learned of the increased

1. Ellet's Report, July 23, 1862, *ORN*, XIX, 46; Ellet to Stanton, July 25, 1862, *ORA*, XV, 529–30; Halleck to Ellet, August 1, 1862, *ibid.*, XVII, Pt. 2, p. 149; Clarke, ed., *Warfare along the Mississippi*, 55.

2. Ellet to Brooks, August 1, Ellet to Stanton, September 28, 1862, *ORA*, XVII, Pt. 2, pp. 148–49, 241–42; Brooks to Ellet, August 16, 1862, in Crandall and Newell, *Ram Fleet*, 120–21.

trade, and while waiting for answers from Stanton, he pieced together enough volunteers to man four rams—*Lioness, Monarch, Sampson,* and *Switzerland*—and joined Lieutenant Commander Phelps in a reconnaissance up the Yazoo River. Colonel Charles R. Woods of the 76th Ohio joined the expedition with two regiments of infantry, a company of cavalry, and a section of light artillery. Phelps intended to reconnoiter in force and brought the ironclads *Benton* and *Mound City,* the gunboat *General Bragg,* and Ellet's four rams.[3]

At 2 A.M. on August 18, the expedition crawled along at night and came upon the riverboat *Fairplay,* lying about twenty river miles above Vicksburg at Milliken's Bend. Phelps detailed a boarding party who clambered aboard and discovered the cabins filled with muskets, ammunition, howitzers, and small arms—all scheduled to be unloaded at daylight and transported by land to Little Rock. Colonel Woods took a detachment ashore, captured the encampment of the 31st Louisiana Infantry, and chased the regiment nine miles inland. Ellet participated as a bystander during the operation, but for the first time since assuming command of the Ram Fleet, he witnessed a well-coordinated affair involving both branches of the service.

On August 19 Phelps started up the Yazoo with *Benton* and *Mound City,* Ellet occupying the rear with *Monarch, Lioness,* and *Sampson* and carrying a detachment of one hundred infantry under Major Peter Dister of the 58th Ohio. At Snyder's Bluff, twenty miles up the Yazoo, an unfinished Confederate battery opened on the flotilla. Phelps drove the workers away with his 8- and 9-inch Dahlgrens, capturing six guns and 7,000 pounds of powder. Before blowing up the fort, he transferred a 24-pounder brass howitzer and a 12-pounder brass fieldpiece to *Monarch.*

On the morning of August 20, Phelps continued up the Yazoo and took the squadron to the mouth of the Sunflower. Finding the river low, he detached two shallow-draft rams—*Lioness* and *Sampson*—and sent them upstream under Lieutenant Crandall. Four miles below Lake George, the rams encountered shoal water and stopped. Crandall scanned the lake and noticed "a number of fine gunboats," but being unable to ascend farther, he returned to the squadron and reported the enemy entrapped by low water but perfectly safe. Phelps returned to the mouth of the Yazoo and detached *General Bragg* and *Monarch*

---

3. Phelps's Report, August 22, 1862, *ORN,* XXIII, 296.

to keep an eye on Vicksburg. Ellet returned to Helena where he found his nephew Charlie waiting with the repaired *Lancaster*. Charlie wanted action, so Ellet sent him downriver to join *Monarch* off the Yazoo.

For the first time since the formation of the Ram Fleet, Ellet found working with the navy an unexpected pleasure. Prior to witnessing the attack of the Ram Fleet at Memphis, Phelps had been quite critical of the independent outfit—one he considered unnecessary and inappropriate—and though he still had doubts about its usefulness, he expressed his "high appreciation of the hearty and zealous cooperation of all engaged" and gave special praise to Ellet. Both officers made an important observation. Moving a strike force of infantry and cavalry from place to place by boat made good tactical sense.[4]

In the weeks that followed, guerrilla activity increased, and barely a day passed without an incident occurring on one side of the river or the other. Down the deep, muddy river, transports carried Union reinforcements and munitions needed for strengthening and equipping both branches of the service. From St. Louis to Vicksburg stretched eight hundred miles of waterway, wandering snake-like over treacherous shoals and through tortuous bends, passing directly through territory where bands of cavalry—some not attached to any particular unit—wandered the banks and waited in ambush. The attacks became so prevalent that no number of gunboats sufficed to bring them to an end, and the lightly armed rams presented tantalizing targets for batteries hidden in the woods and supported by sharpshooters. When a ram was attacked, a few rounds from its brass fieldpieces usually scattered the bushwhackers, but the enemy always fired first and caused the greatest damage. Being constantly on guard kept the crews skittish, and if the hazards became too great, men simply deserted and returned to civilian occupations.[5]

On September 19, while convoying two army transports from Milliken's Bend to Helena, Medical Cadet Ellet learned from a fugitive black that seven hundred grayclads with three fieldpieces waited in ambush at the bend above Bolivar, Mississippi. He lashed both transports to *Queen of the West* and moved all his guns to starboard. He then posted sharpshooters behind bales of hay and cotton layered on *Queen*'s deck. The enemy had spread out along the bank, and the fight

---

4. Phelps to Foote, May 28, Phelps's Report, June 9, August 23, 1862, *ibid.*, 109, 135, 296–97; Ellet's Report, August 26, 1862, *ORA*, XIII, 244–45.

5. Clarke, ed., *Warfare along the Mississippi*, 56.

lasted twenty minutes. Canister and roundshot riddled *Queen*, but Lieutenant Charles M. Callahan replied with the ram's fieldpieces and kept up a steady fire until the vessels passed out of range. Ellet expected more trouble at the next bend, but the sharp firefight at Bolivar discouraged the bushwhackers from pursuing the vessels upriver. Alfred Ellet used the skirmish to remind Stanton that his remedy for eliminating guerrilla attacks had not been addressed.[6]

Ellet never felt constrained by army or navy rules and regulations, nor by their traditional usages, and being an enterprising individual, he looked for new ways to conduct warfare along the Mississippi. To pursue and disperse guerrillas, he envisioned a riverine force of mounted men capable of moving quickly from place to place—one independent of army commands and naval operations. He suggested such a force to Stanton, who at the moment was so consumed by General Robert E. Lee's invasion of Maryland that he had no time to consider Ellet's suggestion.[7]

Leaving *Queen of the West, Lancaster,* and *Sampson* under the command of his nineteen-year-old nephew, Ellet took the rest of the fleet to Cairo for repairs. Before departing from Helena he considered disposing of his stern-wheelers—*Mingo, Lioness,* and *Fulton*—chiefly to rid himself of "worthless parties" and retain the most reliable boatmen for duty on his four best rams. Later, when Stanton refused to add an ironclad to the Ram Fleet, Ellet would change his mind and only dispose of *Mingo*. In the meantime, he waited for answers from the War Department. Two issues bothered him most. "I am sorry the secretary seems inclined to ignore the question of prize money," Ellet wrote Captain Brooks, his quartermaster. On the other matter, he warned that if Stanton decided "to transfer the Ram Fleet over to the navy, it will promptly close my services. . . . I never will permit myself to be made subject to Davis, after what has occurred between us."[8]

Ellet waited a month before pestering Stanton with the same proposals. All he wanted was an answer. His request for an ironclad ram had been ignored, and having learned from informants that the enemy had started to construct more gunboats at Yazoo City, he now asked the secretary for permission to build at least two ironclads. He argued

---

6. Ellet to Stanton, October 14, Charles R. Ellet to Alfred Ellet, September 20, 1862, *ORN*, XXIII, 365–66.

7. Crandall and Newell, *Ram Fleet*, 126.

8. Ellet to Brooks, August 30, 1862, Alfred W. Ellet Papers, Crandall Collection, ISHL.

that if *Queen* had been an ironclad ram when it butted *Arkansas* at Vicksburg, the enemy vessel "would never again have left her anchorage." Two weeks later he tried again to communicate with the secretary. Then, after failing to obtain a leave to visit Stanton in Washington, Ellet asked Captain Brooks to go to the War Department and speak with the secretary directly. In addition to ironclads, he wanted officers of higher rank to command his rams, and a second-in-command— preferably his nephew, nineteen-year-old Charlie Ellet. He also asked that Captain Asgill Conner's company of the 18th Illinois be detached for service with the Ram Fleet, and that Sergeant Bartlett, Corporal Edward C. Ellet, and Private E. W. Sutherland all be promoted to lieutenant for gallant conduct.[9]

Other delays frustrated Ellet. Half his fleet had been detained at Mound City for repairs while the shipyards worked on Grant's transports. He began to wonder if Stanton had lost interest in the Ram Fleet, and when he learned that Davis had been recalled to Washington and would be replaced by Acting Rear Admiral David Dixon Porter, he decided to quit bothering the secretary and become more active. "My boats are now all in good repair," he wrote, "and I shall resume my efforts to break up these bands [of guerrillas] immediately."[10]

Ellet expressed no surprise at Davis's removal, but he knew Porter only by reputation. He also knew that William D. Porter, the deposed commander of *Essex,* was the brother of the new admiral. This made Ellet circumspect and a trifle uneasy, though he would have preferred almost anyone other than Davis. He also found it curious that Porter had been elevated from commander to acting rear admiral, skipping two grades in a service that traditionally respected seniority, but he had no problem requesting the promotion of his nephew from medical cadet to colonel.

Now forty-nine, Porter had joined the navy in 1829. He had criticized its administration for many years, and like his brother, always seemed to be involved in a controversy. Because of the marvelous fighting reputation of his father during the War of 1812, he still had many friends and sup-

9. Ellet to Stanton, September 28, 1862, *ORA,* XVII, Pt. 2, pp. 241–42; Halleck to Grant, September 18, 1862, *ORN,* XXIII, 362; Ellet to Stanton, October 7, 12, 1862, Alfred Ellet Papers, Crandall Collection, ISHL; Ellet to Stanton, November 4, 1862, Ellet Papers, DUL.

10. Ellet to Stanton, October 14, 1862, *ORA,* XVII, Pt. 2, p. 277; Welles to Porter, October 1, 1862, *ORN,* XXIII, 388.

porters in the Navy Department. Though Secretary Welles did not entirely trust Porter, he recognized the admiral's outstanding leadership abilities and his "great energy." Despite Porter's "excessive and sometimes over-scrupulous ambition," Welles classified him as "brave and daring like all his family," but in the back of his mind he wondered how, "with this mixture of good and bad traits," he would succeed.[11]

Porter had already established himself as a fighter, having commanded the Mortar Flotilla during Farragut's attack on Forts Jackson and St. Philip. He had also brought the mortars to Vicksburg and was on the opposite side of the peninsula when Ellet and Davis met Farragut's squadron above the city. Porter, however, had never crossed the peninsula to meet Ellet, so they did not know each other. Ellet naturally wondered what to expect of the new admiral. For the answer, he would not have long to wait.[12]

On October 2 the War Department transferred all its gunboats to the navy. Ellet enjoyed some comfort when he learned the orders of transfer did not include the Ram Fleet. For two weeks he looked for Porter's arrival, wondering whether his small command had simply been forgotten or whether word would come to disband what his detractors called a "costly and troublesome unit."

Porter arrived at Cairo on October 15 and found Ellet waiting to see him. The admiral knew very little about the Ram Fleet, since Welles had never mentioned it. He looked at the rams and decided he could use them for their speed because his cumbersome ironclads could make only a few knots against the current, but he showed no enthusiasm for retaining the boats' intemperate volunteers and suggested they be replaced by navy men. Since Ellet had heard nothing from Stanton, he thought it safer to attach himself to Porter than be left without a command. Puzzled by the situation, Porter wrote Welles, "Colonel Ellet has received no instructions yet to turn [the Ram Fleet] over to the Navy, and is now waiting to be informed what he shall do with them. He is desirous to remain in command of them, but I do not see how that can be done very well without interfering with the naval organization." A week later, after another conversation with Ellet, Porter endorsed the concept of organizing a mobile marine brigade to disperse guerrillas ambushing military transports, and since

11. Welles, *Diary,* I, 157–58.

12. Chester G. Hearn, *Admiral David Dixon Porter: The Civil War Years* (Annapolis, 1996), 81–137 *passim.*

Ellet had conceived the idea, he saw no reason why the colonel should not head it—as long as the unit reported to the navy.[13]

Welles assured Porter that the act turning the War Department's gunboats over to the navy "included" the Ram Fleet, and he so informed Stanton. As Welles's note landed on Stanton's desk, Ellet's correspondence asking for ranking officers, Captain Conner's company, and the promotion of Medical Cadet Ellet to second-in-command reached the War Department. The sudden realization that his personal navy had just been expropriated by Welles jolted Stanton into action, and on October 20 he wrote Ellet, "The Ram fleet was not included in the transfer of the Gunboat fleet to the Navy Department. You will retain command . . . until further orders."[14]

While waiting for Stanton and Welles to reach a decision on the Ram Fleet, Ellet remained in touch with Porter and renewed his suggestion that a mobile marine force be established to deal with guerrilla attacks along the rivers. Porter's commanders verified that the bothersome bands were everywhere, and the admiral could see the wisdom of organizing a force to eliminate the problem. On October 25 he advised Ellet that while he did not have the authority to issue orders to the Ram Fleet, he strongly suggested that if the Confederate ironclads at Yazoo City should come down the river, he would want the rams to be ready to engage them. As a sweetener, he added that he had endorsed the idea of forming a "Naval Brigade" and intended to place Ellet at the head of it. Content with his new relationship with the navy, Ellet promised full cooperation as long as he "retain[ed] command of the Ram Fleet."[15]

Welles's attempt to blend the Ram Fleet into Porter's Mississippi Squadron spurred Stanton into action to save it for himself—after all, he had financed it. On November 1 Lincoln signed Ellet's appointment to brigadier general, and Stanton invited his new brigade commander to Washington for a conference. The secretary intended to move with speed. He reviewed all of Ellet's unanswered correspondence, and when the general arrived Stanton quickly got to the point, conferring on issues

13. General Orders No. 150, October 2, Davis to Welles, October 15, Welles's Office Records, Vol. 191½, p. 3, Porter to Welles, October 18, 21, 1862, *ORN*, XXIII, 388, 395, 396, 418, 428–29; Porter, *Naval History*, 331–33.

14. Welles's Endorsement, n.d., Stanton to Ellet, October 20, Welles to Stanton, October 21, 1862, *ORN*, XXIII, 418, 427, 429.

15. Porter to Welles, October 21, Welles to Stanton, October 31, Ellet to Porter, October 21, Porter to Ellet, October 25, 1862, *ibid.*, 428–29, 429–30, 445.

concerning the appointment of subordinate officers and discussing plans for organizing a marine brigade. If Stanton voiced any reservations about elevating a nineteen-year-old medical cadet to the rank of colonel, he left no record of it. Porter endorsed the promotion, which pleased the general, and Charlie Ellet obtained the post of second-in-command. The general promptly placed his nephew in charge of the Ram Fleet and obtained approval from Stanton to elevate Assistant Surgeon John W. Lawrence to major to act as second-in-command to Charlie.[16]

By placing his nephew in command of the Ram Fleet, the general freed himself to concentrate on forming the Mississippi Marine Brigade—a unit approved by Stanton and recommended by Admiral Porter. Ellet asked that Captain Warren D. Crandall, who had commanded *Lioness*, be made assistant adjutant general and reassigned from the 59th Illinois. Stanton agreed and Crandall proceeded to St. Louis, where he set up a recruiting office at 109 North 3rd Street. On November 14 the XIV Army Corps detached Captain George Currie, who had commanded *Mingo,* from the 59th Illinois and ordered him to rejoin the Ram Fleet at Cairo. Ellet also got another wish. General Halleck transferred Captain Conner's Company K, 18th Illinois, to the Ram Fleet, though Ellet planned to retain the unit for the Mississippi Marine Brigade. During Ellet's meetings with Stanton, his thoughts had not been fully developed, but he intended to commission seven more boats and recruit 1,500 men, dividing them into artillery, infantry, and cavalry. Ellet believed his new brigade, combined with the Ram Fleet, would bring to an end guerrilla activity anywhere it sprouted along the rivers.[17]

On November 7—about the time Stanton concluded the reorganization of the Ram Fleet—President Lincoln grew tired of the bickering between Stanton and Welles and issued an executive order, directing that "Brigadier-General Ellet report to Rear-Admiral Porter for instructions, and act under his direction until otherwise ordered by the War Department." Assistant Navy Secretary Gustavus Vasa Fox, a per-

16. Stanton to Ellet, November 6, 1862, Alfred Ellet Papers, Crandall Collection, ISHL; Porter to Welles, October 21, 1862, Ellet Papers, NA, also in Porter Papers, NA; *Washington, D.C., Evening Star,* March 12, 1892; Ellet to Stanton, November 4, 1862, Ellet Papers, DUL.

17. Special Order No. 16, November 14, 1862, George E. Currie Letters, CMU; Halleck to Ellet, December 11, 1862, *ORA,* XVII, Pt. 2, p. 398; Welles's Office Records, Vol. 191½, p. 3, in *ORN,* XXIII, 396.

sonal friend of Porter's, attended the cabinet meeting debate over the control of Ellet's command. When it ended, he elatedly wrote Porter, "Stanton lost his temper, so we beat him. The cool man always wins." On the subject of the Mississippi Marine Brigade, Fox added, "The proposition is yours, and I presume the War Department will fit it out and act in good faith. I must confess to [having] little confidence . . . in this arrangement. If Ellet is the right kind of man all will go well, and if it goes wrong, Stanton will say it arose from placing him under a Navy officer [because] Western people have no confidence in them." Whether General Ellet, who had little military experience, could manage a brigade scattered over the Mississippi watershed while his young nephew commanded the Ram Fleet had yet to be determined, but on November 8 this peculiar arrangement received the approval of the president and for the moment satisfied Porter. Ellet expressed his disapproval to his sister, writing, "Porter is a fool bent on empire building."[18]

Porter often recalled his long years of labor as a midshipman in the peacetime navy of the 1830s. Like Charles Rivers Ellet, he, too, had been a bright young man with plenty of spunk and a touch of rashness. The difference was that now, with a war in progress, Ellet had already made colonel after only a few months of service.

The admiral preferred officers full of youthful vitality and willing to take risks—not the "old fogies" who had saturated the captain's list at the beginning of the war—but he had no inkling what to expect from this youngster who had leapt from medical cadet to colonel. Knowing that Charlie Ellet had never received a minute of formal naval training, Porter wondered how the young man would respond to orders. With General Ellet devoted to organizing the Mississippi Marine Brigade at St. Louis, Porter dispatched a message to the colonel asking how soon the Ram Fleet could be made ready for service. "I expect a rise in the rivers soon," Porter declared, "and propose ascending the Arkansas." Ellet promptly replied that *Lancaster* and *Fulton* would be "ready for immediate service" and *Lioness* available as soon as it was coaled. Charlie Ellet passed his first test—a simple one of responding to orders

18. Lincoln's Executive Order, November 7, 1862, Roy P. Basler, ed., *The Collected Works of Abraham Lincoln* (9 vols.; New Brunswick, N.J., 1953), V, 490; Stanton to Ellet, November 8, 1862, *ORN*, XXIII, 468, 469; Robert Means Thompson and Richard Wainwright, eds., *The Confidential Correspondence of Gustavus Vasa Fox, Asst. Secretary of the Navy, 1861–1865* (2 vols.; Freeport, N.Y., 1972), II, 147–48 [hereinafter cited as *Fox Correspondence*]; Ellet to sister Mary, December 16, 1862, Ellet Papers, UM.

from someone other than his uncle—but General Grant was facing a command dilemma and Porter's plans were about to be changed.[19]

Ever anxious to open the entire Mississippi, the president authorized Major General John A. McClernand to raise regiments in the Old Northwest and create a command large enough to operate against Vicksburg. Lincoln believed that Grant had been rescued by McClernand at Shiloh, and he operated under the misconception that a separate army commanded by the Illinois politician might bring the war in the west to an end.

Grant learned of the scheme through the newspapers, and realizing that McClernand ranked Sherman, he immediately sought ways to shelter his favorite corps commander from the onerous duty of reporting to a political general. He quickly contrived a plan to grab McClernand's fresh regiments as they dribbled into Memphis, place them temporarily under Sherman's command, and conduct a quick campaign requiring a complicated pincer movement to capture Vicksburg, thereby nullifying any need for McClernand. In early December Grant conferred with Porter, as he needed the cooperation of the navy. This meeting changed Porter's plans for utilizing the Ram Fleet on the Arkansas River.[20]

To concentrate on organizing and recruiting the Mississippi Marine Brigade, General Ellet remained in St. Louis and virtually extricated himself from the Ram Fleet, leaving the day-to-day affairs entirely in the hands of his nephew. With Grant conspiring with Sherman and Porter to capture Vicksburg, General Ellet was about to miss an opportunity to participate in a badly bungled campaign. Grant put the plan of attack together so rapidly that it is doubtful whether any of the Ellets knew of it. The responsibility for the Ram Fleet's participation devolved upon Charles Rivers Ellet, and how well the nineteen-year-old colonel could command a flotilla composed of weakly armed vessels and unreliable crews was about to be tested.[21]

19. *Fox Correspondence,* II, 91–92; Porter to Ellet, November 28, Ellet to Porter, November 29, 1862, *ORN,* XXIII, 513.

20. William T. Sherman, *Memoirs of General W. T. Sherman* (2 vols.; New York, 1875), I, 309–10; Porter to Fox, November 12, 1862, *Fox Correspondence,* II, 150; Grant to Halleck, December 5, *ORA,* XVII, Pt. 1, p. 472; Halleck to Grant, December 7, Sherman to Porter, December 8, Grant to McClernand, December 18, 1862, *ibid.,* Pt. 2, pp. 473, 392, 425.

21. Ellet to Halleck, December 13, 1862, *ORN,* XXIII, 630; Grant to Halleck, December 5, 1862, *ORA,* XVII, Pt. 1, p. 472; Sherman to Porter, December 8, 1862, *ibid.,* Pt. 2, p. 392; Ulysses S. Grant, *Personal Memoirs of U. S. Grant* (2 vols.; New York, 1885–86), I, 26–31.

CHAPTER 5

CHARLIE ELLET AND THE ADMIRAL

Early in December, Colonel Charles Rivers Ellet's problems had just begun. Instead of the original nine vessels fitted out by his father, he now had only seven. Uncle Alfred had decommissioned *Sampson* and *Mingo* and turned them over to the army quartermaster to be used as transports. To the plus side, the other seven vessels had been recently repaired, and by December 4 some of the original captains had been replaced by more reliable men promoted to higher grades:

Switzerland, Major John W. Sutherland
Queen of the West, Captain Edwin W. Sutherland
Monarch, Lieutenant Eleazer W. Bartlett
Lancaster, Lieutenant William F. Warren
Lioness, First Master Thomas O'Reilly
T. D. Horner, First Master Robert Dalzell
Dick Fulton, First Master S. Cadman[1]

1. Ellet to Porter, December 4, 1862, *ORN*, XXIII, 532.

For a while, General Ellet attempted to coordinate the operation of the fleet from St. Louis, but the transfer of orders back and forth between Cairo and St. Louis became cumbersome. Though Colonel Ellet responded to Porter's orders promptly, he did not always follow them exactly, and the admiral lacked confidence in the former medical cadet. On November 24 Porter ordered him to send *Switzerland* and *Queen of the West* downriver to join Captain Walke's squadron. The colonel detached the rams but remained at Cairo. With Grant's movement on Vicksburg about to commence, Porter preferred to have General Ellet on hand and advised him that the navy was moving down to Memphis and to leave St. Louis and "come on and follow down with the rams." The general declared himself too busy with recruiting problems. From Ellet's reply, Porter concluded that the Mississippi Marine Brigade, from lack of interest emanating from the War Department, might not "from present appearances" be raised at all.[2]

During October and November, Confederates had been busy mining Yazoo River channels, fortifying the banks, and patrolling the shore with infantry and cavalry. Informants also warned of more rams under construction at Yazoo City. Captain Walke's small detachment at the mouth of the Yazoo observed increased activity but felt powerless to stop it. For Sherman's attack on the bluffs of Vicksburg to succeed, the lower section of the river must be cleared of torpedoes and the enemy's batteries neutralized. Without waiting for General Ellet, or issuing his directive through Colonel Ellet, Porter sent *Lioness* to the Yazoo with orders to report to Walke. By circumventing the colonel, Porter displayed his annoyance at the general's refusal to leave St. Louis and showed his reluctance to transmit orders through the general's young nephew. This nettled Charlie Ellet, who described himself as "diligently posting himself on military ways" and "submitted [to the snub] with good grace."[3]

Neither of the Ellets understood the involvement of the navy in Grant's campaign—nor the urgency—because Porter did not tell them. Sherman intended to run his transports into the Yazoo, ascend the bluffs northeast of Vicksburg, form a juncture with Grant—who in-

2. C. R. Ellet to A. W. Ellet, November 23, Ellet to Porter, November 26, Porter to C. R. Ellet, November 24, Porter to A. W. Ellet, December 11, Porter to Welles, December 12, 1862, *ibid.*, 503, 507, 502, 541, 543.

3. Walke to Porter, December 8, 13, Porter to O'Reilly, December 12, 1862, *ibid.*, 540, 546, 542; Crandall and Newell, *Ram Fleet,* 143.

tended to bring his force from Holly Springs to Jackson by an overland route—and assault the town from its weakly defended rear. Sherman's transports, however, could not be brought safely up the Yazoo until the navy removed the torpedoes. So on the morning of December 12, Walke, who had been recovering from malaria, detached the USS *Cairo*, Lieutenant Thomas O. Selfridge, the USS *Pittsburg*, Lieutenant William R. Hoel, and two tinclads, *Marmora* and *Signal*, as mine-sweepers. He also sent *Queen of the West* to give protection to the tinclads while they swept the channel.

During the trip up the Yazoo, the tinclads passed over a section of mines and came under fire from the enemy's sharpshooters. Selfridge, rushing into the action, strayed across two torpedoes that blew a hole through the forecastle near *Cairo*'s port forward gun. Selfridge ran the ironclad ashore and it settled in about twelve minutes, leaving its upperworks exposed. While *Marmora* and *Signal* circulated to search for other torpedoes, *Queen of the West* rescued *Cairo*'s crew, and when the ironclad slipped off the bank into deeper water, *Queen* butted and battered the chimneys and jackstaffs until *Cairo* could not be seen in her watery grave.[4]

The squadron returned to the mouth of the Yazoo and reported the loss of *Cairo* to Walke, who promptly dispatched *Marmora* to carry the bad news to Porter. With Sherman making final preparations for shipping his corps from Memphis and Helena to the Yazoo, Porter now faced the dual responsibility of securing good landing places for the army's transports and clearing the waterways of submerged mines—a task interrupted by the sinking of *Cairo* and one which the admiral did not want repeated. On December 20 he ordered Lieutenant Commander William Gwin to take the ironclad *Benton*, the gunboats *Lexington* and *Tyler*, the tinclads *Signal*, *Romeo*, and *Juliet*, and the rams *Queen of the West* and *Lioness* back up the river with instructions to stay there until all torpedoes had been removed and sites selected for landing Sherman's corps. Acting Ensign Symmes Browne of *Benton* approved of having the rams accompany the expedition be-

---

4. Walke's Report, Fentress's Report, Selfridge's Report, and Hoel's Report, December 13, Sutherland's Report, December 15, Ellet's Report, December 20, 1862, *ORN*, XXIII, 546–47, 548, 549–50, 550–51, 553–54, 554–55. See also Edwin Cole Bearss, *Hardluck Ironclad: The Sinking and Salvage of the "Cairo"* (Baton Rouge, 1980), 97–101, and Thomas O. Selfridge, Jr., *Memoirs of Thomas O. Selfridge, Jr., Rear Admiral, U.S.N.* (New York and London, 1924), 75.

cause each carried "two 12-lbr. brass pieces mounted on the upper deck, which were very effective on the high banks where we cannot reach the enemy."[5]

Reaching the Yazoo on December 23, Gwin found that Walke, still ailing with malaria, had already sent Lieutenant Commander John G. Walker back up the river to remove the torpedoes. Walke warned Gwin that Walker's detachment had met with frequent attacks from both sides of the river and encountered heavy resistance from batteries mounted on Drumgould's Bluff.

On the 24th Gwin met Walker's detachment descending the Yazoo and explained that Sherman's expeditionary force was en route to attack Vicksburg. Walker reported mysterious buoys off Lieutenant Colonel W. A. Johnson's plantation and the river heavily seeded with torpedoes downstream from Drumgould's Bluff. He agreed to remove them while Gwin staked out landing sites, but asked assistance in repelling grayclads firing from woods and canebrakes along both sides of the river. Gwin ordered Captain Sutherland to join Walker's squadron and deploy *Queen* to provide a covering fire.

During the ascent, *Queen of the West* crossed over a torpedo wire but could not stop to drag it up because of fierce musket fire from the nearby shore. Sutherland replied with his brass pieces, and Gwin's gunboats shelled the woods, enabling details to move about in yawls and begin the hazardous chore of snipping cables attached to torpedoes. *Queen of the West, Tyler,* and *Juliet* attempted to protect the dragging operation as cutter crews moved carefully upstream, but enemy resistance stiffened and the minesweepers never progressed farther than a few miles above Johnson's Landing. For three days the squadron remained at work, each morning discovering more torpedoes planted during the night, and each day facing another fusillade of fire from Rebels tucked behind trees and horse artillery roving the banks. Finally, on the afternoon of the 26th, Sherman's transports entered the Yazoo, and the men of *Queen of the West,* working with grappling hooks above the mouth of Chickasaw Bayou, sighted the convoy ascending the river. By then, Sutherland had consumed seventy-eight boxes of am-

5. Walke to Porter, December 13, Porter to Gwin, December 20, Walker to Walke, December 23, 570–71, 1862, *ORN,* XXIII, 555, 567–69; Sutherland to Ellet, January 4, 1863, *ORA,* XVII, Pt. 1, p. 664; John D. Milligan, ed., *From the Fresh Water Navy, 1861–64: The Letters of Acting Master's Mate Henry R. Browne and Acting Ensign Symmes Browne* (Annapolis, 1970), 125.

munition, but he doubted whether any of it caused harm to the enemy.[6]

On December 26 Sherman landed at Chickasaw Bayou, and on the 27th, when the Confederates slowed his advance, the general began looking for another approach to the enemy's flank. Once again Porter sent ironclads upriver, this time to feign an attack on Drumgould's Bluff while *Signal* and *Queen of the West* made a reconnaissance above Chickasaw Bayou. Lieutenant Commander Elias K. Owen led the mission, only to discover new batteries being mounted below the bluff. Undecided on what course of action to take, and because *Queen* had nearly exhausted its coal, Owen sent Captain Sutherland back to Porter to request new instructions.[7]

Porter wanted the river cleared to Drumgould's Bluff to enable Sherman to move out of the wetlands of the bayou and onto firmer ground farther up the Yazoo. On December 30, following the disastrous attack the previous morning, it became evident that the campaign would fail unless Sherman could flank the enemy. Porter called a meeting of his commanders to ask for suggestions. Colonel Charles Rivers Ellet presented a plan for clearing the Yazoo of torpedoes above Drumgould's Bluff. He suggested attaching a strong framework of sixty-five-foot spars to the bow of *Lioness,* strengthening it with heavy transverse and diagonal braces, and tying the lattices together with a thirty-five-foot crosspiece at the tips of the spars. With iron rods one and one-half inches in diameter and ten feet long driven through the crosspiece every few feet, the apparatus resembled a huge rake but with the rod tips bent to form a hook. Ellet believed the hooks would latch onto the cords connected to torpedoes and either explode the devices or rip them loose from their moorings. If the device exploded, it would be too far from the vessel to cause serious damage, and if the rake was destroyed, Ellet believed he could replace it quickly. With Porter's approval, the colonel set a crew to work building the apparatus, and on the morning of December 31 he began the work of fitting it to *Lioness.*

That night Porter and Sherman planned to sneak quietly upriver

---

6. Porter's Report, December 27, 1862, Log of *Benton, ORN,* XXIII, 572–73, 674–75; Sherman to Rawlins, January 3, Sutherland to Ellet, January 4, 1863, *ORA,* XVII, Pt. 1, pp. 606, 664. For an account of the navy's minesweeping operations, see Edwin Cole Bearss, *The Vicksburg Campaign* (3 vols.; Dayton, Ohio, 1985–86), I, 139–42, 164–65.

7. Owen to Porter, December 28, 1862, *ORN,* XXIII, 583, 584.

and make one final assault on the enemy's flank at Snyder's Bluff. When Porter learned the rake had been fitted to *Lioness,* he approached Ellet with a desperate proposal, asking if the colonel would be willing to blow up a raft the enemy had moored across the Yazoo at Snyder's Bluff. Ellet agreed and found thirty-five volunteers willing to accompany him. Porter sent up a barge containing fifteen barrels of gunpowder, and Ellet lashed it to *Lioness.* He took the point position at the head of the fleet and waited for orders to advance. That night, fog so thick that a person could see no farther than a few feet blanketed the river, making movement impossible, and in the morning rain fell in torrents, drenching the already slippery banks to such an extent that Sherman called off the attack. Ellet's mission of raking the river of torpedoes never materialized, and had *Lioness* reached the raft at Snyder's Bluff, the ram and its barge would probably have been blown to pieces by the batteries on the bluffs.[8]

Though Ellet never enjoyed the opportunity to test his ingenious apparatus under fire, Porter observed that the young colonel displayed a great deal more zeal "in carrying out his orders" than the admiral originally anticipated. Not only had Ellet acted with speed and energy, he also demonstrated great imagination in overcoming obstacles. In a letter to Welles, Porter gave the colonel high marks for daring, writing, "This desperate duty he took upon himself cheerfully, and no doubt would have performed it well had the opportunity occurred . . . or lost his life or his vessel." Though Welles had always been skeptical about the usefulness of the Ram Fleet, he probably felt much better when Porter added, "I have great confidence in the commander of the rams and those under him, and take this opportunity to state to the department how highly I appreciate [Colonel Ellet] and his associates." In the months ahead, Porter would find cause to remember this moment as the high-water mark in his relations with the Ellets.[9]

Grant's 45,000 men never made the march to Jackson, Mississippi, though a few of them got as far as Oxford. General Van Dorn destroyed Grant's Holly Springs supply depot, and Brigadier General Nathan Bedford Forrest wreaked havoc on the Mobile and Ohio Railroad supply

---

8. C. R. Ellet to A. W. Ellet, January 3, 1863, *ORA,* XVII, Pt. 1, pp. 662–63. For the account of Sherman's repulse at Chickasaw Bluffs, see Bearss, *The Vicksburg Campaign,* I, 143–229.

9. Porter to Welles, January 5, 1863, Ellet Papers, NA; Porter to Welles, January 3, 1863, *ORN,* XXIII, 604–5.

line linking Jackson, Tennessee, with Columbus and Hickman, Kentucky. After this catastrophe, Sherman's 32,000 men found it impossible to scale the rain-soaked cliffs at Walnut Hills without Grant's help. The campaign ended in an embarrassing defeat for the Union army, and Sherman, much to his dismay, had the awkward chore of explaining the disaster to General McClernand, who arrived at Milliken's Bend on the morning of January 2—just in time to witness Sherman's withdrawal.[10]

The daily rains and swamplike conditions impeded Sherman's attack, and because of the weather and topography of the area, he could never get his forces synchronized for a concerted assault on any point. An attack higher up the Yazoo would have been preferable, but difficulties in clearing the river of torpedoes made the effort treacherous. Constant attacks by infantry posted in the woods on both sides of the river created unsafe conditions for wire cutters attempting to clear the channel of torpedoes, and because neither the navy nor the Ram Fleet carried a large number of marines, there were never enough men to go ashore and drive away the enemy. General Alfred Ellet had anticipated difficulties of this type when he lobbied the War Department for authorization to form the Mississippi Marine Brigade. This deficiency forced Sherman to land his corps below Drumgould's Bluff—a poor choice for launching winter operations but, under the timetable established by Grant, his only choice. In the latter days of December 1862, General Ellet had not yet formed the Mississippi Marine Brigade, and because of recruiting difficulties, two months would pass before he did.[11]

On January 4, Major General McClernand assumed command of the military force assembled at Milliken's Bend. He reorganized Sherman's right wing of the Army of the Tennessee, and to wash away the stain of the fiasco at Vicksburg, he gave Brigadier General George W. Morgan command of the XIII Corps, Sherman command of the XV Corps, and renamed his newly acquired forces the Army of the Mississippi. With the formalities over, McClernand conferred with Sherman and Porter and decided to abandon further operations at Vicksburg. To keep the army busy, Sherman supported McClernand's expedition against Fort Hindman at Arkansas Post, a village about fifty miles up the Arkansas River. Porter agreed to supply gunboats for the

---

10. Grant to Halleck, December 26, Grant to Kelton, December 25, 1862, Sherman to Rawlins, January 3, Sherman to Halleck, January 5, 1863, *ORA,* XVII, Pt. 1, pp. 477–78, 610, 613.

11. Ellet to Porter, January 7, 1863, *ORN,* XXIV, 141.

operation, but it seemed strange to him that McClernand would divert his entire force to Arkansas Post when Lincoln, Stanton, Halleck, and Grant all expected him to operate against Vicksburg.[12]

Porter planned to take three ironclads, four gunboats, and seven tinclads on the expedition, leaving a few vessels at the mouth of the Yazoo together with the rams *Queen of the West* and *Lancaster*. At the admiral's request, Colonel Ellet transferred to *Monarch* with instructions to join the flotilla at the mouth of White River—not to participate in the fight, but to tow coal barges. *Switzerland* could not join the expedition because thirty-two of her crew had become stricken with smallpox. Ellet did not object to the ignominy of serving as a towboat so long as it brought him close to the action.[13]

On January 4 the squadron departed from Milliken's Bend. On the 8th the flotilla entered White River cutoff, and on the afternoon of the 9th it steamed into the Arkansas River. At dusk McClernand's transports tied to the bank four miles below Fort Hindman. Some of the infantry disembarked, cooked rations, and pitched tents. No reconnaissance had been ordered, and McClernand made the mistake of landing his force near a large swamp that had to be crossed to reach the enemy's flank.[14]

Early in the summer of 1862 Confederate engineers decided to build a fort on the Arkansas below Little Rock but needed to find a rise of ground above flood stage. The village of Arkansas Post, located on the north bank of the river, offered several topographical advantages compared with other sites. It was on elevated ground at a horseshoe bend, difficult to assault from the rear, and partially surrounded by swampy terrain. They named the earthwork Fort Hindman, and to cover every field of fire they made it a square, full-bastioned work with exterior scarps running one hundred yards in length into parapeted salient angles. The earthwork mounted fourteen guns, ranging from 8- and 9-inch columbiads in iron-armored casemates to 10-pounder Parrotts and 6-pounder smoothbores mounted on field carriages. On the night McClernand landed his 32,000 bluecoats, Brigadier General

12. General Order No. 1, January 4, 1863, *ORA*, XVII, Pt. 2, p. 534; Sherman to Rawlins, January 4, 1863, McClernand's Report, January 20, 1863, *ibid.*, Pt. 1, pp. 612, 705; Hearn, *Admiral Porter*, 165–67.

13. Porter to Ellet, January 4, 8, Ellet to Porter, January 7, 1863, *ORN*, XXIV, 98, 101, 138.

14. Porter to Welles, January 11, 1863, *ibid.*, 107; Hearn, *Admiral Porter*, 168–69.

Thomas J. Churchill, commanding Fort Hindman, counted about 5,000 men.[15]

McClernand launched his attack on January 10, but the men became mired in swamps. They never reached the fort and that night returned to their encampment by the river. The next morning they tried again, and once again Porter moved his ironclads up to the fort. This time the ironclads all but knocked Fort Hindman to pieces, disabling three heavy guns and forcing its surrender. During the action Ellet remained out of range, sitting atop the deck of his vessel where he could watch Porter's ironclads crumble the casemates of the fort. His instructions were to watch for enemy rams, and if any should appear, to advance through the fire and sink them, but no ram appeared and Ellet remained a spectator. By the time Sherman and Morgan got their corps through the swampy gullies and slashed timber, the fight on the river was over but muskets still rattled in the rear.

At 4 P.M., learning that Morgan's troops had been checked at the rifle pits in the rear, Porter called up Ellet. He sent *Monarch,* together with the tinclads *Rattler* and *Glide,* above the fort with men from the 7th Kentucky to cut off the garrison's escape and destroy any enemy vessels. Ten miles above Arkansas Post *Monarch* went aground after cutting off the enemy's retreat, but Ellet felt a twinge of chagrin when the tinclads passed and destroyed a ferry attempting to run off with forty grayclads.[16]

McClernand dispatched his battle report to Washington and claimed a great victory, barely mentioning the part played by the navy. While the general enjoyed his moment of triumph, Grant arrived at Memphis and learned that McClernand had removed his army from the vicinity of Vicksburg. Annoyed that McClernand had taken both corps to Arkansas Post, Grant called the action a "wild goose chase" and ordered all the troops back to Milliken's Bend.[17]

In the aftermath of the Arkansas Post expedition, Charlie Ellet complained to his uncle about the frustrations of command. *Horner*

15. McClernand's Report, January 20, Jenny's Report, n.d., 1863, *ORA,* XVII, Pt. 1, pp. 705, 760; Faust, *HTI,* 23.

16. Porter to Welles, January 11, 13, Porter's Congratulatory Order, n.d., and Ellet's Report, January 12, 1863, *ORN,* XXIV, 108, 119, 118, 120; C. R. Ellet to sister, January 13, 1863, Ellet Papers, UM; Hearn, *Admiral Porter,* 170–71.

17. McClernand's Report, January 20, 1863, *ORA,* XVII, Pt. 1, pp. 705–9; Sherman, *Memoirs,* I, 302–3; Grant to Halleck, January 11, 14, 1863, *ORN,* XXIV, 106, 165–66.

had arrived from Cairo with two Parrotts for *Monarch,* but they could not be mounted because they came without carriages. "Whose idea was this?" the colonel asked, urging his uncle to exercise more care and exertion in supplying guns. On the matter of coal he complained about being forced to borrow from the navy, and when receiving his own supply, howled that Porter "seized" it, forcing the rams to cut green timber or burn fence rails. "It appears to me," Charlie Ellet grumbled, "that our quartermasters have been very remiss in their duty. . . . It is going to tend still more to draw us into the Navy." On the subject of the Mississippi Marine Brigade—which had kept the general tied to his recruiting office at St. Louis—the colonel suggested that the "honor and profit . . . beckoning you on" should be turned over to others. "My own advice would be for you to come at once with every man you can raise. . . . Now is the time for the brigade to act; 400 men could be used with great effect down here." In closing, Colonel Ellet added, "send [my communications] to the Secretary of War, to show him that I have not failed to keep my promise to do my best."[18]

Two weeks later, on January 29, Porter wrote Alfred Ellet and, using words sounding much like those of the general's nephew, urged him to bring down three hundred men with horses to break up guerrilla warfare on the river. On February 18, having heard nothing from the general, he wrote once more, "When shall I see you and the brigade? What I would give to have you here now." Porter offered his full support and as an extra inducement added, "There is a glorious chance for you to operate in parties consisting of two or three thousand men and three or four fieldpieces." The admiral had become so frustrated waiting for Ellet that he offered to provide officers to boost the recruiting effort, and thinking he might stir a little family rivalry, declared, "I admire bravery whenever it is connected with judgment; that is the reason I shove your nephew into all kinds of scrapes."[19]

Alfred Ellet, however, did not want to abandon his recruiting chores until he had his full complement of men and a new flotilla of boats for the Mississippi Marine Brigade. He dallied at St. Louis, letting his nephew run the Ram Fleet and respond to Porter's orders. The admiral had tested the colonel's bravery and admired it. Now he would test the young man's judgment.

18. C. R. Ellet to A. W. Ellet, January 14, 1863, *ORN,* XXIV, 166.
19. Porter to Ellet, January 29, February 18, 1863, *ibid.,* 209, 424.

CHAPTER 6

THE CAPTURE OF
QUEEN OF THE WEST

On January 24 Porter returned with his squadron to the Vicksburg area and found eleven enemy steamers in the Yazoo bringing down supplies and provisions under the misconception that the Union navy had departed altogether. The presence of twenty-seven vessels of the Mississippi Squadron, which included the rams *Queen of the West, Monarch, Lioness, Lancaster,* and *Horner,* forced the supply boats to scurry back up the Yazoo. Porter had little expectation of catching the enemy steamers, but he worried that during his absence the enemy had raised the sunken *Cairo.* On the 27th he ordered *Queen of the West, Lancaster,* and the tinclad *Rattler* upriver to investigate. Aside from picket fire, the detail observed no activity in the vicinity of *Cairo*'s watery grave, so they returned and reported that the high stage of the river impeded any salvage operation.[1]

1. Porter's Report, January 16, 24, Porter to Smith and Smith's Report, January 27, 1863, *ORN,* XXIV, 172–73, 189, 203.

Another five riverboats laden with supplies for Vicksburg lay below the town, stopped by batteries of the 1st Illinois Light Artillery posted across De Soto Point near the cut of Williams's canal. On January 24 the steamer *City of Vicksburg* built up a head of steam, raced past the Illinois batteries, and reached the safety of Vicksburg with only slight damage. Two steamers followed but turned back when fired upon by the artillery. Annoyed that *City of Vicksburg* lay like a sitting duck at the landing, Porter asked Colonel Ellet if he thought a ram could destroy her. Always anxious to display a little recklessness, Ellet replied that *he* could.[2]

Because the mission involved great risks—and because young Ellet tended to flirt with death—Porter took the precaution of issuing carefully composed instructions. For the attack on *City of Vicksburg,* he selected *Queen of the West,* the fastest and most durable of Ellet's rams. He ordered the attack to be made at night, and to prevent a telltale show of sparks from flowing out the chimneys and warning the enemy, he instructed Ellet to have a large bed of coals burning under the boilers before he cast off. *Queen* was to be kept darkened except for the three tiny lights used for identification, and those were to be shielded until approaching the Union batteries posted at the lower end of the canal. Once under way, the ram was to proceed slowly and quietly around De Soto Point, hugging the right bank.

City of Vicksburg lay at the same moorage previously occupied by *Arkansas,* and even in the dark Ellet knew exactly where to find it. Porter emphasized the importance of keeping *Queen* concealed until rounding the point, at which time Ellet must then open his engines and steer the ram so as to strike *Vicksburg* twenty feet forward of her wheel. After stoving in the boat's port quarter, *Queen*'s gunners must be ready to fire shells into the stricken vessel's machinery and shoot flaming turpentine balls into its upperworks. Then, Porter warned, *Queen*'s crew "must look out for themselves" and press with full speed downriver. "If you get disabled," he added, "drift down until abreast of our batteries, and [a] small army steamer [*De Soto*] will go to your assistance." Knowing the mission had equal odds of turning into a disaster for Ellet and his crew, Porter asked General Grant to have men watching for the

2. Scates to Sherman, Sherman to McClernand, January 24, 1863, *ORA,* XXIV, Pt. 3, pp. 9–10.

ram and to advise him immediately should *City of Vicksburg* depart from her moorage prior to the attack.[3]

During the afternoon of February 1, Ellet called for volunteers, accepting in one instance a man from *Lancaster,* First Master James D. Thompson, who had recently been placed under arrest for insubordination. That evening, with every hand he could borrow, Ellet put the men to work arranging two thicknesses of cotton bales behind the bulwarks and around the decks. To safeguard the helmsman, he moved the wheel to a protected area behind the bulwarks. The work lasted late into the night, and the ram did not get under way until 4:30 A.M. The vessel started downstream, keeping close to the right bank, but the helmsman complained that he could not see to handle the wheel from its new location. Ellet lay to and lost more than hour returning the wheel to the pilothouse.[4]

By the time *Queen* rounded De Soto Point, the first rays of sunlight illuminated the river, and Ellet had lost the chance to slip past the Confederate batteries. Up on the bluffs the alarm brought men rushing to their guns, and a few minutes after *Queen* sprinted around the point, heavy guns opened on the ram. Running with the current, *Queen* moved so swiftly that only three shots struck her. Using the advantage of daylight, Ellet observed that if he followed Porter's heading, he would be on an oblique angle and only strike *Vicksburg* a glancing blow. Instead of crossing the river as he rounded the point, he kept to the west bank until nearly opposite the steamer, then helmed over hard to port and cut directly across.

Ellet experienced the same difficulties in striking *City of Vicksburg* as had "Dirty Bill" Porter in *Essex* and his uncle in *Queen* in their attempt to ram *Arkansas.* But now the river had reached flood stage and the eddies below the city flowed more swiftly. Ignoring fire from the batteries, Ellet headed straight for the forward port quarter of the steamer. At the moment of impact a powerful eddy caught *Queen*'s stern and swung it partially sideways. The ram lost momentum but managed to cut away *Vicksburg*'s cookhouse and demolish its cabin.

---

3. Porter to Ellet, February 1, 1863, *ibid.,* Pt. 1, p. 337; Porter to Grant, February 1, 1863, *ORN,* XXIV, 217.

4. Ellet to Porter, February 2, 1863, *ORN,* XXIV, 219, 220; Crandall and Newell, *Ram Fleet,* 155, 160. Crandall claims that Edwin W. Sutherland was not on board *Queen of the West* during the attack, but Ellet named him as present and as captain.

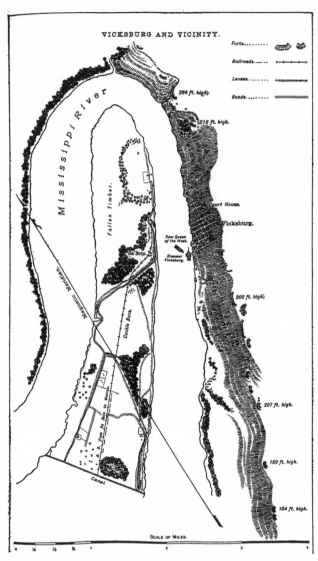

Sketch showing where Queen of the West *rammed* City of Vicksburg. *Colonel Currie located a 20-pounder Parrott near De Soto opposite Vicksburg and fired into the city during General Grant's siege in June and July of 1863.*

Reprinted from *ORN*

After failing to crush *Vicksburg*'s hull, Ellet signaled Sergeant James H. Campbell, the gun captain, to fire the piece filled with turpentine balls. *Vicksburg*'s upperworks burst into flame, but the Rebel crew went to work and quickly extinguished the blaze.

Shells from the city's batteries began to strike *Queen*, setting bales of cotton near the starboard wheel afire. A shot discharged from *Queen*'s forward gun sprayed sparks into cotton on another section of the deck and started a second fire. Flames spread rapidly, smoke filled the engine room, and the engineers spilled onto the deck. "I saw that if I attempted to run into the *City of Vicksburg* again," Ellet declared, "my boat would certainly be burned." After shouting for Captain Sutherland to take *Queen* downriver, Ellet put every available man to work knocking burning bales into the river and hosing down the fires. With shells dropping all about the vessel, Sutherland backed into the current and angled downriver toward the opposite shore.[5]

Queen's escape from under Vicksburg's batteries ranked among those rare episodes of miraculous deliverance. Hundreds of Vicksburg residents, gathered on the bluffs to watch the Confederate artillery sink the ram, admitted afterwards that its escape, "although a mortifying sight, was yet a magnificent one." With the vessel aflame, every gun on the hill fired plunging projectiles into the blazing ram. Twelve shots struck the boat, knocking the cabin to pieces, and two penetrated the hull just above the waterline. During its escape *Queen* passed two regiments of sharpshooters posted in rifle pits. The grayclads kept up a fierce fire but merely embedded their bullets in the ram's wall of cotton. When Ellet spotted *De Soto* waiting to provide assistance, he knew *Queen* was out of danger and ordered Sutherland to tie up at Biggs's plantation. After making a quick assessment of damage, he found no one seriously hurt and only one gun destroyed.[6]

Ellet believed his attack had failed, but *City of Vicksburg*'s crew inspected the boat and reported it sinking. The port wheel had been crushed by the blow, and a hole punched in the vessel's side. The crew kept the pumps going until enough empty barges could be lashed abeam to keep the boat afloat. Repair crews attempted to save the craft but were only able to salvage the machinery.[7]

5. C. R. Ellet to Porter, C. R. Ellet to A. W. Ellet, February 2, 1863, *ORN*, XXIV, 219–20.

6. *Mobile Advertiser*, February 3, 1863; Ellet to Porter, February 2, 1863, *ORN*, XXIV, 219–20.

7. Porter to Welles, February 8, 1863, *ORN*, XXIV, 222.

Porter praised Ellet for his courageous attempt to ram *City of Vicksburg,* but he privately disapproved of the colonel's attack being made during daylight. In reporting the action to the Navy Department, Porter wrote, "I cannot speak too highly of this gallant and daring officer. The only trouble I have is to hold him in and keep him out of danger. He will undertake anything I wish him to without asking questions, and these are the kind of men I like to command."[8]

Porter quickly appreciated the importance of having *Queen of the West* below Vicksburg. It gave him the means for attacking Confederate shipping all the way down to Port Hudson, where the advances of Admiral Farragut's squadron had been stopped. An observer in Vicksburg lamented, after seeing commodity prices escalate the following day, "The worst that has befallen this place, and perhaps the entire Confederacy, since the arrival of the Yankee army on the peninsula across the river, is the interference of our communication with Red River." Ellet also demonstrated that a vessel could pass Vicksburg's batteries, making it feasible for Porter to order down another. Had *Queen of the West* been lost, however, Porter would have been subject to criticism for sending a lightly armed riverboat, without support and commanded by a youngster, against a heavily fortified position.[9]

Porter believed that if he succeeded in blockading Vicksburg from below while maintaining control of the Yazoo, the Confederates would eventually deplete their supplies. He decided to send *Queen of the West* down to the mouth of the Red River on a commerce-destroying mission and promised Ellet reinforcements at the earliest opportunity. At 1 P.M. on February 2, the colonel reported the ram back in fighting trim and shoved off Biggs's landing to begin his mission of destruction. Several miles downriver he passed his first hurdle, running the batteries at Warrenton so quickly that only two shells nipped the upperworks of the ram.[10]

At Grand Gulf, fifty miles south of Vicksburg, Colonel Ellet entered Big Black and attempted to destroy the vital bridge spanning the river. After navigating the mouth, he found the waterway too narrow and winding to make the ascent, so he ordered *Queen* back to the Mississippi. By then the alarm had spread that a Union ram had passed

8. Porter to Welles, February 2, 1863, *ibid.,* 217–18.

9. *Ibid.,* 218; *Mobile Advertiser,* February 5, 1863.

10. Porter to Welles, February 2, 1863, *ORN,* XXIV, 218, 222; C. R. Ellet to A. W. Ellet, February 5, 1863, *ORA,* XXIV, Pt. 1, pp. 337–38.

Warrenton's batteries. Lieutenant General John C. Pemberton, commanding forces in Mississippi and East Louisiana, reacted with speed and sent a telegram to Natchez ordering that a fast steamer be dispatched to Red River to warn away all shipping. On the way up the Red, Pemberton's courier stopped three steamboats coming down—*Eleanor, Red Chief,* and *Era No. 2*—and turned them back.[11]

At midnight *Queen of the West* reached Natchez and landed across the river at Vidalia. Ellet threw out pickets and sent a search party into the village to gather information and take, if possible, a few prisoners. Finding the townsfolk surprised by his visit, Ellet mistakenly concluded that Natchez was not connected to Vicksburg by telegraph and failed to destroy the city's line. Instead, his men chased Colonel Zebulon York, on leave from the Army of Northern Virginia, into the woods, fired two shots, and missed.[12]

Ellet recalled his marines and at 3 A.M., February 3, Captain Sutherland once more cast off and continued down the river. At dawn *Queen* passed silent batteries on Ellis Cliffs and steamed down to the mouth of Red River. Finding no evidence of enemy shipping, Sutherland ventured another fifteen miles down the Mississippi before sighting the side-wheeler *A. W. Baker* approaching from below. *Baker*'s pilot had not been warned of *Queen*'s descent and whistled for the ram to pass to starboard. The pilot decided he did not like the looks of the ram, and when *Queen* refused to give way, he steered for the shore and grounded near the bank. Seven Confederate officers jumped overboard, swam ashore, and escaped into the woods, but a number of civilians, including several ladies, were captured and taken on board *Queen. Baker* carried no supplies, having just transported a load of salt and bacon to the Port Hudson garrison.

As Ellet's marines climbed on board *Baker,* the steamer *Moro* rounded into view upriver. *Moro*'s pilot seemed unconcerned by *Queen*'s presence until a single shot across the bow forced him to come alongside. Ellet took the prize to a landing and found the steamboat laden with 110,000 pounds of pork, 500 live hogs, and a large quantity of salt for Port Hudson. With his bunkers low, Ellet decided to return to Biggs's plantation for coal. For the trip upriver he placed Captain Asgill Conner in charge of the two prizes.

11. C. R. Ellet to A. W. Ellet, February 5, 1863, *ORA*, XXIV, Pt. 1, p. 338; Ferguson to Pemberton, February 3, 1863, *ibid.*, Pt. 3, p. 615.

12. C. R. Ellet to A. W. Ellet, February 5, 1863, *ibid.*, Pt. 1, p. 338.

Ellet stopped briefly at the mouth of Red River to put ashore his civilian prisoners, and while disembarking them the steamboat *Berwick Bay* stumbled upon *Queen*. Loaded with a large cargo of commissary stores for Port Hudson, *Berwick Bay* carried an extra treasure, forty bales of cotton, and this induced Ellet to dally a little longer and go on a scout up the Red. Burning a little more coal, he wasted the balance of the day without sighting another vessel. When night fell he started back up the Mississippi, urging Captain Conner to stay in sight with all three prizes. The procession moved so slowly that Ellet feared he would run out of fuel, so he ordered Conner to burn the vessels, lamenting that he had not allowed himself enough time to transfer the cargoes.

On the morning of February 5, Ellet disembarked his prisoners before passing Warrenton and sent them under guard to Young's Point, the headquarters of Sherman's corps. Then, keeping the boilers well fired, he made a dash past Warrenton's batteries. More guns had been added since *Queen* passed below, and with a strong current restricting the ram's speed, Sutherland hugged the west bank. Once again a few shots ripped through *Queen*'s upperworks but caused little damage. A few minutes later *Queen* pulled to Biggs's landing, and Ellet advised Porter of his safe return.[13]

Ellet's three prizes and short jaunt up Red River did not go unnoticed by Confederate authorities. At Port Hudson, Major General Franklin Gardner retained the steamer *Dr. Beatty* after he learned of the capture of *A. W. Baker*. Brigadier General Henry H. Sibley, commanding Confederate forces on the Atchafalaya, learned from Ellet's prisoners that three steamboats had been captured and ordered a company of cavalry and a cannon from the Valverde Texas Artillery to the mouth of the Red.[14]

Charlie Ellet needed coal as much for ballast as for fuel, and his concern for *Queen*'s safety escalated when Confederates began emplacing guns opposite Biggs's plantation. He concocted all sorts of schemes to get coal down to his vessel, on one occasion volunteering to run upriver in *De Soto* to obtain a supply. Porter vetoed the suggestion as too risky, reminding Ellet that *De Soto* would make less than four miles an hour traveling against the current, placing it under Vicksburg's batter-

13. *Ibid.*; Porter to Welles, February 5, 1863, *ORN*, XXIV, 222–23.

14. Gardner to Waddy, February 5, Sibley to Gardner, February 4, 1863, *ORN*, XXIV, 224–25.

ies for up to an hour. Ellet then went to General Sherman to suggest that a barge filled with coal be floated downriver after dark. Sherman agreed and asked Porter to do it, adding, "Colonel Ellet seems to be full of energy and resources" and whenever he "needs assistance which I can give, tell him to call on me."[15]

On the night of February 7, Porter drifted a barge containing 20,000 pounds of coal ten miles downriver to where Ellet, using *De Soto,* intercepted the cargo and hauled it into a slough. With coal enough to last him a month, and anxious to capitalize on *Queen*'s recent success, the colonel worked through the night filling the ram's bunkers. He also wanted heavier guns, and Sherman gave him two 30-pounder Parrotts emplaced at the lower mouth of the canal. Ellet then requested the use of *De Soto* as a coal tender, and because Sherman had little use for the vessel, he told Ellet to take it. Instead of mounting both 30-pounders on *Queen,* he put one on *De Soto,* promising Porter that he would turn the vessel into a cottonclad. Then, thinking himself well prepared for another raid, he asked Porter for orders. By then Ellet had converted *Queen* from an unarmed ram to a lightly armed gunboat carrying one 30-pounder and one 20-pounder Parrott, four 12-pounder howitzers, a large supply of ordnance stores, and a complete set of surgeon's operating instruments.[16]

Porter intended to send an ironclad below Vicksburg to cooperate with *Queen of the West,* and he believed that the two vessels, acting together, could interdict commerce as far as Port Hudson on the Mississippi and Alexandria on Red River. The success of this strategy depended upon Ellet's judicious management of *Queen,* and Porter's orders emphasized that the colonel should take only carefully calculated risks.

The admiral directed Ellet to depart at night, taking *Queen of the West, De Soto,* and the coal barge past the batteries at Warrenton with all lights concealed. On reaching Red River, Ellet was to remain near the mouth and watch for the smoke of descending steamboats. If *Queen* captured a prize, Porter did not want the conquest signalized by a burning hulk floating downriver. He ordered Ellet to break up the machinery and anchor the vessel before torching it.

15. Porter to Ellet, February 5, Sherman to Porter, February 6, 1863, *ibid.,* 371, 240.

16. Porter to Welles, February 8, Sherman to Porter, February 5, Sherman to Ellet, February 6, Ellet to Porter, February 6, 8, 1863, *ibid.,* 222, 371, 372, 373–74; Crandall and Newell, *Ram Fleet,* 178.

Porter did not expect Ellet's second raid to catch the Confederates as unprepared as the first, and he warned, "there is one vessel, the [*William H.*] *Webb,* that you must look out for. If you get the first crack at her, you will sink her, and if she gets the first crack at you she will sink you." Knowing that Ellet never received any formal naval training, he explained in great detail how to protect the vessel from an enemy ram and how best to defend the vessel against boarding attempts.

Knowing the inability of *De Soto* to protect itself, Porter admonished Ellet to always keep it in sight and to not go off on a chase unless the tender "will be perfectly safe." He suggested that once all the coal had been removed from the barge, Ellet should lash *De Soto* to *Queen,* but at the smallest chance of the vessel's falling into the hands of the enemy, the colonel must "destroy her at once."

Porter mentioned nothing about raiding up Red River, but he did suggest reconnoitering Port Hudson and destroying all small boats, wharf boats, and barges on the Mississippi. Part of the West Gulf Blockading Squadron lay at anchor below the batteries at Port Hudson, and Porter suggested that Ellet make an effort to communicate across the bend with Admiral Farragut.

Knowing Ellet's risk-taking proclivities, Porter summarized his instructions by adding: "The great object is to destroy all you can of the enemy's stores and provisions and get your vessel back safe. Pass all batteries at night if the canal is opened. I will keep you supplied with coal. Keep your pilot house well supplied with hand grenades, etc., in case the enemy should get on your upper decks. Do not show your colors along the river unless necessary in action."[17]

Ellet planned to depart from Biggs's landing on the night of February 8, but a flange broke on *De Soto*'s steampipe and forced a twenty-four-hour delay. The time lost should have worked to Ellet's advantage because it enabled Porter to reach the colonel with an important message, which read, "Don't be surprised to see the [ironclad] *Indianola* below. Don't mistake her for a rebel; she looks something like the *Chillicothe.*" Ellet replied, "I shall certainly start this evening . . . [and] take every precaution to avoid a collision with the *Indianola.*" In his earlier order, Porter had made no mention of detaching an ironclad, and it is not altogether certain that Ellet *wanted* a companion.[18]

17. Porter to Ellet, February 8, 1863, *ORN,* XXIV, 374.

18. Porter to Ellet, Ellet to Porter, February 10, 1863, *ibid.,* 370, 371. *Indianola* reached Porter's squadron about February 7.

At nightfall on February 10, Ellet's engineers stoked the fireboxes on *Queen of the West* and *De Soto,* and by 9 P.M. they had smoke and sparks under control and plenty of steam. With the coal barge lashed to *Queen,* Ellet gave orders to cast off, and the men went to quarters as the vessels approached Warrenton. A reporter from the *New York Tribune* who had attached himself to the Ram Fleet wrote, "The suspense was terrible. We were at point-blank range, the night was fine," and he wondered, "why they did not fire?"[19]

At daybreak Ellet's squadron passed Grand Gulf and stopped at Taylor's Point, a plantation once owned by former president Zachary Taylor. Thinking that title now rested with Jefferson Davis, Ellet intended to seize enough cotton to build breastworks on *De Soto* and to encourage a few blacks to enlist as laborers. Learning that Taylor had sold the property to a planter from Kentucky, Ellet appropriated the cotton but not the slaves.

Thirty miles below Taylor Point, *Queen* demonstrated off Natchez, but Ellet did not land. Porter would have preferred for Ellet to have passed and gone about his business instead of attracting unneeded attention. After wasting two hours parading off the city, the ram and the steamer departed for Old River, the Mississippi's former channel before the current created a more direct path by cutting across the base of a large peninsula. For Ellet, Old River had advantages because both the Red and Atchafalaya Rivers flowed into it, and he could station his vessels to intercept any riverboat plying either waterway. The Atchafalaya, just as important as Red River, connected the Mississippi and Red Rivers to Berwick Bay and provided another route for supplying Port Hudson and Vicksburg.

At nightfall on February 11, Ellet moored *Queen* at the mouth of Old River and sent *De Soto* about a mile ahead to perform picket duty. At daylight, he left *De Soto* and the coal barge to watch for Rebel shipping and started down the Atchafalaya. Lookouts spotted a train of twelve army wagons moving along the bank and guarded by a squad of soldiers. Ellet led a force ashore, and the enemy fled. *Queen*'s marines spent the morning smashing wagons, turning mules loose, and throwing harnesses and supplies into the river. At midday Ellet continued down the Atchafalaya, looking for two transports reported by blacks to

---

19. Ellet's Report, February 21, 1863, *ibid.,* 383–84; *New York Tribune,* February 15, 1863, quoted in Gosnell, *Guns on the Western Waters,* 179.

be at Simmesport. Too much time had been lost, and the small garrison at Simmesport had scrambled on board the boats and skedaddled down the river. When *Queen* arrived the town appeared to be deserted, and Ellet had to settle for destroying seventy barrels of beef left on the wharf. From mail confiscated at the local post office he learned that a Union force under Major General Nathaniel P. Banks had recently occupied Berwick Bay and the mouth of the Atchafalaya. While Ellet dallied at Simmesport, Confederate cavalry quietly watched from the bayou as men from *Queen* plundered the town.

Ellet recalled his men and made a quick pass down the river looking for the two reported transports. Along the way he spotted a wagon train carting supplies of the Valverde Artillery away from Simmesport. When *Queen* opened fire, the teamsters drove their wagons into the swamps and fled. The marines landed and wasted more time wading through the quagmire to pick through the abandoned supplies. They found one wagon filled with ammunition and stores, and since the contents had not been damaged, they set it afire.

As evening approached, Ellet started back up the river, only to be fired upon by a group of civilians who lay hidden behind the levee close to where the first wagon train had been captured. The marines returned fire, and the 30-pounder Parrott sprayed the levee with canister. The guerrillas ducked below the bank and dispersed, but during the brief skirmish a minié ball struck James D. Thompson, first master of the ram, through the knee.[20]

Prior to leaving Biggs's plantation, Thompson had a premonition of death. He had written General Ellet asking that if he were killed, the money due him should be forwarded to his fiancée in Illinois. The ship's surgeon, Dr. David S. Booth, did what he could to repair Thompson's shattered knee. Though the injury did not appear to be mortal, it resembled the wound that killed Charles Ellet, Jr., and Thompson needed better medical attention than he could get on the ram.[21]

Had Charlie Ellet followed orders, he would have gone back to the Mississippi, but at daybreak on the morning of February 13 a civilian came on board and volunteered the names of the men who had fired

20. Ellet's Report, February 21, 1863, *ORN*, XXIV, 384; *Chicago Tribune,* March 1, 1863; John W. Lister Diary, February 10, 1863, John W. Lister Papers, Crandall Collection, ISHL.

21. Thompson to A. W. Ellet, February 1, 1863, Alfred Ellet Papers, Crandall Collection, ISHL; Lister Diary, February 11, 1863, Lister Papers, *ibid.*

on *Queen*. Enraged by Thompson's injury, Ellet returned to the site of the ambush and captured three plantation owners. He allowed them to remove their personal belongings and then organized a detail to burn their homes, barns, sugar mills, and other buildings.[22]

Ellet then made another mistake. When Porter sent *Queen* back to Red River, he clearly specified that the ram should remain near the mouth, and he mentioned nothing about excursions down the Atchafalaya. The colonel recalled those orders as he returned to the mouth of the Red and expressed his intention to go down the Mississippi and communicate with Farragut, but then he changed his mind. Instead, on the afternoon of the 13th, he started up Red River with *De Soto* and the coal barge. Forty miles later he settled for the night at the mouth of Black River.[23]

Ellet had no difficulty collecting intelligence because local inhabitants seemed to be more than willing to share information. Eighty-five miles above the mouth of Red River, Confederates had built an earthwork at Gordon's (Barbin's) Landing and named it Fort Taylor. Another fort had been built at Harrisonburg on the Ouachita River, and Ellet could not decide which to attack. A civilian informed him that the steamer *Louisville* had just passed down the Black and gone up the Red laden with a 32-pounder for *William H. Webb,* which they reported at Alexandria. Ellet decided he had better capture *Louisville* before it delivered the gun. Besides, he learned of other boats on the upper Red, and this induced him to venture at least as far as Fort Taylor.[24]

Early on the 14th Ellet cast off and, with *De Soto* following, started up the winding Red River. None of *Queen*'s pilots had ever been on the Red, and with the sluggish *De Soto* bucking the current, the two vessels proceeded at a slow and cautious pace. At 10 A.M. *Queen*'s lookout warned of smoke ahead, and several minutes later the steamboat *Era No. 5* rounded the bend. The skipper, finding himself confronted by a Union ram, attempted to turn the vessel around. Ellet ordered a warning shot fired, but the gunner aimed at the boat and sent a projectile crashing into the vessel's stern, where it passed through the

22. Ellet's Report, February 21, 1863, *ORN*, XXIV, 384.

23. Porter to Ellet, February 8, 1863, *ibid.,* 374; Gosnell, *Guns on the Western Waters,* 184.

24. Ellet's Report, February 21, 1863, *ORN*, XXIV, 384; *Chicago Tribune*, March 1, 1863; Bearss, *The Vicksburg Campaign,* I, 639. Fort Taylor eventually became Fort De Russy.

cookroom, demolished a stove, and wounded the cook. Passengers waving white handkerchiefs came running to the deck, and Ellet took possession of the boat.

The 150-ton *Era No. 5* belonged to the Red River Packet Company and made a fine prize. The boat carried 4,500 bushels of corn for the Confederate quartermaster at Little Rock and had on board two lieutenants and seventeen privates of the 27th Louisiana Infantry. Ellet sent his marines on board and, with *Era No. 5* following, resumed his ascent of the Red. Fifteen miles below Fort Taylor he paroled the privates and sent them ashore with all but one of the passengers—a German Jew named Elsasser who carried $32,000 in Confederate money and whom the colonel erroneously suspected of being a Rebel quartermaster. Ellet made one other error. He freed a Confederate brigadier general dressed in civilian clothes who claimed to be a noncombatant. Then, rather than destroy his fine prize, Ellet manned it with a small crew, attached it to his flotilla, and left the vessel and the barge under guard below while *Queen* and *De Soto* reconnoitered the defenses of Fort Taylor.[25]

Captain John Kelso commanded Fort Taylor, and boats passing upriver had alerted him of *Queen*'s ascent. Below the fort the river formed a bend, and during the day Kelso made certain that the garrison had carefully bracketed their cannon on the point. Suspecting that *Queen* would attack at night, he also arranged for a warehouse to be set afire below the fort so the position of an enemy vessel would be outlined by the blaze.[26]

Ellet arrived below the bend at sundown, and over the treetops he could see the smoke of several steamers stoking up their fireboxes. Leaving *De Soto* behind the bend, he ordered the pilot to move ahead slowly, and show no more than the bow of *Queen* around the point. As the ram crept forward, Ellet observed the fort about a quarter mile away. He liked the arrangement because he believed that if the fort gave him trouble, he could easily back and take shelter behind the bend. The current, however, created eddies and a great deal of turbulence as it whipped around the point, and the direction of the water flow became difficult to see as night approached.[27]

25. Ellet's Report, February 21, 1863, *ORN*, XXIV, 384; Gosnell, *Guns on the Western Waters,* 184–85; Crandall and Newell, *Ram Fleet,* 170.

26. Kelso's Report, February 15, 1863, *ORA,* XXIV, Pt. 1, p. 348.

27. Ellet's Report, February 21, 1863, *ORN*, XXIV, 384; Gosnell, *Guns on the Western Waters,* 185.

Not knowing what resistance to expect from Fort Taylor, Ellet went after the steamers, opening with two shots from the bow gun on a fleeing riverboat. Kelso answered with his four 32-pounders, sending three shells into the water beside the ram and drenching the crew. Ellet reacted swiftly, ordering Second Pilot Thomas W. Garvey to back *Queen* around the point and withdraw downriver. Being unfamiliar with the bars, Garvey ran aground about sixty yards from the point, exactly where Kelso's gunners had fixed their range of fire. During the next few minutes *Queen*'s three pilots worked frantically to back off the shoal. Three 32-pounder shells hurtled over the protective bales of cotton and crashed into the deck between the chimneys. One engine stopped when a shot carried away the regulating lever. Fragments of exploding shells swept the decks. Below one shell nipped off the steam escape pipe and another fractured the steam chest, driving the engineers and firemen topside and the prisoners aft. Men grabbed cotton bales, tumbled them into the river, and used them to raft down to *De Soto*. Ellet lost all control of the crew when they abandoned the vessel without waiting for orders. He had made a grave error by not shifting Thompson, the wounded master, to *De Soto* before engaging the fort, and when he attempted to have him removed by the yawl, he found it gone.

Ellet signaled for *De Soto* to come up and take off the men who had been scalded, but the little steamer stayed behind the point and sent its yawl. As soon as the boat bumped against the ram, Ellet scrambled into it with his men and reached *De Soto* safely. Only the injured Thompson remained on board *Queen,* and Ellet wanted him saved from capture. Lieutenant John L. Tuthill and Third Master J. C. Duncan volunteered to go back to *Queen* with a small detail and attempt to get the vessel off the bar. If unable to do so, they promised to remove Thompson and any casualties still on board and, if attacked, burn the boat. Ellet approved the mission, and the pair departed in the yawl.[28]

Tuthill and his volunteers encountered problems once on board *Queen*. The pitch-black decks and passageways had become so obscured by steam and blocked by debris that Thompson could not be moved. As the rescue team fumbled about the boat, they heard faint

28. Ellet's Report, February 21, 1863, *OR N*, XXIV, 384–85; *Chicago Tribune*, March 3, 1863; Gosnell, *Guns on the Western Waters*, 186–87; *Cincinnati Daily Commercial*, March 4, 1863.

sounds from upriver and observed the dim outline of three skiffs pulling toward the ram. From shore, Kelso's men had observed the abandonment of *Queen,* and the captain had hurriedly organized a detail to capture the stricken vessel. From the skiffs came calls for surrender. Tuthill dropped into the yawl with several men, and without waiting for the others, pushed off. Duncan surrendered with twelve men, including First Master Thompson, who was too badly wounded to leave Ellet's cabin and died a few days later.[29]

When Tuthill reached *De Soto* and explained how his detail had been attacked, Ellet considered running the steamer alongside *Queen* and recapturing her. After further thought, he decided that doing so would jeopardize his only chance of escape. Confederates roving the banks made repeated calls for *De Soto* to surrender, and Ellet, fearing that the enemy might be closing in from all sides, set *De Soto* adrift. On the way downriver the steamer picked up men afloat on bales of cotton and hauled them on board. Then, as fog began to settle on the river, *De Soto*'s pilots lost sight of the banks and struck a shoal that sheared off the boat's rudder. Ellet formed a work party and pushed the steamer off the bar, but the boat had no steerage and could only be navigated by alternating the use of her paddle wheels. At 10 P.M. *De Soto* drifted up to *Era No. 5* and tied beside her.

Having no means of defense, Ellet had but one choice—to get back to Biggs's plantation as quickly as possible. *Era No. 5* provided his only means of escape, so he transferred all his men to the prize and dispatched a detail to torch *De Soto.* The incendiaries distributed red-hot coals and soon had the vessel in flames. Much to Ellet's annoyance, he found his coal barge aground. Instead of pausing to transfer coal to the bunkers of *Era No. 5,* he set the barge afire, an act of desperation he would regret a few hours later.[30]

For the veterans of the Red River raid, the situation now became a race for survival. By leaving *Queen of the West* in the hands of the enemy, Ellet made a tragic and costly mistake, but because he had left Thompson, a wounded man, on board, he could not burn the vessel. Ellet's surviving marines were exchanged a few days later at Port

29. Ellet's Report, February 21, 1863, *ORN,* XXIV, 385; Kelso's Report, February 15, 1863, *ORA,* XXIV, Pt. 1, p. 348; *Cincinnati Daily Commercial,* March 4, 1863; Bearss, *The Vicksburg Campaign,* I, 642–43.

30. Ellet's Report, February 21, 1863, *ORN,* XXIV, 385; *Cincinnati Daily Commercial,* March 4, 1863; Gosnell, *Guns on the Western Waters,* 188–89.

Hudson, but the Confederates did not know what to do with *Queen*'s civilian crew and ushered most of them off to different prisons. Porter deserved a share of the blame for sending a nineteen-year-old medical cadet on a mission that could test the skills and training of a professional naval officer.

Ellet ordered *Era No. 5* into the current and once again took his chances with the fog. With poor visibility and a treacherous channel to navigate, Ellet had reason to believe he might never reach the Mississippi. By morning, some very angry Confederates with fast boats would be nipping at his heels.[31]

31. Hoffman to Grant, April 9, Breese to Rawlins, April 20, Hoffman to Bonneville, May 23, 1863, *ORA,* Ser. 2, III, 457, 499, 694; Gosnell, *Guns on the Western Waters,* 188–89.

CHAPTER 7

THE ESCAPE OF *ERA NO. 5*

On February 12, two days before Ellet abandoned *Queen of the West,* Admiral Porter issued orders to Lieutenant Commander George Brown directing him to lash two coal barges alongside the ironclad *Indianola* and run her past the Vicksburg batteries. The admiral explained his reasons for sending *Indianola* below—first, to protect *Queen* and *De Soto* from *Webb,* the enemy's so-called ram, and second, to go up Red River and destroy the enemy's shipping and stores. "Ellet and yourself will consult together what is best to be done, and whatever you undertake try and have no failure. When you have not the means of certain success, undertake nothing; a failure is equal to defeat"—good advice he had neglected to give Ellet. Because Brown came from a tinclad, Porter explained an ironclad's method for engaging Confederate vessels, using solid shot against rams and shrapnel against cottonclads. He reiterated the importance of Ellet's communicating with Farragut and closed by saying, "Make your calculations to get back here with plenty of coal on board."[1]

---

1. Porter to Brown, February 12, 1863, *ORN,* XXIV, 376–77.

Fog on the river delayed Brown's departure until the night of February 13, and just before midnight he caught the Vicksburg batteries napping. Counting only eighteen shots as *Indianola* coasted by, Brown tied up four miles below Warrenton and reported his successful passage to the admiral. In the morning Porter dispatched a message to Welles expressing great expectations for the success of the two vessels, writing, "This gives us entire control of the Mississippi, except at Vicksburg and Port Hudson, and cuts off all the supplies and troops from Texas."[2]

At 5:20 A.M. on February 14, Brown cast off from the Louisiana shore and, hauling both of his barges, started downriver in search of *Queen* and *De Soto*. He expected to find both vessels off the mouth of Red River. At almost the same moment, Ellet had departed from the mouth of Black River, captured *Era No. 5,* and proceeded upstream to reconnoiter Fort Taylor. Had Ellet returned to the mouth of the Red in compliance with Porter's orders, the prospects for all the vessels involved in the mission would have vastly improved, but from that moment on, everything went wrong.

Brown made good progress traveling with the current until February 15, when storms followed by fog forced him to anchor a few miles below Natchez. Ellet encountered the same storms early that morning as *Era No. 5* descended the Red. A correspondent traveling with Ellet wrote, "The night was a terrible one—thunder, lightning, rain, and fog," and he doubted whether any fool aside from Ellet would attempt to run down the snake-like river in an unfamiliar boat under such horrid conditions. To lighten the vessel, the panicked crew worked through the night throwing *Era*'s cargo of corn overboard. By daylight they discovered the error of their act when engineers reported their fuel depleted, and the last of the corn went into the fireboxes.[3]

At daybreak *Era No. 5* entered the Mississippi, and with rain falling and fog blanketing the valley, the vessel turned upriver. Ellet wanted to put some distance between himself and the speedy *Webb*—rated at fourteen miles an hour when running against the current—but logs and debris drifting down the swollen river knocked paddles off *Era*'s side wheels and cut her speed. When the corn gave out, Ellet tied up at

2. Brown to Porter, February 18, Porter to Welles, February 14, 1863, *ibid.*, 377–78, 375–76.

3. Brown to Porter, February 18, Ellet's Report, February 11, 1863, *ibid.*, 378, 385; Crandall and Newell, *Ram Fleet,* 172.

Union Point and sent a detail ashore to cut wood. They returned with a few cords so saturated with water that the boilers could not make enough steam to propel the vessel more than two miles an hour against the current.

When opposite Ellis Cliffs, Pilot Garvey—who had backed *Queen* onto a bar at Fort Taylor—ran *Era* aground in less than two feet of water. Four hours passed while carpenters went ashore to cut a tree and fashion a spar for shoving her off. Had it not been for a dense fog, batteries on Ellis Cliffs or guerrillas roving the banks could have made quick work of capturing the steamboat. While aground, Ellet learned that the pilot had recently made disloyal statements. Arresting Garvey came at an opportune moment. The allegation enabled Ellet to later claim that "the loss of the *Queen* was due to the deliberate treachery of her pilot."

Once they were again under way, the boat's starboard wheel, which had already been damaged by drift, began "dropping to pieces." Ellet paused to confer with his officers. He suggested two options. The first alternative—to abandon *Era No. 5*, seize skiffs and dugouts from nearby plantations, attempt to sneak by the batteries of Port Hudson, and join Farragut's squadron fifty miles downriver—attracted little interest. The officers preferred to take their chances with the crippled steamer, even though they all expected to be captured, so Ellet put the vessel into the hands of Pilot McKay and resumed the torturous voyage to Biggs's landing.[4]

On the morning of February 16, as *Era No. 5* approached Natchez, the lookout discerned the dim outline of a gunboat directly ahead. Suspecting that *Webb* had passed during the night, the men steeled themselves for the inevitability of being blown out of the water, rammed, or captured. As *Era* drew closer, it became apparent through a break in the fog that the vessel was not *Webb* but an ironclad. At that moment a lookout on *Indianola* spotted *Era*, and thinking the vessel might be *Webb*, raised the alarm. Ellet ordered the whistle blown and came abeam the ironclad. The reporter for the *New York Tribune* probably spoke for the entire crew when he wrote, "You may be sure that no men ever witnessed a more welcome sight than this same good steamer *Indianola*. It was a miraculous escape . . . [for] from the depths of despair we were raised to the heights of exaltation. We, some

4. Ellet to Porter, February 11, 1863, *ORN,* XXIV, 385; *Cincinnati Daily Commercial,* March 4, 1863; Gosnell, *Guns on the Western Waters,* 188–89.

of us, [were] hatless, bootless and coatless. All of us were hungry. We had eaten nothing for the last 48 hours but a little stale and sour corn-meal, found in the bottom of a barrel"—a condition the crew of *Indianola* promptly corrected by sharing their food and clothing with *Queen*'s survivors.[5]

Ellet met with Brown and, feeling much safer, discussed methods for disposing of *Webb*. Brown suggested going back up the Red, de-stroying the water batteries at Fort Taylor, and if possible, either recov-ering or destroying *Queen of the West*. Ellet helped himself to *Indianola*'s coal and agreed to lead the way, providing Brown would wait until carpenters repaired *Era*'s paddles. At 4:30 P.M. both vessels headed downriver, and forty minutes later *Era*'s lookout reported the dim outline of *Webb* moving through the fog off Ellis Cliffs. Ellet rounded to and whistled a warning signal to *Indianola*. Brown cleared for action, and on board *Era*, Ellet's engineers connected a hot-water hose to the boilers and prepared for a lively engagement.[6]

Lieutenant Colonel William S. Lovell, commanding *Webb*, had no intention of being ripped apart by the two 11-inch and two 9-inch Dahlgrens mounted in *Indianola*. He had been given no time to pro-tect his boilers, and his crew consisted of last-minute volunteers. He had little means of defense other than four 12-pounders and a detach-ment of a hundred soldiers pooled from two separate commands. After passing Fort Taylor on the morning of February 15 and finding *Queen of the West* in possession of Captain Kelso, Lovell learned that Ellet had burned *De Soto* and escaped in *Era No. 5*, so he "pushed on with all speed" through the fog. Before reaching the Mississippi he picked up nine men in a boat from *Queen*, who informed him that Ellet might be joined by an ironclad.[7]

On the afternoon of February 16, Lovell stopped at Ellis Cliffs and learned that another gunboat had passed Vicksburg on the night of the 13th. Forewarned, he proceeded with more caution. About 5:10 P.M., when lookouts on *Webb* and *Era No. 5* simultaneously sighted each

5. Brown to Porter, February 18, Ellet to Porter, February 11, 1863, *ORN*, XXIV, 378, 385; Gosnell, *Guns on the Western Waters*, 190.

6. Brown to Porter, February 18, Ellet to Porter, February 11, 1863, *ORN*, XXIV, 378, 385.

7. Statistical Data of Ships, *ibid.*, Ser. 2, I, 107, 271; Lovell to Pemberton, February 28, 1863, *ORA*, XXIV, Pt. 1, p. 346.

other, each correctly surmised the other's identity. When Ellet came about and headed upriver, Lovell took up the chase, but he changed his mind as soon as he sighted the tips of *Indianola*'s chimneys jutting above the fog. Brown fired two shots from his 11-inch bow guns and missed with both. *Webb* backed, came about, and minutes later vanished in the fog. Lovell took the vessel back up Red River and met two steamers coming down to pursue *Era No. 5*. Wisely, he turned them back.[8]

Indianola and *Era No. 5* anchored at the mouth of Red River, and Ellet went on board the ironclad to discuss operations. Brown changed his mind about attempting to recover *Queen* after he learned it had been towed up to Norman's Landing to be repaired, and Ellet, not happy with his flimsy steamboat, decided to return to Biggs's landing. He seized 170 bales of cotton to protect his machinery and started the slow voyage upriver. Perfectly confident he could defend *Indianola* against both *Queen* and *Webb*, Brown decided to blockade the Red. He bid Ellet good-bye, and in parting handed the colonel a report asking Porter to send down another gunboat.[9]

Ellet enjoyed a slow but uneventful trip upriver until he stopped at St. Joseph, Louisiana, and seized the mail. One of the letters disclosed that Colonel William Wirt Adams's veteran cavalry had moved to Grand Gulf with two pieces of artillery and intended to destroy *Era No. 5* as it passed. Ellet took what precautions he could, and sure enough, as the steamboat approached Grand Gulf, two 6-pounders opened and fired thirty-six shots. One hit a cotton bale and bounded into the water. The others all missed.[10]

The Confederates had planned another reception for *Era No. 5* at Palmyra Island, below New Carthage. Ellet chose to go around the island by taking the Louisiana side but ran into a hail of small-arms fire from the bank. He then tried the Mississippi side, but cavalry hidden in the woods opened fire in a determined effort to force *Era* back to the other side of the island. Suddenly the boiler fires died, forcing Ellet to let the boat drift downriver while stokers cleaned the furnaces. With

8. Lovell to Pemberton, February 28, 1863, *ORA,* XXIV, Pt. 1, p. 346; Brown to Porter, February 18, Ellet to Porter, February 11, 1863, *ORN,* XXIV, 378, 385.

9. Brown to Porter, February 18, Ellet to Porter, February 11, 1863, *ORN,* XXIV, 378–79, 385–86.

10. Ellet to Porter, February 11, 1863, *ibid.,* 385–86.

good pressure restored, *Era* ran by the sharpshooters and passed Palmyra Island, only to be met by a three-gun battery hidden in the woods on the Louisiana side. Enemy artillery fired forty-six rounds but never hit the vessel.[11]

At nightfall on February 21, *Era No. 5* approached the dangerous stretch of river below Warrenton, and Ellet hoped to slip by unnoticed. The batteries had been alerted, and as soon as the vessel came in range, two 20-pounder Parrotts opened on the darkened *Era*. Ellet counted twenty-four shots, but none of them struck the steamboat. He tied up at Biggs's landing and forwarded his report and Brown's to Porter.[12]

The admiral read the reports in the morning and in a sour mood advised Welles, "The best calculations are liable to be upset, and mine have been disarranged by the capture of *Queen of the West* up the Red River." He found it embarrassing to explain what happened and grumbled:

> That vessel grounded under the guns of a battery, which she foolishly engaged, and received a shot through her boilers and steam drum, which drove most of her people overboard.
>
> Had the commander of the *Queen of the West* waited patiently, he would, in less than twenty-four hours, have been joined by the *Indianola*. . . . This is a serious disappointment to us [above Vicksburg], as we calculated certainly on starving out the garrison at Port Hudson by merely blockading the mouth of Red River. My plans were well laid, only badly executed. I can give orders, but I cannot give officers good judgment. The *Indianola* is now there by herself. Whether the commander will have the good sense not to be surprised, remains to be seen.[13]

Porter could not communicate with Brown. On one hand he worried that *Indianola* would be captured because it could only make two miles an hour against the current, but on the other hand he depended "on that vessel alone for carrying out my cherished plan of cutting off supplies [for] Port Hudson and Vicksburg." He predicted that *Queen of the West* would be repaired and commissioned by the enemy, and if so, make trouble for *Indianola*. But then he contradicted himself by condemning Ellet's rams as "fit for nothing but towboats."[14]

11. *Ibid.*, 386; Gosnell, *Guns on the Western Waters,* 191–92.
12. Ellet to Porter, February 11, 1863, *ORN,* XXIV, 386; Gosnell, *Guns on the Western Waters,* 191–92.
13. Porter to Welles, February 22, 1863, *ORN,* XXIV, 382–83.
14. *Ibid.*

Colonel Ellet crossed the peninsula on the morning of February 23 and reported to the admiral in person. By then Porter had cooled down, and because he personally liked the reckless youngster, he informed Welles that while Ellet had lost his ram, great service had been done by destroying $200,000 in Confederate property. Though he regretted that *Queen* had been lost, he admitted that Ellet could not have destroyed the vessel with wounded men on board. The colonel told Porter that *Queen,* though captured, would "not be worth anything for some time to the rebels, and is much used up," and that it could no longer serve as a ram, "being too weak and shattered." Porter wanted to believe Ellet's statement, but he had doubts.[15]

On the 23rd Porter closed the investigation of *Queen's* loss after speaking with Ellet, but at the mouth of Red River the ripple effect of the ram's capture had begun. Two days earlier Lieutenant Commander Brown wisely decided against ascending the Red after being informed that *Queen* had been repaired, manned, and readied for service. He became more alarmed when told that *Webb* and four cottonclads had been fitted out with boarding parties for the purpose of capturing *Indianola.* Brown abandoned his post and started up the Mississippi, making two miles an hour. He lost more time by stopping to collect cotton to barricade his decks. With *Indianola's* bunkers full, Brown could have cut his two barges loose and hastened his withdrawal, but he had a ninety-mile lead and worried that if Porter sent down another gunboat, it might need coal.[16]

On the morning of February 24 *Indianola* passed Grand Gulf, but by late afternoon it became evident from smoke far downriver that several vessels were advancing in hot pursuit. By nightfall he could see them—*Queen of the West, William H. Webb,* and two cottonclads, *Dr. Beatty* and *Grand Era,* both filled with men. By then Brown had no hope of outrunning his pursuers, so at a point twenty-five miles from Biggs's landing he cleared for action. At Palmyra Island he came about and stood down the river to meet the enemy with his 11-inch Dahlgrens. Having the coal barges lashed alongside gave him extra protection, and he depended upon them to protect his beams.[17]

Brown observed *Queen* in the lead. The moon provided good light for ramming but poor illumination for aiming big guns. At 150

15. Porter to Welles, February 23, 1863, *ibid.,* 383.
16. Brown's Report, May 28, 1863, *ibid.,* 380.
17. *Ibid.;* Mixer to Welles, April 26, 1863, *ibid.,* 393–94.

yards, *Indianola* opened with the 11-inch bow guns. Both shots missed, so Brown swung sideways to avoid a head-on blow. *Queen* crashed into the barge lashed to the ironclad's port beam, knocked men to the deck, and became entangled.

While the forward gun crews reloaded, Brown faced the bow of the vessel back downriver and sighted *Webb* seventy-five yards away and bearing down under a full press of steam. Once more the Dahlgrens roared and again both shots missed. Head-on, the two vessel collided, stoving in eight feet of *Webb*'s bow. Aside from everyone being knocked to the deck, *Indianola* remained uninjured, but the concussion jarred both *Queen* and the portside barge loose. In passing, *Webb* ripped away the barge on the ironclad's starboard side, thereby exposing both of *Indianola*'s vulnerable beams.

Queen stood upriver and came about for another ramming run, and once again Brown attempted to meet the attack head-on. *Queen* struck *Indianola* on the forward quarter, glanced off, and absorbed two shots from the ironclad's stern guns. *Queen* circled once more, and this time struck *Indianola* behind the starboard wheelhouse, shattering planks and ripping away armor. Brown made a futile effort to escape, but *Webb* observed *Indianola* pulling away and sped toward the ironclad's unarmored stern. Brown's gunners got one Dahlgren loaded, fired at point-blank range, and missed again. *Webb* crashed into *Indianola*'s stern, started the ironclad's timbers, and crushed the starboard rudder. The vessel began to fill, and Brown made a frantic attempt to scuttle it. The time for taking such drastic action had passed. When two cottonclads bearing boarders appeared off the beam, he surrendered, and a short distance above Hurricane Island, *Indianola* settled in ten feet of water. Given time, the Confederates knew they could raise her.[18]

On the night of February 24 Porter heard the occasional rumble of heavy naval guns, and in the morning he learned that *Queen* had tied up at Warrenton. Being an analytical person, he reasoned that *Indianola* had been either captured or sunk, and a short time later his fears were confirmed. From the admiral's point of view, the disaster reflected back upon Ellet's recklessness, and in a telegram to Welles he complained that the loss "can be traced to a noncompliance with my

18. Brown to Welles, May 28, Mixer to Welles, April 26, 1863, *ibid.*, 380–81, 394–95; Brand to Gardner, February 26, Brent's Report, February 25, 1863, *ORA*, XXIV, Pt. 1, pp. 363–64, 365–68.

instructions." Welles replied that the ironclad "must be destroyed unless the attempt . . . involves still greater risks." Porter decided not to risk any more vessels on a mission already badly bumbled and personally embarrassing. None of his ironclads could cope with the speed and maneuverability of *Queen* or *Webb*. Railing against both Ellet and Brown, Porter wrote, "There is no use to conceal the fact, but this has, in my opinion, been the most humiliating affair that has occurred during this rebellion, and after taking so much trouble to make matters sure, it almost disheartens me, and [discourages me from] sending off any expedition, unless I go with it."[19]

Before the Confederates could mount an effort to raise *Indianola*, Porter conceived a plan he hoped would scare away a salvage party. On the morning of February 25 he set details to work building a dummy ironclad out of a flatboat, and by adding logs, extended its length to three hundred feet. Carpenters added a huge casemate forward and inside mounted an enormous "Quaker" gun. After adding immense wheelhouses and a pilothouse, the men built two chimneys out of barrels and seated them on pots of burning tar and oakum. With the whole structure smeared with tar and named "Black Terror," painters inscribed on the wheelhouses, "Deluded People, Cave In!"[20]

At 11 P.M. on the 25th, a tug towed the creature down to De Soto Point and turned it loose at the bend. Vicksburg's batteries opened with a long, sustained bombardment that did no observable damage. Convinced that "Black Terror" was indeed a dangerous ironclad, Major General Carter L. Stevenson, commander at Vicksburg, became alarmed and dispatched a courier to *Indianola*'s work party with orders to blow it up. He also sent word to Warrenton that *Queen* should leave immediately and escape down the river. *Queen* departed in a hurry, but while warning *Webb* and *Dr. Beatty*, accidentally crashed into *Grand Era* before all four vessels cleared for Red River.[21]

"Black Terror" grounded below the mouth of Williams's canal, but General Sherman's men gave her a push, and off it went again. By nightfall on the 26th, a detail left behind to salvage *Indianola*'s guns

19. Porter to Welles, February 27, Welles to Porter, March 2, 1863, *ORN*, XXIV, 388, 389, 390; Gosnell, *Guns on the Western Waters*, 199.

20. Hasler's Report, February 25, 1863, *ORN*, XXIV, 395–96; Richard S. West, Jr., *The Second Admiral: A Life of David Dixon Porter* (New York, 1937), 216–17.

21. Pemberton to Stevenson, February 27, Pemberton to Cooper, February 28, 1863, *ORN*, XXIV, 409, 410; Gosnell, *Guns on the Western Waters*, 199–200.

believed they spied "Black Terror" lying just around the upper bend. Spooked by their imaginations, they burst one of the ironclad's 11-inch Dahlgrens and spiked the other three guns. Placing a charge of powder inside the casemate, they struck a match and fled. After the explosion erupted, the detail disappeared into the woods. On March 1 Colonel Adams tried to reconstruct events leading up to the destruction of *Indianola* from men of the salvage detail who straggled into Grand Gulf. He concluded that the whole affair had been a hoax and blamed the loss of *Indianola* on the workers, who had saved nothing on the ironclad but "the wine and liquor stores."[22]

On March 5 the *Vicksburg Whig* mirthfully scolded Pemberton and Stevenson, who, "thinking that this monster would take the *Indianola* immediately issued orders to blow her up." Two days later the *Richmond Examiner* picked up the story and added, "Laugh and hold your sides lest you die of a surfeit of derision. . . . Blown up because, forsooth, a flat boat or mud scow, with a small house taken from a back garden of a plantation put on top of it, is floated down the river, before the frightened eyes of the Partisan Rangers."[23]

The chain of events that started when Porter sent Colonel Ellet on a mission to the mouth of Red River ended on the night of February 26, 1863, with the destruction of *Indianola*. The Confederates returned and attempted to raise the vessel but never did. *Queen of the West* remained in Rebel hands, but the ram never again became a factor in the Confederacy's defense of the river.

On the night of February 28, Reuben Townsend, Samuel Weaver, and David E. Hooper, all members of *Queen*'s former crew, eased *Era No. 5* into the Mississippi, cut holes in her hull, and turned her loose in the river. They got "a good ducking" because they failed to secure their boat. Charles Rivers Ellet lost a little esteem in the eyes of Admiral Porter, but this did not disturb the young colonel or make him more cautious. He still commanded six rams, and he intended to keep them busy.[24]

22. Porter's Report, n.d., Pemberton to Cooper, February 28, Adams to Reeve, March 1, 1863, *ORN*, XXIV, 397, 410, 411. *Indianola* was finally raised by a Union salvage team, refloated on January 5, 1865, and sold at Mound City, Illinois. See Bearss, *The Vicksburg Campaign*, I, 678.

23. *Vicksburg Whig*, March 5, 1863; *Richmond Examiner*, March 7, 1863.

24. David E. Hooper's Diary, February 28, 1863, David E. Hooper Papers, Crandall Collection, ISHL.

CHAPTER 8

EXPEDITIONS ABOVE VICKSBURG

Unlike General Ellet, Admiral Porter viewed the Ram Fleet not as a fighting unit but rather as a weak flotilla of utility vessels useful as dispatch or patrol boats, and on occasion, for special missions. On February 3, the day after *Queen of the West* attempted to sink *City of Vicksburg,* Porter decided that a ram could deal with guerrilla raids in the vicinity of Greenville, Mississippi, and sent *Monarch,* commanded by Captain Edwin W. Sutherland, upriver with a battalion of marines. He intended for *Monarch* to relieve the gunboat *Tyler,* which Porter believed could be put to better use in the Yazoo. Aware of the lax discipline among some members of the Ram Fleet, Porter ordered Sutherland to arrest any of *Monarch's* men who commit "outrages on the inhabitants or [their] property," and if they refused to obey orders, to "fire upon them" until they did.[1]

The admiral had already begun circulating notices along the river warning guerrillas that if they were captured in the act of firing upon

1. Porter to Sutherland, February 3, 1863, *ORN,* XXIV, 231.

unarmed vessels, they would be treated as "highwaymen and assassins" and given no quarter. If caught in the act of pillaging, levying contribution, or burning the cotton of inhabitants, they could be tried and hanged. By practicing a little vigilance, Sutherland should have no trouble carrying out his mission. On the subject of cotton, however, Porter had recently empowered his squadron to confiscate every bale "belonging to the so-called Confederate Government," and because this carried an implication of prize money, the temptation to seize cotton, wherever found, tantalized members of the Ram Fleet.[2]

Sending *Monarch* to Greenville involved more than a routine patrol to ward off guerrillas. Captain Sutherland had recently married Widow Harris, who lived at nearby Skipworth Landing, and Porter cautioned him to not relieve *Tyler* until after attending "to your own affairs" and to be prudent when visiting ashore. "The widow was a noted rebel," one observer recalled, and "such an alliance boded no good for the Captain, though he was regarded as an officer of undoubted loyalty." General Ellet, however, viewed the marriage with suspicion. He ordered nephew Charlie to not allow Sutherland's bride aboard the rams one moment longer than necessary for her to obtain passage to the North "or wherever else she may wish to go."[3]

Sutherland spent a few days honeymooning with his wife at Skipworth Landing and on February 9 moved his command over to Greenville. He found evidence of a Rebel hideout in a church by the river, but the guerrillas had fled with their horses, leaving their sick and wounded in a nearby hospital. Sutherland could not bring himself to burn either the church or the hospital, so he decided to steam over to Cyprus Bend where the ram *Dick Fulton* had been fired upon and disabled. When Porter learned of Sutherland's change of plans, he wrote, "If possible get those fieldpieces that are firing on our vessels [and] if you catch any of the party who fired on unarmed vessels hang them to the nearest tree."[4]

At Cyprus Bend Sutherland found no enemy or fieldpieces, so on February 14 he returned to Greenville. By then word had circulated through the area that the captain had taken a wife who lived at

2. Porter to Welles, February 1, Porter to Sutherland, February 13, 1863, Porter's Notice, n.d., *ibid.*, 214, 356, 365.

3. Porter to Sutherland, February 3, 1863, *ibid.*, 231; Crandall and Newell, *Ram Fleet,* 228–29; Alfred Ellet to C. R. Ellet, February 2, 1863, Ellet Papers, UM.

4. Smith to Porter, February 10, Sutherland's Report, February 11, Porter to Sutherland, February 13, 1863, *ORN,* XXIV, 337, 352, 360.

Skipworth Landing. Feeling that Sutherland might not be as hard-hearted as other Union officers, a woman of Greenville approached the captain pleading that he not destroy the town. Sutherland replied that he would not do so unless fired upon first. In his report to Porter, he claimed that the woman acted as an emissary for Confederate lieutenant colonel Samuel W. Ferguson, who proposed meeting under a flag of truce in the morning.[5]

The meeting between Sutherland and Ferguson produced two different versions. Ferguson, who commanded a detachment in the Yazoo Delta, claimed that Sutherland had asked for the meeting for the purpose of condemning Porter's orders and to be "spared the pain and mortification of having to perpetuate such barbarities." Ferguson brought several officers to the meeting, but Sutherland came alone. Ferguson read all the letters in Sutherland's possession. Then, in private talks, Ferguson concluded that the real object of Sutherland's visit was to resign from the Ram Fleet if a commission could be secured from the Confederacy. "He spoke very freely of his disgust at his present service," Ferguson reported, "and even said, 'Should I, by what influence I possess, be allowed to resign, I would not like to remain inactive during the war.'" Ferguson recommended accepting Sutherland's offer, provided *Monarch* was included in the deal. The ram could destroy a number of enemy boats and cut off supplies to Grant's army before the Union navy could respond.[6]

Sutherland knew he must report his meeting with Ferguson to Porter, but he also had to explain why they met at all. He claimed that Ferguson asked for the meeting to denounce Porter's threat to hang guerrillas and to demand an explanation for why the *Tyler* had shelled the town, "frightened women and children," shot at a sick Methodist minister, and "failed to give good and valid reasons for doing it." Ferguson also said he would burn all the Confederate cotton to keep it from falling into Union hands, and if necessary, would "run up the black flag," and follow with swift reprisals if Sutherland attempted to carry out Porter's edicts. He also promised to "hang every negro" caught "going to or coming off our boats."[7]

Sutherland had placed himself in the awkward position of trying to

5. Sutherland to Ferguson, February 14, Sutherland's Report, February 16, 1863, *ibid.*, 360, 361.

6. Ferguson to Reeve, February 15, 1863, *ORA*, XXIV, Pt. 3, p. 626.

7. Sutherland's Report, February 16, 1863, *ORN*, XXIV, 361.

delude both Porter and his own shipmates. The admiral was already suspicious of Sutherland's marriage to the Harris woman, but arrangements such as this during wartime were not entirely anomalous, and while waiting for an answer from Ferguson, Sutherland had no reason to suspect that circumstances were working against him. On February 13, however, Porter learned that Ferguson had moved about eight hundred grayclads to the vicinity of Greenville and urged Grant to send enough force to "clean out that country." Grant, looking for a useful way to employ his idle army, agreed to detach a unit from Brigadier General Andrew J. Smith's division if the navy would provide gunboats. Porter explained that *Monarch* was already on site, so on February 16 Brigadier General Stephen G. Burbridge's command made a surprise appearance off Greenville.[8]

Burbridge informed Sutherland that he intended to land about two miles above Greenville, and the captain had no alternative but to render assistance. Anxious to keep an eye on the general, Sutherland followed him eight miles inland to Deer Creek, where the brigade camped. Then he returned to his vessel. Sutherland had personal reasons for wanting Ferguson to escape, so he dispatched a message to Burbridge claiming that the detachment left behind at Greenville seemed to be "utterly demoralized" and urged the general to return. In explaining his action to Porter, Sutherland embellished his report by claiming that Burbridge's column was "one continuous line of stragglers, pillaging every house within 2 or 3 miles of the road. Arriving at my vessel I shelled the men away from the houses in reach of my guns" to keep them from "taking jewelry from the persons of women and toys of little children." Burbridge returned to Greenville, not because of Sutherland's urging but because Ferguson had moved farther inland. Contrary to Sutherland's claims, Burbridge reported good discipline and "very little straggling."[9]

On February 18, after hearing of a small Confederate force at Cypress Bend, Arkansas, Burbridge moved his brigade across the river and sent a detachment of the 6th Missouri Cavalry on a reconnaissance. For two days the 6th Missouri chased a small force of southerners from point to point and finally drove them inland. In the meantime, Ferguson re-

8. Porter to Grant, McClernand to Porter, February 15, Sutherland's Report, February 20, 1863, *ibid.*, 359–60, 361.

9. Sutherland's Report, February 20, 1863, *ibid.*, 361–62; Burbridge's Report, February 27, 1863, *ORA,* XXIV, Pt. 1, pp. 350, 352.

turned to Greenville, so Burbridge reembarked his brigade and took it back across the river to pursue the grayclads. By then Ferguson had received permission from General Pemberton to pursue negotiations with Sutherland for the purpose of securing his defection and obtaining the ram.[10]

Burbridge landed at Greenville on the morning of February 23 and learned that Colonel Ferguson had again withdrawn to Deer Creek. The general started his column in pursuit but found every bridge burned. While details rebuilt bridges, Union cavalry roamed the countryside looking for Ferguson, but all they encountered were small detachments waiting in ambush to fire a few volleys and vanish. Burbridge returned to Greenville with 325 head of livestock and about fifty prisoners, most of whom escaped when a small force of grayclads surprised the guards. Without realizing that he was praising a potential traitor, Burbridge wrote, "To Captain Sutherland, of the steam ram *Monarch,* I am indebted for many acts of courtesy. . . . His ram was with my transports from the time we reached Greenville until our return."[11]

Most of Burbridge's jaunts up and down the river were made at Sutherland's suggestion. They were useless wild goose chases that accomplished nothing, and the grayclads always managed to be several hours ahead of Burbridge's probes. On February 26 the Union forces departed on their transports, and Colonel Ferguson returned to Deer Creek.

With Burbridge's brigade out of the way, Ferguson dispatched a letter to Sutherland suggesting they meet under a flag of truce at Greenville. Sutherland never received the message. He had convoyed Burbridge back to Young's Point and on February 27 reported his return to Porter. Had Sutherland remained another twenty-four hours at Greenville, both he and his ram would probably have served out the remainder of the war in the Confederate army. Instead, Charlie Ellet became suspicious of Sutherland's frequent communications with the enemy under a flag of truce and the "coming and going to the vessel of the rebel wife." After talking to members of the crew, he removed the captain from command of *Monarch.* Instead of cashiering Sutherland, the young colonel sent him to St. Louis and directed him to report to

10. Burbridge's Report, February 27, 1863, *ORA,* XXIV, Pt. 1, pp. 350–51; Pemberton to Ferguson, February 21, 1863, *ibid.,* Pt. 3, p. 637.

11. Burbridge's Report, February 27, 1863, *ibid.,* Pt. 1, pp. 350–52.

General Ellet for service in the Mississippi Marine Brigade. Uncle Alfred was having a difficult time obtaining officers for his new squadron of boats, and Sutherland escaped further inquiry.[12]

In early February, at the time Porter sent *Queen of the West* on a solo mission to Red River and *Monarch* to Greenville, the admiral and General Grant began to hatch new schemes to flank Vicksburg by sending an expedition through the Yazoo Delta. This would enable Grant to land soldiers above the Yazoo River batteries at Haynes's and Snyder's Bluffs, attack Vicksburg's outer defenses from the rear, and secure a safe lodgment for landing the army. Porter intended to send a second detachment up the Yazoo to operate below Drumgould's Bluff, believing the two squadrons, each firing from opposite angles, would either pound the Confederate batteries into submission or drive the gunners away.[13]

With the Mississippi River running high above flood stage, water had inundated the Yazoo Delta and swelled the waterways emptying into the Yazoo River. Grant and Porter believed that light-draft boats could be floated into Yazoo Pass if engineers cut the levee at Delta, Mississippi, a small town located on the east bank of the river about six river miles below Helena, Arkansas. If the boats could navigate Yazoo Pass, they might reach the deeper Coldwater River, move into the Tallahatchie, and finally into the Yazoo.

On February 6 Porter placed Lieutenant Commander Watson Smith in charge of the expedition and detached two ironclads, *Chillicothe* and *Baron De Kalb*, and the tinclads *Rattler, Romeo, Forest Rose, Signal,* and *Marmora*. Grant provided about a hundred soldiers for each vessel and promised more if the expedition penetrated Yazoo Pass. On February 7 Porter learned that Acting Master George W. Brown and Lieutenant Colonel James H. Wilson had cut the levee, opened a channel seventy-five yards wide into the Delta, and gotten *Forest Rose* through Moon Lake to the mouth of Old Pass, where they found four fathoms of water.[14]

With sufficient depth to bring in his squadron, Brown entered Yazoo Pass on February 20 and sent word to Porter that obstructions

12. *Ibid.;* Ferguson to Sutherland, February 25, Ferguson to Reeve, February 28, Sutherland to Porter, February 27, 1863, *ORN,* XXIV, 363, 365.

13. Porter to Smith, February 6, Porter to Greer, February 27, 1863, *ORN,* XXIV, 244, 261.

14. Porter to Smith, February 6, Smith to Porter, November 2, Brown to Porter, February 4, 7, 1863, *ibid.,* 244, 245, 249, 251. *Baron De Kalb,* one of the "City Class Series" built by James Eads, was first named *St. Louis* but renamed on September 8, 1862, because there was already a sloop-of-war in the navy by the same name.

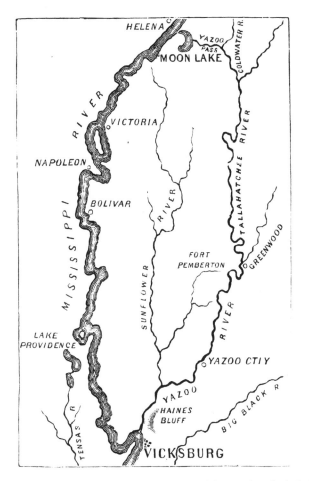

*The Mississippi and Yazoo Delta area above Vicksburg, where both the Ram
Fleet and the Mississippi Marine Brigade staged many of their operations*

Reprinted from Charles Carlton Coffin, *Marching to Victory*
(New York: Harper and Brothers, 1889)

had been cleared to the Coldwater. Eight days later, twenty-two of
Grant's transports arrived with 5,000 troops from the XIII Army
Corps under Brigadier General Leonard F. Ross. Smith took the lead
in *Chillicothe* and the expedition got under way, crawling slowly down
the Coldwater.[15]

15. Brown to Porter, November 2, 1863, *ibid.*, 245–46.

Ahead of the transports came the tinclad *Petrel,* the ram *Lioness,* commanded by First Master Thomas O'Reilly, and the recently repaired *Dick Fulton,* commanded by First Master S. Cadman. In going through Yazoo Pass the rams' high cabins and tall chimneys became entangled in willows overhanging the narrow and tortuous streams. The boats stopped frequently while men used axes and pikes to hack away branches overstretching the upper decks, and on the second day into the pass, a limb crashed upon the deck of *Lioness* and killed one member of its crew. By the time the rams reached the Coldwater, neither of them was in condition for service, having lost their chimneys and damaged their wheels. The flotilla stopped while *Lioness, Fulton,* and the transports in the rear column made repairs. *Lioness* entered Yazoo Pass with thirteen days' supplies, *Fulton* with only seven. By the time the rams reached the Coldwater, *Fulton* had lost the use of one of its boilers and fallen to the back of the column. On the Coldwater traveling became a little easier, but at night the flotilla stopped while *Petrel* and *Lioness* paddled ahead gathering cotton to protect sharpshooters on the upper decks. Neither vessel had been protected properly before entering the Delta, and Smith admitted, "I cannot do much for the rams, excepting to pack cotton forward."[16]

On March 10 the long column entered the Tallahatchie. Much time had been lost, giving the enemy ample time to take defensive measures. *Lioness* took the lead and probed ahead, its fieldpieces moved forward as a precaution against attack. Downriver smoke curled skyward, and the crew came to quarters. As the ram rounded a bend, lookouts reported a small side-wheeler, the steamer *Thirty-Fifth Parallel,* loaded with cotton and tied to a wharf. Its crew had gone ashore to burn dozens of bales still waiting to be loaded. *Lioness* advanced, firing several shots to induce the steamer to surrender, but its crew cut the vessel loose and attempted to escape. Being much faster than the cotton-laden steamer, *Lioness* closed rapidly, firing as it approached. *Parallel's* crew pretended to surrender by hoisting white flags but used the time to set the vessel on fire. They eased to the bank and fled into the woods. *Chillicothe* and *De Kalb* heard the firing and rushed down in support, only to find *Parallel* a mass of flames with *Lioness* lying off and watching.[17]

16. Smith to Porter, November 2, February 26, March 2, 3, 1863, *ibid.,* 246, 260, 261, 263; Crandall and Newell, *Ram Fleet,* 190.

17. Brown to Porter, November 2, 1863, Log of *Chillicothe, ORN,* XXIV, 246, 693; Crandall and Newell, *Ram Fleet,* 191.

During the past two weeks the enemy had responded to the navy's flanking movement by throwing up Fort Pemberton, an earthen and cotton-bale work located on a sharp S-curve near Greenwood and three miles west of where the Yalobusha joins the Tallahatchie to form the Yazoo. They placed obstructions across the river above the work and kept scouting bands of infantry roving the banks to harass the flotilla and retard its progress. By the time Union vessels began spilling into the Tallahatchie, Fort Pemberton mounted seven guns, all bearing up the river. Stretched across the river above the fort and acting as a barrier lay the scuttled *Star of the West*—the steamer that had drawn, on the night of January 9, 1861, the first cannon shots of the war when it entered the harbor of Charleston, South Carolina, to reinforce Fort Sumter. None of these defensive measures had been started at the time the Union squadron entered the Delta.[18]

At 9 A.M. on March 11 *Lioness* continued down the Tallahatchie, followed once again by the long column. On the previous night blacks had warned Smith that the Rebels were building an earthwork some twenty miles downriver, and in the morning when *Lioness* nosed around the upper bend, Fort Pemberton came suddenly in sight nine hundred yards away. With General Ross on board, Smith edged *Chillicothe* forward to make a quick reconnaissance, but as soon as the vessel rounded the bend, the fort opened with five guns, damaging the forward casemate of the ironclad, knocking off plates, and driving in the casemate's 9-inch white pine backing.[19]

Because army transports had not arrived, Smith waited until the following morning before resuming the attack. At 11:25 A.M. he brought up *De Kalb* and with *Chillicothe* swung around the bend. Smith kept *Lioness* handy to ram *Star of the West* after the ironclads silenced the fort's guns. *Baron De Kalb* opened with its rifled 42-pounders and *Chillicothe* with its two 11-inch Dahlgrens. Ninety minutes later both vessels ran out of ammunition. Smith had no way of knowing that Fort Pemberton was running short of projectiles for their rifled 32-pounder, and if *Lioness* had made its ramming run promptly at 1:00 P.M., *Star of the West* might have been shoved aside

18. Brown to Pemberton, February 9, 17, Loring to Pemberton, February 21, 1863, *ORN*, XXIV, 294, 295, 296; Loring to Memminger, March 22, 1863, *ORA*, XXIV, Pt. 1, p. 415.

19. Smith to Porter, November 2, 1863, Log of *Chillicothe*, *ORN*, XXIV, 246, 693. Fort Pemberton was also called Fort Greenwood.

enough to allow the Union flotilla to pass. *Chillicothe,* however, received another mauling from Fort Pemberton's battery. After the fighting, word reached Smith that reinforcements were on the way. He withdrew to wait for their arrival and set the crews to work buttressing the damaged casemates with cotton. On March 13 the two ironclads battled the fort once more, only to be beaten off again.[20]

When reinforcements—a brigade commanded by Brigadier General Isaac F. Quinby—did not arrive, Smith suffered from a condition Porter described as "softening of the brain" and turned the squadron over to Lieutenant Commander James P. Foster. A week passed before Quinby reached the Tallahatchie, and by then Fort Pemberton had mounted two more guns—including an 8-inch naval gun—and filled its rifle pits with reinforcements. Quinby took one look at the flooded lowlands and decided against mounting a land attack. On March 23 Foster made one more attempt to silence Fort Pemberton, but failed. By then the fort had become too strong, and Foster, separated by two hundred miles of unprotected communications, gave up the enterprise and withdrew.[21]

The squadron had no alternative but to retrace its route through Yazoo Pass, and on April 10, when the flotilla reached Helena, every vessel bore the scars of its journey into the Tallahatchie. The men of *Lioness* and *Fulton* had been for several days out of supplies, living, as did those aboard *Chillicothe* and many of the vessels of the navy, off the army's generosity. The two rams came out of the pass in virtually unserviceable condition, and *Lioness* had drawn the disdain of naval observers as being a vessel that burned too much coal. Both rams returned with large amounts of confiscated cotton—a windfall that helped pay for their trip. Porter turned the bales over to naval authorities at Milliken's Bend, leaving the matter of prize money to be determined at a later date.[22]

After the Yazoo Pass fiasco, Porter could find little use for the two rams. *Dick Fulton* became a tow vessel, and though the admiral some-

20. Smith to Porter, March 13, November 2, 1863, *ORN,* XXIV, 273–74, 247.

21. Pemberton to Fuller, April 17, 1863, *ORA,* XXIV, Pt. 3, pp. 721–22; Quinby to McPherson, March 21, 1863, *ibid.,* Pt. 1, p. 407; Smith to Porter, March 22, Foster to Porter, March 18, April 13, 1863, *ORN,* XXIV, 285, 284, 283; Porter, "Journal of Occurrences," I, 532, Porter Papers, LC.

22. Smith to Porter, March 7, 16, Foster to Commanding Officer, April 10, 1863, *ORN,* XXIV, 264, 278, 291; Porter, "Journal of Occurrences," I, 534–35, Porter Papers, LC.

times added the ram to a convoy of transports, it never participated in another important expedition. *Lioness,* however, still had a future.[23]

Before the Yazoo Pass expedition, *Lioness* had been engaged with *Horner* in bringing down provisions and stores from Cairo, and *Monarch* and *Fulton* had been operating near Greenville, Mississippi. Porter never again used any of the four vessels on a meaningful mission, though they continued on patrols and often engaged in convoying Grant's transports. *Switzerland* and *Lancaster,* however, were about to undergo a severe test, but not with Porter's knowledge.[24]

23. Porter to Welles, May 8, 1863, *ORN,* XXIV, 658.
24. Porter to Welles, February 8, Selfridge to Porter, February 19, Porter to Welles, April 6, May 8, 1863, *ibid.,* 324, 425, 532, 658.

CHAPTER 9

"RASH, AMBITIOUS, EVEN INSUBORDINATE . . ."

With the section of the Mississippi River between Vicksburg and Port Hudson once again open to Confederate commerce, Secretary Welles worried that *Indianola* might still be salvaged by the Confederacy, and if joined by *Webb* and *Queen,* pose a threat to Farragut's squadron below Port Hudson. Farragut, however, recognized the importance of blockading Red River. For several weeks he had been pressing General Banks to cooperate in capturing Port Hudson, thereby opening the Mississippi to Union gunboats, but the general was preoccupied with mounting an expedition up the Atchafalaya River from Berwick Bay.[1]

Frustrated by Banks's temporizing, Farragut resolved to run Port Hudson's batteries and reclaim control of the central Mississippi. To

1. Welles to Farragut, March 2, Banks to Halleck, February 28, 1863, *ORN,* XIX, 645, 640.

one of his officers he declared, "The time has come; there can be no more delay. I must go—army or no army."[2]

Running past Port Hudson involved the same risks as passing Vicksburg, but Farragut would have to take his chances against a much stronger current. Annoyed daily by the steady delivery of supplies to Port Hudson, he could sit and watch no longer. After *Queen of the West* tied to the landing to deposit a cargo, Farragut's impatience peaked, and he finally induced Banks to occupy the Rebels' attention so he could move seven of his oceangoing ships above Port Hudson. On the night of March 14 Banks launched a feeble and poorly coordinated diversion. Farragut made his run but lost the USS *Mississippi*. Port Hudson's batteries stopped the squadron at the bend below the town, and all the vessels turned back but *Hartford* and *Albatross,* which came through the fire lashed together. By then *Queen of the West* had withdrawn, but Colonel Ellet's reckless raid up Red River continued to take its toll.[3]

Separated from his squadron, Farragut proceeded with *Hartford* and *Albatross* to Red River, where he picked up two of Ellet's crew from *Queen of the West.* They had been hiding in the woods for several weeks and informed Farragut of the destruction of *Indianola.* Confederate shipping had all fled up Red River, so Farragut got under way on the morning of March 17 and headed for Vicksburg. Two days later he anchored below Warrenton and sent a message to Grant, suggesting a joint meeting with Porter and asking for coal.[4]

Porter, however, had taken General Sherman on a flanking expedition, this one into Steele's Bayou, and had not been heard from since. Farragut dispatched his secretary, Edward C. Gabaudan, to locate the admiral and open communications. While Farragut waited, Grant responded to his request and on the night of March 21 sent down a coal barge. In the morning Farragut learned from Grant that Porter might be gone indefinitely, so he explained his reasons for coming to Vicksburg. He told Grant that he intended to ask Porter for two rams

2. Quoted from Alfred T. Mahan, *Admiral Farragut* (New York, 1892), 211, with no date.

3. Farragut's Report, March 16, Alden's Journal, March 14, 1863, *ORN,* XIX, 665–68, 768. See also Charles Lee Lewis, *David Glasgow Farragut: Our First Admiral* (Annapolis, 1943), 165–82.

4. Farragut to Welles, March 19, Farragut to Grant, March 20, 1863, Log of *Hartford, ORN,* XX, 3–4, 5, 763–64.

and an ironclad to strengthen the blockade of Red River. He had some doubts whether *Hartford* and *Albatross,* the latter being a small gunboat, could hold the river against *Webb, Queen, Dr. Beatty,* and *Grand Era* while at the same time keeping a sharp watch on all the other crossing points along the Mississippi.[5]

On March 22, while Farragut probed Grant for support, General Ellet arrived at Young's Point from St. Louis with the Mississippi Marine Brigade and learned unofficially from Charlie of the admiral's request for two rams. In Porter's absence, Captain Walke looked after the Mississippi Squadron, and when General Ellet asked for a copy of Farragut's letter, Walke refused. Not to be brushed aside so easily, Ellet dispatched a note to Farragut asking if he could be of service. A squad of marines, guided by a young man who lived in Vicksburg, volunteered to carry the message across the peninsula. Wading through sloughs with water up to their armpits and crawling over huge piles of drift thrown up by the flooded river, the mud-smeared men hailed a boat, and after much questioning, finally delivered the note to the admiral. Farragut assumed the general had authority to act on his own and on March 23 invited him to come on board *Hartford* for a conference.[6]

There being no moon, General Ellet felt strongly that two rams could be sent down to Farragut without risk, and he walked eleven miles across the peninsula to express his willingness to provide them. Farragut stressed that he did not wish to interfere with Porter's command, but having two rams would be most "gratifying."[7]

Ellet recrossed the peninsula and advised Walke that he intended to send *Switzerland* and *Lancaster* down to Farragut during the night and urged the captain to include a gunboat. With the recent loss of *Indianola* still hanging like a dark cloud over the Mississippi Squadron, Walke would not risk another disaster, especially during Porter's absence. He never had much confidence in the Ram Fleet and refused to participate, but he wished Ellet good luck.[8]

5. Grant to Farragut, March 21, 1863, *ORA,* XXIV, Pt. 3, p. 123; Farragut to Grant, March 22, 1863, *ORN,* XX, 9–10.

6. Ellet to Walke, Ellet to Farragut and Foltz, March 22, Farragut to Ellet, May 23, Ellet's Report, May 13, 1863, *ORN,* XX, 13, 12, 52–53; Sanford, "Recollections of the Ram Fleet," Civil War Collection, MHS; Clarke, ed., *Warfare along the Mississippi,* 71–75.

7. Farragut to Ellet, March 23, Ellet's Report, May 13, *ORN,* XX, 14, 53.

8. Ellet to Walke, Walke to Ellet, March 24, 1863, *ibid.,* 16.

In the meantime, Farragut shelled Warrenton's bothersome battery and suggested to Grant an amphibious attack to dispose of it. The general had been looking for useful ways to employ his troops and ordered Major General Frederick Steele to make two regiments available for the attack. To transport the infantry across the river, Grant asked Ellet for "ten or twelve small boats." Ellet thought he had a better idea. Since he intended to send down two rams on the night of March 24–25, they would provide better transportation than small boats, and since Farragut had agreed to help with *Albatross* and employ *Hartford* to provide a covering fire, no small boats would be needed.[9]

To lead this dangerous mission, General Ellet picked his nephew, the family daredevil, and on the afternoon of the 24th Colonel Charles Rivers Ellet took command of *Switzerland* and *Lancaster*. The general added two more Ellets to the venture—his son Edward, to go with Charlie, and his nephew John A. Ellet, to command *Lancaster*. With only enough volunteers to man the rams, he made hasty preparations for a late-night passage of Vicksburg's batteries. The crew lashed yawls to the starboard guards for use in an emergency and dangled knotted ropes over the sides for men to cling to if driven from the deck by a ruptured boiler or a broken steampipe. The general warned Charlie not to stop and render assistance if one of the rams became disabled, but to "run on down" because Farragut needed help for "keeping possession of the river between Vicksburg and Port Hudson." After designating the night of March 25–26 for the Warrenton attack, Alfred Ellet explained to Charlie the importance of having both rams available for the joint operation. Because on past occasions his nephew had not kept him informed, the general added, "Report to me [at] every convenient opportunity."[10]

Colonel Ellet had limited time to prepare for the late-night run. The crews worked in darkness loading stores and provisions. Time passed quickly, and not until 4:30 A.M. on the 25th did the rams weigh anchor and get under way. With lights extinguished, *Switzerland,* commanded by Major John W. Lawrence, took the lead, and *Lancaster,* commanded by cousin John Ellet, followed close behind. To keep noise to a minimum, the vessels drifted with the current, but to keep

<hr />

9. Grant to Farragut, Farragut to Grant, Grant to Steele, March 23, Grant to Ellet, Crandall to Grant, March 24, 1863, *ORA*, XXIV, Pt. 3, pp. 131, 132, 133, 136–37.

10. A. W. Ellet to C. R. Ellet, March 24, 1863, *ORN*, XX, 17.

the bows faced downriver, the wheels needed to be turned at times. A light westerly wind blew the slightest sound across the peninsula and into the faces of sentinels watching the river at Vicksburg's Water Battery. From time to time the rams' escape pipes released a noisy burst of steam, and minutes before the vessels rounded De Soto Point, enemy signal lights flashed from one battery to the next. "Concealment was useless," Colonel Ellet declared. "[Dawn] was beginning to break, and I saw if we were to pass at all, it was to be done at once." Though the colonel still had the option of aborting the mission, he had confidence in the speed of his rams, and with the boilers registering 160 pounds of steam, he ordered *Switzerland* full ahead.[11]

The Water Battery opened on *Switzerland* as it rounded the point. The first fifteen shots landed in the water, but as the ram closed range and approached the Wyman's Hill batteries, enemy fire became more intense and accurate. "Shot after shot struck my boat," Charlie Ellet reported, "tearing everything to pieces." He looked aft and observed *Lancaster*, two hundred yards to the rear, steaming steadily through a hail of shot, with splinters flying off its deck as shots ripped through the upperworks. Three-quarters of a mile below the point, a 10-inch shell plunged through *Switzerland*'s boiler deck and punched a hole in the center boiler. A cloud of steam gushed through the hatchways, filling the pilothouse with hot, suffocating vapor. With the engines stopped, Ellet made the pilots stand at their posts to keep the ram drifting with the current. As the steam cleared, he could distinctly hear the cheering of Rebels, and he looked back just in time to witness an explosion on *Lancaster*. Moments later the ram sank, bow first. Knowing that all the guns would now be directed on *Switzerland*, Ellet ordered the crew to take cover in "as secure a position as possible."[12]

General Ellet had crossed the peninsula early that morning and posted himself on the bank with Captain Crandall. There he waited in "indescribable torture" for his son and two nephews to come into sight. When he heard the enemy cheering, he knew they had encountered trouble. Sensing that a disaster had occurred, he and Crandall jumped into a yawl and began pulling into the river. *Switzerland* drifted into view, stern first, with steam still pouring from the hatches. Ellet spotted his son Edward, standing on the hurricane deck with

11. C. R. Ellet's Report, J. A. Ellet's Report, March 25, 1863, *ibid.*, 19, 20–21.
12. C. R. Ellet's Report, Walke's Report, March 25, 1863, *ibid.*, 20, 18–19.

Charlie, both of them shouting for him to go back, that they were all uninjured. Ignoring their advice, General Ellet jumped on board the ram as it floated by the last Vicksburg battery. With a tow from *Albatross*, *Switzerland* came to anchor off Brown & Johnson's Landing. Taking a quick count, Ellet found one engineer scalded and five of the crew missing and presumed drowned. Several minutes later, after pulling through a storm of grape and shell, John Ellet came alongside in a yawl with some of *Lancaster*'s survivors. The general finally relaxed. He had lost a ram but none of his family.[13]

Lancaster's misfortunes began when a shot from one of the upper batteries passed through both chimneys. Five minutes later another shot struck under the pilothouse, carried away the steps, and sliced off the foot of the reserve helmsman, who waited by the steps to be called if needed. Most of the shots from the Water Battery ineffectually riddled the ram's upperworks, and just about the time John Ellet believed he could safely pass the city, a shot exploded the steam drum and enveloped the vessel "in a terrible cloud" of hot vapor. Most of the crew sought shelter in the bow, where a breeze protected them from the steam. A heavy projectile plunged through the vulnerable stern, passed diagonally through the vessel, and pierced the bottom of the hull beneath where they stood. The vessel began to rapidly fill, but Andrew J. Dennis, the pilot, stayed at the wheel and attempted to con the vessel ashore. After a shot demolished the wheel, John Ellet went below with Dennis to operate the tiller ropes by hand. They found the vessel filling with water, and on returning to deck noticed that the ram had spun around in an eddy and lay almost motionless under Vicksburg's Marine Hospital Battery. John Ellet ordered the yawls cut loose and the vessel abandoned. Moments later *Lancaster* sank near the lower end of the canal. Ellet saved all but one person, Orderly Sergeant William H. McDonald, who attempted to swim ashore and drowned.[14]

At 5:15 A.M., on hearing the first firing from above, Farragut ordered *Hartford* to open on Warrenton's batteries. He passed them at 7:15 and continued upriver just in time to see *Lancaster* sink and *Switzerland* adrift. Why Colonel Ellet waited until dawn's early light to pass Vicksburg puzzled Farragut, because doing so had never been the

13. C. R. Ellet's Report, March 25, 1863, *ibid.*, 20; Alfred Ellet to wife, Sara, March 26, 1863, Ellet Papers, UM.

14. J. A. Ellet's Report, March 25, 1863, *ORN*, XX, 22.

admiral's intention, and he blamed the general—not the colonel—for sending down the rams in "broad daylight."[15]

On the evening of the 25th Porter emerged from an unsuccessful flanking movement up Steele's Bayou only to be vexed by another disaster, the loss of *Lancaster*. Furious, he wrote General Ellet, asking by what authority had the rams been sent past Vicksburg "in open day, and without taking any precautions to guard their hulls?" The general considered the letter impertinent, but he replied temperately, explaining the mission as a reaction to "an urgent request from Admiral Farragut," and accepted full responsibility for the consequences. Porter also demanded to know the names of the persons responsible for the vessels. When he learned that Charles Rivers Ellet had led the mission, and another Ellet the *Lancaster*, he said he could have predicted the outcome. As one historian observed, "Rash, ambitious, even insubordinate, are adjectives that come to mind when one describes the Ellets, but no one could suggest that they lacked courage."[16]

Farragut intervened and wrote Porter, first to exonerate himself from any intention "to interfere with your command," and second to defend General Ellet, who, by responding to a consensus of senior officers, had merely acted "in accordance with your wishes if you were present." Though Farragut concurred that Colonel Ellet should not have attempted to make the run during daylight, he still made it plain to Porter that he needed two rams and an ironclad to maintain the blockade of Red River. Without reinforcements, he could not personally drop below Port Hudson and resume command of his squadron. Porter agreed to part only with *Switzerland,* but he warned Farragut to not let Colonel Ellet get out of sight "or he will go off on a cruise somewhere before you know it, and then get the ship into trouble."[17]

When Mary Ellet Cabell, Charlie's sister, learned that Porter had considered placing her brother under arrest for disobeying orders, she wrote, "I have nothing to say of Porter—he is a bad, base man & you

15. Stevenson to Memminger, March 25, Stevenson to Pemberton, March 25, 1863, *ORA*, XXIV, Pt. 1, p. 480; Farragut to Porter, March 25, 1863, Log of *Hartford, ORN,* XX, 25, 764.

16. Porter to Ellet, Ellet to Porter, March 25, 1863, *ORN,* XX, 23; Milligan, *Gunboats down the Mississippi,* 145.

17. Farragut to Porter, March 25, Porter to Farragut, March 26, 1863, *ORN,* XX, 24–25, 29.

have everything to fear from his . . . cunning. My blood boils to think that you have to fight friends as well as the enemies of the country you are dying to save."[18]

On March 28 General Ellet placed his nephew, Lieutenant Colonel John A. Ellet, in charge of *Switzerland* and sent him downriver to hasten repairs on the ram. While men worked around the clock repairing *Switzerland*'s boilers, Porter floated down a barge laden with provisions. The crew fired the boilers on the night of the 29th, and by midday on the 30th they had the bunkers filled and the bulwarks reinforced with cotton bales. Charles Rivers Ellet remained in command of the Ram Fleet but returned to Milliken's Bend with his uncle. John Ellet shoved off before dawn on the morning of the 31st and, accompanied by Company G, 101st Illinois, began the descent to rendezvous with *Hartford* and *Albatross* below Warrenton. Upriver, *City of Vicksburg* broke from her moorings and floated by Warrenton about the same time. A patrol set her on fire, and the burning derelict passed by *Hartford* a few minutes before *Switzerland* arrived.[19]

At 6:00 A.M. on March 31 Farragut signaled *Switzerland* to take the lead and get under way—followed by *Albatross* and *Hartford*. During the admiral's twelve-day stay below Vicksburg, Brigadier General John S. Bowen, commanding Grand Gulf, used the time to add heavy guns to his two main batteries. He waited patiently for *Hartford*'s descent, but Farragut next stopped at Hurricane Island to look for the remnants of *Indianola*. He found nothing and concluded that recent floods had pushed the ironclad into deeper water. Before passing Grand Gulf, Farragut next stopped at New Carthage to wait for darkness. General Bowen had posted sentinels along the banks with rockets to warn of the approach of the vessels, but after Farragut failed to arrive when expected, the lookouts left their posts for dinner. At 7:35 P.M. *Switzerland* nosed around the bend and came in view of the battery at Point of Rocks. The watch sounded the alarm, and men rushed back to their pieces. Helped along by a six-mile-an-hour current and a very dark night, *Switzerland* steamed down the stem of the river, rounded the bend at Point of Rocks, and though struck twice, reached safety with

18. Mary Ellet to C. R. Ellet, April 4, 1863, Cabell-Ellet Papers, UV.

19. A. W. Ellet to J. A. Ellet, March 28, Porter to Farragut, March 26, 1863, Log of *Hartford*, *ORN*, XX, 28, 31, 765; Crandall and Newell, *Ram Fleet*, 228.

only slight damage. *Albatross* ran the batteries without being hit, but a shot struck *Hartford* and killed one man.[20]

Farragut anchored for the night a few miles below Grand Gulf and resumed the downward journey at daylight. On April 1 *Switzerland* destroyed two flatboats at St. Catherine's Bend and at nightfall joined *Hartford* and *Albatross* at the mouth of Red River. In the morning Ellet sent men ashore to do a little foraging. They returned with a boat filled with provisions, ammunition, and three live hogs, warning that "the 'rebs' anticipated 'gobbling up' our three vessels without trouble."[21]

Farragut took measures to protect his vessels from the type of attack that had captured *Indianola*. To guard against enemy rams, he ordered a raft of cypress logs slung around each vessel, and he made the gun crews sleep at their stations. The precautions were not entirely necessary. When General Banks's army started up the Atchafalaya River, they came across *Queen of the West* and destroyed it, thereby eliminating the greatest threat to Farragut's vessels.[22]

From time to time Farragut steamed down to the bend above Port Hudson to communicate by land with the squadron posted below the town's batteries. *Switzerland* went along to rid the Mississippi of small boats used to carry supplies across the river, but Farragut never let Ellet out of sight for any length of time. A month passed, and the admiral grew tired of performing blockade duty. General Banks had brought a portion of his army across the river and wanted naval support for his expedition to Alexandria, Louisiana. Farragut could not take *Hartford* up Red River. Nor would he risk sending *Albatross,* a small gunboat, or *Switzerland,* which carried only light fieldpieces. The ram made one quick reconnaissance up Red River to Fort De Russy (formerly Fort Taylor), but Farragut specifically forbade Ellet from venturing farther. During *Switzerland*'s brief absence, Farragut learned that on April 16 Porter's squadron had passed Vicksburg and

20. Gabaudan to Morris, April 13, J. A. Ellet's Report, May 20, Farragut to Welles, April 6, 1863, Log of *Hartford*, *ORN,* XX, 36, 41, 48, 765; Bowen to Memminger, March 27, 1863, *ORA,* XXIV, Pt. 3, pp. 693–94. See also John A. Ellet's Journal, 1–2, Ellet Papers, NA.

21. John Ellet's Journal, 3, Ellet Papers, NA.

22. Alfred T. Mahan, *The Gulf and Inland Waters* (New York, 1901), 152; Banks to Grant, April 23, Pemberton to Cooper, April 21, 1863, *ORA,* XXIV, Pt. 3, pp. 224, 773.

anchored at New Carthage, twenty river miles above Grand Gulf. What Banks needed were durable light-draft gunboats, so Farragut detached *Switzerland* and sent Ellet upriver to urge Porter to send down his ironclads.[23]

At 5:30 P.M. on May 2, John Ellet found Porter already below Grand Gulf and delivered Farragut's and Banks's messages. Grant had landed troops at Bruinsburg on April 30, and most of the army had already moved inland. Porter needed to make a decision—could he drop down the river and support Banks, or must he remain off Bruinsburg to aid Grant? His answer came early on the morning of May 3 when the Rebels abandoned Grand Gulf and blew up the fort, leaving the river open from the canal cut below Vicksburg to Port Hudson. With Grand Gulf eliminated, Porter conferred with Grant and, with the general's blessing, formed a squadron to support Banks. At noon he started down the Mississippi, taking the ironclads *Benton, Lafayette,* and *Pittsburg,* the gunboat *General Price,* the tug *Ivy,* and the ram *Switzerland.*[24]

At 1 A.M. on May 4 Porter found Farragut off Red River and exchanged signals. The two admirals met on *Hartford,* and after a brief conference Porter agreed to take his squadron up to Alexandria and support Banks. Farragut detached *Arizona* and *Estrella*—two gunboats that had come up the Atchafalaya from Berwick Bay—and *Albatross.* He also returned *Switzerland,* and at daylight Porter started up Red River. Ellet took the lead, stopping briefly at abandoned Fort De Russy to remove a raft that had been anchored and strung across the river. The squadron reached Alexandria on the morning of May 7 and took possession of the town. Banks arrived that evening, a little too late to claim victory.[25]

Porter left the town in Banks's possession and began working back down the Red, sending *Switzerland* and his two light-drafts up the larger tributaries to destroy stores and river commerce. Along the sixty-five-mile stretch of Black River to Trinity, Ellet found the landings

23. Ellet's Report, May 20, Farragut to J. A. Ellet, April 29, May 1, 1863, *ORN,* XX, 42, 68–69. 69–70; John Ellet's Journal, 15, Ellet Papers, NA.

24. Porter to Welles, May 3, 7, 1863, Log of *Carondelet, ORN,* XXIV, 626–27, 645, 692; J. A. Ellet to A. W. Ellet, May 20, 1863, *ibid.,* XX, 41–42.

25. Farragut to Porter, Porter to Farragut, May 4, J. A. Ellet to A. W. Ellet, May 20, 1863, *ibid.,* XX, 76, 42; Farragut to Welles, May 4, 1863, Farragut Papers, USNAM; Farragut to Welles, May 7, 1863, *ORN,* XXIV, 645.

stacked with bacon, sugar, molasses, salt, tobacco, and saltpeter—all waiting for shipment to Port Hudson. Moving into the Ouachita, Ellet reached as far as Harrisonburg before being stopped at Fort Beauregard, an earthwork with one 42-pounder, two 32-pounders, and twelve fieldpieces, all well protected. Unlike cousin Charles, who might have tried to force a passage, John Ellet waited for *Pittsburg, Arizona,* and *Price* to try their guns on the fort, but the defenders held the line. Ellet steamed back down to the Red to report the problem to Porter, who recalled the squadron and sent *Switzerland* back to Alexandria to cooperate with Brigadier General Godfrey Weitzel. Weitzel had been left behind with two brigades after Banks started his army to Simmesport in preparation for the investment of Port Hudson.[26]

On May 14 Weitzel learned that an undetermined number of grayclads had returned to an area twenty miles upstream from Alexandria. He sent two companies of horsemen to reconnoiter and learned that Colonel W. P. Lane's 1st Texas Partisan Regiment of one thousand dismounted cavalry and several pieces of light artillery had entered the area. Believing he could trap the unit, Weitzel placed a combined force of three hundred infantry, cavalry, and artillery on *Switzerland* and sent them upriver to flank Lane's force. Because of the low stage of the river, and having no experienced pilots, Ellet had to sound his way over the falls above Alexandria. By the time he reached the deeper water above, the enemy spotted the ram and abandoned their cotton breastworks.[27]

When Porter assimilated the Ram Fleet, he had already formed the opinion that the boats were best suited as transports. With most of the Mississippi now in control of the Union navy, and with no enemy gunboats on the river, the rams had become an obsolete weapon. When General Weitzel put an armed force on *Switzerland* to attack the enemy movement by water instead of by land, he applied the ram in its most useful way. This system for transporting a strike force by water had already been approved by Porter and organized by General Ellet under the name of the Mississippi Marine Brigade. The brigade, however, did not include *Switzerland,* which remained part of the Ram Fleet, and *Switzerland* would be isolated from both commands until after Vicksburg surrendered.

26. J. A. Ellet to A. W. Ellet, May 20, 1863, *ORN*, XX, 42.
27. *Ibid.,* 43; Weitzel to Irwin, May 18, 19, 1863, *ORA*, XXVI, Pt. 1, pp. 35–36, 38.

On May 20 John Ellet took the vessel back to the mouth of Red River and went to work repairing the boat's boilers. He lay there until June 3, when Captain Walke sent the ram to Simmesport on a reconnaissance. Greeted by a battery of guns from Colonel Joseph Phillips's 3rd Arizona Regiment, *Switzerland* stood off and returned the fire. Struck seven times—including two shots at the waterline, two setting the cotton bulwarks ablaze, and another severing the steampipe—Ellet gave up the fight and, while making repairs, limped toward the mouth of Red River with one killed and two wounded. Observing Walke approaching on *Lafayette*, Ellet explained the situation, and both vessels returned to Simmesport to finish the fight. Walke brought *Lafayette*'s heavy guns to bear and chased away the enemy. According to a correspondent from the *Memphis Bulletin* who witnessed the fight, Walke and Ellet sent men ashore and "burned the place." Both officers omitted any incendiary actions from their reports.[28]

For a while, John Ellet's fighting came to an end. *Switzerland*'s boilers seeped, the hull leaked, and by the time the vessel reached Vicksburg on July 5, the paddle wheels were so badly damaged that the boat could no longer travel far. Had Alfred Ellet not formed the Mississippi Marine Brigade and brought it to Vicksburg in late March, the war would have been over for the Ellets. Instead, the fighting was just beginning for one of the most unlikely task forces ever organized for riverine war.[29]

28. Walke to Porter, June 4, Ellet to Walke, June 3, 1862, *ORN,* XXV, 154–55, 155–56; Walke to Palmer, June 3, 1863, *ibid.,* XX, 220; J. B. Bingham to *Memphis Bulletin,* June 11, 1863, Ellet Papers, NA.

29. Andrews to Palmer, May 18, 1863, *ORA,* XXVI, Pt. 1, p. 493; J. A. Ellet to C. A. Ellet, May 20, 1863, *ORN,* XX, 43; J. A. Ellet to A. W. Ellet, July 5, 1863, *ibid.,* XXV, 227.

CHAPTER 10

THE MISSISSIPPI MARINE BRIGADE

Though the surviving vessels of the Ram Fleet continued to operate, General Ellet lost interest in the command and concentrated all of his efforts on forming the Mississippi Marine Brigade. When he experienced recruiting difficulties, he became desperate enough to ask General Halleck for permission to enlist convalescents recovering in St. Louis hospitals. The request sounded radical, but on December 21, 1862, Stanton gave approval, believing that soldiers unable to march could serve effectively on boats. Captains James R. Crandall and William H. Wright immediately distributed handbills as far east as the Department of the Ohio, which read:

MISSISSIPPI MARINE BRIGADE
SOLDIERING MADE EASY!
NO HARD MARCHING!
NO CARRYING KNAPSACKS!
There will be but very little
marching for any of the troops.

They will be provided on the
Boats with good cooks and bedding.[1]

Another handbill, even more enticing, announced:

> The proposed service is especially attractive to old soldiers. It has the
> following advantages:
> 1. There are no trenches to dig.
> 2. There are no rebel houses to guard.
> 3. There is no picket duty to perform.
> 4. There is no danger of camps in the mud, but always a chance to
>   sleep under cover.
> 5. There is no chance of short rations.
> 6. The command will always be kept together.[2]

Recovering veterans, however, found neither the $100 enlistment
bonus nor the peculiar service especially attractive. Convalescents were
not ideal candidates for filling the ranks of an amphibious strike force
composed of infantry, cavalry, and artillery, so on February 11, 1863,
Stanton solved the problem by transferring to the Marine Brigade
men of the 59th and 63rd Illinois and, from the Ram Fleet, Company
K of the 18th Illinois. Lieutenant Colonel Currie, who once commanded the ram *Mingo,* herded the new command of horse marines
into Benton Barracks on the Fair Grounds in northwestern St. Louis
and drilled them while General Ellet concentrated on outfitting his
new flotilla.[3]

Both Stanton, who financed the Mississippi Marine Brigade, and
Porter, who endorsed its formation, had waited since November 8,
1862, for Ellet to organize the unit. Before joining the Ram Fleet the
general had never been a boatman, and his entire career afloat began in
June 1862 when he took command of the ram *Monarch.* Since then, he
had spent most of his time at anchor or ashore. Unlike Charles, his deceased older brother, Alfred Ellet never received a good education,
having devoted the better part of his forty-two years to a life of farming. His great height and enormous physique made him a commanding

1. Crandall and Newell, *Ram Fleet,* 256.
2. Newsclip, n.d., in Crandall Collection, ISHL.
3. Ellet to Halleck, December 20, Halleck to Ellet, December 21, 1862, *ORA,* Ser.
3, II, 952–53; Special Order No. 60, February 11, 1863, quoted in Crandall and Newell,
Ram Fleet, 166; Clarke, ed., *Warfare along the Mississippi,* 60–62.

figure, and nobody questioned his skill as a horseman, but as a general commanding a brigade he had not been tested.[4]

While organizing the unit, Ellet left most of the work to others. Captain James C. Brooks, the Ram Fleet's quartermaster and fiscal agent, became responsible for outfitting seven new boats and spent $350,000 doing so. After much trouble, he purchased five large New Orleans packets at Louisville and New Albany—*Autocrat, B. J. Adams, Baltic, Diana,* and *John Raine*—and modified each boat to carry about 125 cavalry, with horses, and 250 infantry. The other two boats were *E. H. Fairchild,* a supply vessel, and *Woodford,* a hospital boat. Ellet expected to command two fleets, but by the time he activated the Mississippi Marine Brigade, four of the vessels of the Ram Fleet had been captured, sunk, or decommissioned, and the others confined by Porter to menial riverine operations.[5]

Brooks stripped the brigade's newly acquired boats and began modifying them by expanding the coal bunkers and protecting the boilers with heavy timbers. He encased the cabins from the lower deck to the hurricane roof with a double thickness of two-inch laminated oak planks loopholed for rifle muskets and cut with large swinging doors for ventilation. He placed semicircular sheets of boiler iron around the pilothouse without inhibiting the view of the pilots. Brooks provided spacious officers' cabins aft and put the men's sleeping quarters inside the intermediate deck with their messroom forward. Each vessel carried a large crane fitted with hooks and pulleys on the forecastle so a railed gateway could be quickly dropped—one wide enough to enable two horses abreast to come and go. To repulse boarders, a hot-water hose connected to the boilers hung ready near the deck. By March 5 Brooks had all the boats ready for service except the hospital ship, *Woodford,* but Ellet still needed men.[6]

Recruiting became the responsibility of Captain Warren D. Crandall, Ellet's assistant adjutant general, and because there was little else for two aides-de-camp to do until the brigade was raised, the general's

4. Welles to Stanton, October 31, Stanton to Ellet, November 8, 1862, *ORN,* XXIII, 428, 469; Crandall and Newell, *Ram Fleet,* 248–49.

5. Brooks's Historical Sketch, November 1, 1865, Brooks to Porter, November 29, Ellet to Halleck, December 13, 1862, *ORN,* XXIII, 277, 514–15, 630–31.

6. Ellet to Stanton, March 4, 1863, *ORA,* Ser. 3, III, 59; Crandall and Newell, *Ram Fleet,* 259.

son, Lieutenant Edward C. Ellet, and his friend, Lieutenant Sanford G. Scarritt, helped. They occupied rooms on the second floor of a building on Third Street near the post office. Captain George Q. White became quartermaster, Captain W. M. Lewis, paymaster, and Major James Robarts, surgeon-in-chief. Headquarters soon became "a veritable beehive" where Crandall, his clerks, and other officers "worked early and late," but not very productively, in their efforts to recruit the brigade. The general never appointed or asked for a chaplain. Had he done so, the periodic intervention of spiritual influence might have suppressed the rowdiness of the brigade.[7]

By mid-December General Ellet realized that if he could not get men transferred from units already in the service, or convalescents from hospitals, he would soon have seven boats and too few troops. Recruiting jaunts to Louisville, Nashville, Cincinnati, and Cleveland produced a few convalescents to serve as boatmen, primarily because Crandall made promises the general, at a later time, would find difficult to keep.[8]

On February 21, 1863, Ellet reviewed his brigade at the Fair Grounds—527 infantry, 368 cavalry, and 140 artillery. His rolls were still short about 500 men. The marines wore traditional army uniforms, the only difference being the caps, which were made with full round tops, broad straight visors, and a wide green band trimmed with gold lace. All the small arms were new, but the artillerists had only received six light field guns.[9]

The general organized his brigade into three sections—a regiment of infantry, a battalion of cavalry, and four batteries of artillery. Off the parade ground units never operated together, each being split about equally among the boats. Nineteen-year-old Colonel Charles Rivers Ellet commanded the infantry regiment, but his executive officer, Lieutenant Colonel Currie, provided the knowledge and experience to guide day-to-day operations. The regiment contained the traditional ten companies, each with a captain, the only exception being Company B, which was led by a lieutenant. Major James M. Hubbard commanded four companies of cavalry and Captain Daniel P. Walling the light artillery. Changes in the roster of officers constantly occurred.

7. Crandall and Newell, *Ram Fleet*, 253, 260.

8. *Ibid.*, 255–56; Ellet to Halleck, December 13, 1862, *ORN*, XXIII, 630.

9. Ellet to Stanton, March 4, 1862, *ORA*, Ser. 3, III, 59; Crandall and Newell, *Ram Fleet*, 258.

General Ellet initially intended that *Autocrat, Adams, Baltic, Diana,* and *Raine* each carry two companies of infantry, one of cavalry, and a battery of light artillery, but he never mustered enough men for a fifth cavalry company or a fifth battery. Almost as an afterthought, the general kept the Ram Fleet in the family by giving it to Lieutenant Colonel John A. Ellet. At the time, John Ellet was off Red River with Farragut and in no position to command anything but the ram *Switzerland.*[10]

At 6 A.M. on March 13, *Autocrat, Adams, Baltic, Diana,* and *Fairchild* cast loose their lines at St. Louis and dropped down to Cairo to coal and provision. Captain Isaac D. Newell, Company A, remained behind with *Raine* to await more recruits. *Woodford,* the hospital boat, remained at Cairo refitting while ministering to a sudden outbreak of smallpox. Two men deserted. Another committed suicide by wrapping himself in a blanket and plunging into the water—a harbinger of things to come.[11]

On March 21, as the boats passed downriver, recruiting received a boost from an unexpected source. At Eunice, Arkansas, fifteen grayclads—"a hard-looking set"—waved a white flag, and *Autocrat* pulled to shore to investigate. The men claimed to be disaffected conscripts, and six of them joined Lieutenant Tobias S. Benson's Company B Infantry. Then, as the boats passed Milliken's Bend, the marines observed thousands upon thousands of Grant's soldiers encamped for miles along the western shore of the river.[12]

When the squadron reached Young's Point the following day, General Ellet learned that Admiral Porter had taken an expedition into Steele's Bayou, so he called upon General Grant. Farragut had just arrived from Port Hudson looking for reinforcements from Porter, and it was at this point that General Ellet committed *Lancaster* and *Switzerland* to a mission that resulted in the sinking of the former and the separation of the latter from the remaining Ram Fleet.[13]

After the unexpected disaster, members of the Marine Brigade reconsidered the terms of their enlistments and became mutinous, forcing General Ellet to wait for Porter before attempting more actions on

---

10. Crandall and Newell, *Ram Fleet,* 260–61. See also Special Orders No. 28, March 26, 1863, *ibid.,* 262–63.

11. *Ibid.,* 261–62.

12. *Ibid.,* 262; Amos W. Bellows Diary, March 21, 1863, Crandall Collection, ISHL.

13. Crandall and Newell, *Ram Fleet,* 262; Bellows Diary, March 25, 1863, Crandall Collection, ISHL.

his own. Weeks of idleness coupled with sickness had already bred problems among the brigade. Widespread dissatisfaction and disorderly conduct erupted simultaneously on *Autocrat, Adams, Baltic,* and *Raine.* After the general promised "no short rations" in recruiting handbills, the men resented being served "two biscuits apiece, with coffee and rice." In an act of apparent collusion, they upset tables and benches in the messrooms and demolished the officers' quarters on every boat. When the officer of the day, Captain Oscar F. Brown, Cavalry Company C, attempted to stop the riot, one of the men punched him in the face. Captain Calvin G. Fisher, commanding *Adams,* distributed revolvers and with help from Brown subdued the troublemakers. Ellet arrested four of the ringleaders and placed them in leg irons connected to 20-pound balls. "It was a severe lesson," Captain Crandall recalled, "but a salutary one to the entire command."[14]

General Ellet also discovered that the captains of the boats tended to move about as they wished, burning coal and taking unauthorized excursions up and down the river. On March 23 he issued orders that the boats were to remain at their station unless threatened, and to not move without specific instructions from the "highest officer of this command present." The message circulated through the squadron a few days before a violent gale swept the river, blowing down the chimneys of *Fairchild,* ripping loose a barge attached to *Diana,* and causing damage to every boat in the brigade.[15]

At this point Porter emerged from Steele's Bayou in a state of vexation over the failure of his expedition. Already irritable, he became incensed when he learned that General Ellet had allowed *Lancaster* and *Switzerland* to run Vicksburg's batteries during daylight. He also learned of the Mississippi Marine Brigade's recent revolt and of other incidents involving disciplinary problems.

Because of the unorthodox affiliation of Ellet's marines with the navy, relations between the admiral and the general had never been smooth, causing Porter, on April 2, to air his concerns with Secretary Welles. What annoyed him was a disrespectful letter from Ellet, who assumed all responsibility for his nephew's rash conduct and forbade any of his officers from taking orders from the navy unless they came

14. Crandall and Newell, *Ram Fleet,* 263–64; Crandall's Logbook, March 27, 1863, Crandall Collection, ISHL.

15. Log of *Diana,* March 28, 1863, CMU; General Orders No. 4, March 23, 1863, *ORN,* XXIV, 524.

through an officer of the Marine Brigade. "I saw from the first," Porter declared, "that the course of General Ellet was adverse to harmonious action; that he was determined to assume authority and disregard my orders." After giving his reasons why, Porter added, "The time has passed when a marine brigade would be of any service on this river, the guerrilla warfare having been put to a stop by the watchfulness of the gunboats."[16]

The admiral's statement, though not entirely true, made it clear that he wanted to shed the brigade and have nothing more to do with the Ellets. "As General Grant is the commander in chief of the Army of the Mississippi, and is here, it is not right to have a military force acting independently of him," Porter argued. "I have already proposed to him that he should employ the Marine Brigade under his directions, as it was very near interfering with some movements he was making." He reminded Welles that Grant needed transports, and if transferred, the boats of the Marine Brigade would satisfy that deficiency. He predicted that Ellet, "with little or no knowledge of military matters," would diminish the usefulness of the Marine Brigade as he had the Ram Fleet, and recommended that the unit be "merged into the army under General Grant, as no longer being needed on this river."[17]

Porter then pounced on General Ellet. Referring to the improper passage of the Vicksburg batteries during daylight by the general's two nephews, Charlie and John Ellet, Porter stated, "I alone have the right to regulate the movements of vessels from these headquarters, and no officer of [a] division can exercise such right excepting [when] I am not within reach and a matter of absolute necessity occurs, which was not the case here." Because Ellet attempted to shield his relatives from the admiral's wrath, Porter accused the general of placing himself "in such antagonism to my authority that I am forced, much to my regret, to suspend you from your command until the Government can take such steps in the matter as they may think proper. I see no prospect of having any harmony of action with your command while you seem to be under impressions adverse to military and naval discipline."[18]

Welles took no action on Porter's request aside from shuffling the problem over to Stanton and asking that the Marine Brigade be either

16. Ellet to Porter, April 1, 1862, *ORN*, XX, 32; Porter to Welles, April 2, 1863, *ibid.*, XXIV, 522–23.

17. Porter to Welles, April 2, 1863, *ibid.*, XXIV, 523–24.

18. *Ibid.*, 525.

abolished or merged into the army. By then Grant had begun his push down the western bank of the Mississippi, and Ellet had spoken to Porter and resolved the imbroglio over command protocol. Neither Grant nor Porter found any time to discuss the matter further.[19]

On April 2 Porter gave General Ellet an opportunity to redeem himself. He ordered the brigade to Greenville, Mississippi, a small river town containing four dry goods stores, one large schoolhouse, a single church, and "15 nice white houses" on a green behind the town. There Colonel Ferguson's grayclads made frequent appearances and annoyed passing transports with three small pieces of artillery.[20]

Ellet attached *Monarch* to the squadron, and during the trip up-river the pilot ran onto a snag and lost two barges. Rebel batteries opened from the banks, and *Lioness* provided covering fire while other boats pulled *Monarch* free. A squad of horse marines trotted ashore and, for their curiosity, received a volley of canister. Withdrawing to the boats, the men informed Ellet of the encounter. Instead of landing his force at Greenville, the general decided to drop a few miles downriver, land near Lake Village on the Arkansas side of the river, and forage rather than fight.

The cavalry disembarked and began a roundabout scout of the adjacent country, intending to enter Lake Village from the rear. General Ellet and Captain Crandall participated in the reconnaissance, but nobody in the group had the faintest idea of what lay ahead. The cavalry started down a rough levee road until they came upon a creek. The riders fanned out to look for a ford, and Crandall, thinking he had come to a shallow stream, plunged into it. Toppling head over heels into the water, he swam for shore, leaving Ellet to recover the horse. Captain Francisco V. De Coster, in another effort elsewhere on the stream, swam his horse to the opposite bank, but no one followed. He continued down the bank in search of a better crossing. Finding none, he returned to the point he had crossed and observed that "the company went off and left me." Abandoned and annoyed, De Coster swam to the other side but lost an hour getting his horse out of the water and up the bank. He returned to the landing late in the afternoon, drawn by smoke from a mansion his comrades had burned. Amos Bellows

19. Welles to Stanton, April 16, 1863, *ibid.*, XX, 548.
20. Porter's orders were originally written on March 26 (see *ibid.*, XXIV, 513), but his most recent orders were verbally issued during a meeting with Ellet on April 2. See also Bellows Diary, March 21, 1863, Crandall Collection, ISHL.

greeted his friend's safe return, but lamented that it was "bad to see such a beautiful building destroyed."[21]

General Ellet never reached Greenville. On April 5 a dispatch boat from Porter found the command at Lake Village Landing and delivered new orders. Partisan rangers and loose companies of Confederate cavalry had been harassing the supply lines of Major General William S. Rosecrans's Army of the Cumberland, and Porter decided that the Mississippi Marine Brigade might find useful employment after all. "The object in sending you," Porter explained, "is to defend the line of the Tennessee River. You will destroy all rafts, flatboats, skiffs, or canoes, and destroy all the means [the Rebels] may have of transporting an army." Knowing the penchant of the undisciplined rascals in the brigade, Porter ordered Ellet to keep his forces "well together and not let them act in detached parties. . . . I am pushing a strong force of gunboats up the Tennessee River," the admiral added, "and your vessels will be able to lie securely under the protection of their guns." Porter also promised to send the rams, and closed by saying, "dispatch is the great object just now."[22]

Had Porter learned of Ellet's misadventures in the creeks and swamps near Lake Village, he might never have sent the Mississippi Marine Brigade on another mission. Once again the general had failed to follow orders. Yet he enjoyed the good fortune of departing with his brigade on an important expedition without ever having to report his activities. Better still, he would be out from under Porter's immediate supervision. Were it not for the importance of rushing support to Rosecrans, the history of the Mississippi Marine Brigade might well have ended in April 1863.[23]

21. Crandall to family, April 6, W. D. Crandall Papers, and Bellows Diary, April 4, 1863, Crandall Collection, ISHL; Crandall and Newell, *Ram Fleet*, 267–68; J. D. Moriarty, "No Time to Hold On," newsclip, MHS.

22. Ellet's Report, [May 29], Porter to Ellet, April 4, 1863, *ORN*, XXIV, 529, 76–77.

23. Porter's Orders, March 26, 1863, *ibid.*, 513–14.

CHAPTER 11

CAMPAIGNING WITH GENERAL ELLET

Porter's dispatch ordering the Mississippi Marine Brigade to the Tennessee River emphasized great haste—something General Ellet still needed to demonstrate as a brigade commander. Though the admiral could be demanding, he could also be reasonable. He knew that Ellet had no Tennessee River pilots and would have to stop at Cairo to hire them. He also knew that if Ellet needed coal or supplies, he could get them there. Aside from that, he expected the general to waste no time, hurry over to the Tennessee, destroy all ferries and flatboats, and make contact with Colonel Abel D. Streight at Fort Henry.[1]

On the morning of April 8, Ellet stopped for a while at Memphis but failed to communicate with the district commander, Major General Stephen A. Hurlbut. He then wasted nine days at Cairo, and during that time the army lost contact with him. Hurlbut, coordinating part of the expedition from Memphis, grumbled, "The Marine Brigade has

1. Porter to Ellet, April 4, 1863, *ORN*, XXIV, 77.

The Mississippi River above Memphis and the lower reaches of the Tennessee
Reprinted from *B&L*

not reported yet. If Ellet has gone up the Tennessee, as directed, he will be in time to co-operate. If not, he should be cashiered for running by me without reporting." Confused by the constant rumors concerning the official status of the Marine Brigade, Hurlbut erroneously believed that it now reported to him. Nonetheless, he asked Brigadier General Grenville M. Dodge to reprimand Ellet—if he "ever reaches the Tennessee River"—for the discourtesy. At the time, Dodge was mounting an expedition from Corinth to beyond Tuscumbia, Alabama, in support of Colonel Streight's projected raid, but he could not move his command from Eastport, Mississippi, until Ellet arrived with Streight's force.[2]

Ellet finally got under way and on April 15 found Colonel Streight waiting for him at Fort Henry with 130,000 rations and 1,250 mules. Ellet lost another two days loading Streight's mules on his boats. By then Lieutenant Commander LeRoy Fitch, who had preceded Ellet down to Eastport, lost patience and complained to Porter's fleet captain, Alexander M. Pennock, that two gunboats had been waiting for more than a week to provide convoy and asked whether the Marine Brigade was actually coming. "If so," Fitch grumbled, "it had better hurry up."[3]

With Confederate cavalry nibbling at his supply lines, General Rosecrans planned to retaliate by sending a large mounted force into Georgia to break up the Western and Alabama Railroad and sever General Braxton Bragg's main supply line. On April 7 he assigned the expedition to Colonel Streight and detailed the 51st and 73rd Indiana, 8th Illinois, 3rd Ohio, and two companies from the 1st Middle Tennessee Cavalry. Rosecrans arranged to mount Streight's infantry on mules and transport the animals on Ellet's boats to Eastport. On April 15 Streight met the Marine Brigade at Fort Henry but was further delayed because his transports had not arrived. As a consequence, Streight's command did not shove off until the morning of the 17th and, escorted by the marines and two tinclads, reached Eastport late on the 19th. The mules demonstrated their disdain for the boat ride by stampeding when they touched land, and many of them escaped into the brush. By the time Streight got his column of mule riders in motion, much time had been lost.

On May 3 Brigadier General Nathan Bedford Forrest's Confederate cavalry caught up with the mule brigade short of its objective and forced Streight to surrender. Whether Ellet could be blamed for contributing to the disaster is questionable, but on April 19 General Dodge implied that the opportunity for a successful mission had been squelched by the loss of surprise caused by the tardiness of the Marine Brigade. Rosecrans had expected Streight to depart from Eastport on

2. Hurlbut's Report, April 14, 1863, *ORA*, XXIII, Pt. 1, p. 242; Hurlbut to Dodge, April 7, 1863, *ibid.*, XXIV, Pt. 3, p. 176.

3. Streight to Dodge, April 18, Fitch to Pennock, April 19, 1863, *ORN*, XXIV, 82–83.

April 16, but he did not reach there until late on the 19th. Some of the time lost could be charged to Ellet—but not all of it.[4]

Part of the brigade's tardiness resulted from Ellet's interpretation of Porter's instructions to destroy enemy shipping on the Tennessee River—a task he preferred to transporting mules. Though Streight had emphasized the importance of getting down to Eastport, Ellet stopped here and there to carry out Porter's orders. He eventually reached Clifton, Tennessee, and spoke with a group of Unionists who had just been burned out of their homes by three hundred grayclads passing through on a mission of destruction. Ellet vowed to retaliate, but he could not lose time chasing after the firebrands until after he delivered Streight to Eastport.[5]

At Eastport, General Dodge decided to use the Marine Brigade to make a demonstration at Savannah, Tennessee, while he advanced his brigade toward Tuscumbia. Before Ellet shoved off on his new assignment he burned Eastport, but in his report he intimated that the town had mysteriously burst into flames. Then, instead of demonstrating at Savannah, he put his scouts ashore and began working both sides of the Tennessee River as the boats advanced downstream toward Clifton. He hoped to test his horse marines against the battalion of grayclads marauding the countryside, but his loosely led detachments spent most of their time burning mills and stores and confiscating cotton, mules, and horses. During these raids the boats worked slowly down the river. Then, on April 23, *Diana* ran into the tug *Cleveland* and sank it. Samuel Henecks, sailing master of *Autocrat,* raised the tug the following day, and the boats continued on to Clifton. By the time Ellet collected his marauding marines, the river had dropped and forced the boats down to Britt's Landing, a few miles above the mouth of Duck River.[6]

On the foggy morning of April 26, Ellet took the lead in *Autocrat*

4. Dodge's Report, April 19, Rosecrans's Report, May 9, 1863, Streight's Report, August 22, Rosecrans to Halleck, April 12, 1864, *ORA,* XXIII, Pt. 1, pp. 244, 281, 286, 292, Pt. 2, p. 232; Ellet's Report, [May 29, 1863], *ORN,* XXIV, 529; John A. Wythe, *Life of Nathan Bedford Forrest* (New York, 1899), 190.

5. Log of *Diana,* April 18, 1863, CMU; Bellows Diary, April 18, 1863, ISHL.

6. Bellows Diary, April 20, 1863, Crandall Collection, ISHL; Ellet's Report, [May 29, 1863], *ORN,* XXIV, 530; Log of *Diana,* April 23, 24, 1863, CMS. For a simple synopsis of Hurlbut's and Rosecrans's joint attacks into Alabama and Georgia, see Bearss, *The Vicksburg Campaign,* II, 134–35. Ellet covered up the accident by reporting that *Diana* had gone aground and was struck by *Cleveland,* causing the latter vessel to sink in shallow water.

and attempted to get over the Duck River shoals. The Duck emptied into the Tennessee from the east, pushing rocks toward the opposite shore and leaving a very narrow channel about fifty yards from the eastern bank. Once a boat entered the swift and narrow current, it had to go straight through without stopping. Anticipating that Ellet's boats would have navigation problems, Major R. M. White of the 6th Texas Cavalry placed four fieldpieces near the head of the shoals and opened as *Autocrat* started down the channel. Along the bank several hundred dismounted cavalry fired carbines at the passing boats, and for several minutes *Autocrat, Diana,* and *Adams* sustained a raking fire. White's artillery opened at almost point-blank range, firing shells through *Autocrat* that sent splinters helter-skelter and exploded out the other side. Minié balls and canister thudded into the oak planking but failed to pierce the heavy layers of laminated wood. Eighty shots struck the pilothouse and smashed its glass. On *Diana,* six shots penetrated the wooden bulwarks, but canister merely splattered against the planking and dribbled into the river.[7]

The marines quickly recovered from the shock and replied with muskets and field artillery double-shotted with canister. Once clear of the shoals, Ellet's signal officer, Lieutenant William F. Warren, waved all boats ashore. Down came the gangways, and much to the enemy's surprise, mounted marines splashed ashore. The Texans limbered up and retired in a hurry, leaving nine killed along the banks. The horse marines located Major White bleeding from a mortal wound at his nearby farmhouse. Others pursued the enemy twelve miles inland, but instead of continuing the chase, they became hungry and spent time stopping at farms, looting homesteads, and raiding smokehouses. At the plantation of Lieutenant Colonel Thomas G. Woodward they discovered that a banquet had been prepared to celebrate "the capture of the Yankees." Instead, the marines raided the colonel's larder and filled their stomachs before returning to the boats. During the skirmish, the brigade lost two killed and one wounded.[8]

7. Ellet's Report, April 30, 1863, *ORA,* XXIII, Pt. 1, pp. 278–79; Log of *Diana,* April 26, 1863, CMU; Crandall and Newell, *Ram Fleet,* 277–78, 280–81; John J. Spilman Diary, April 28, 1863, Crandall Collection, ISHL; News Report from Cairo, April 30, 1863, newsclips in Crandall Collection, ISHL.

8. Ellet's Report, April 30, Warren's Report, April 26, 1863, *ORA,* XXIII, Pt. 1, pp. 278–79, 279–80; C. G. Fisher to Crandall, n.d., C. G. Fisher Letters, Crandall Collection, ISHL; Crandall and Newell, *Ram Fleet,* 280–81.

ELLET'S BRIGADE

At the end of the war, John D. McClain of Company F Infantry met one of Major White's veterans making his way home. After chatting for a while, the Texan admitted that "the worst his command was ever sold out, was in an attack on what they supposed were cattle-boats" passing Duck River shoals. This marked the first time that Ellet's brigade operated exactly the way Porter envisioned by landing "fifteen hundred troops, with field artillery, at a moment's notice." Colonel Woodward's command had been staging partisan raids along the Tennessee River for many months, and the speed at which Ellet's brigade responded to White's attack created quite a shock. The Texans, however, got even. As soon as Ellet departed, White's survivors retaliated on the property of local citizens friendly toward the Union.[9]

For reasons not entirely clear, Ellet reported the skirmish to Stanton on April 30 but made no mention of it to Porter until May 29. By writing Stanton, he probably hoped to garner a little praise by demonstrating the usefulness of his brigade. He also closed his message to Stanton by adding that the river was falling and that his orders from Porter did "not provide for this emergency." Ellet intended to go back to the Mississippi and wanted someone other than Porter to know and approve it.[10]

By not reporting the skirmish to Porter until a month later, Ellet postponed the disclosure of his tardy rendezvous with Colonel Streight's brigade. He also took credit for destroying "a great many flat[boat]s and ferryboats," though no record can be found to verify this statement. In his reports to both Stanton and Porter, Ellet claimed credit for driving off the 6th Texas Cavalry but mentioned nothing about having help from the timberclad *Lexington*. Lieutenant Commander Fitch had been about a mile behind the Marine Brigade with *Lexington* and *Monarch* when he heard artillery fire at the mouth of Duck River. Having much heavier guns than Ellet, Fitch pushed up to the shoals and shelled the banks, throwing the 6th Texas Cavalry into a state of panic. White initiated a confused retreat, and the sudden attack of the Marine Brigade met with little resistance during the twelve-mile chase. Regardless of Ellet's failure to recognize Fitch's participation, the skirmish boosted the

9. McClain to Crandall, June 23, 1887, James D. McClain Papers, Crandall Collection, ISHL; Porter, *Naval History*, 334.

10. Ellet to Stanton, April 30, 1863, *ORA*, XXIII, Pt. 1, pp. 278–79; Ellet to Porter, [May 29, 1863], *ORN*, XXIV, 530.

brigade's confidence and gave the marines the mistaken impression that guerrilla units would not stand and fight.[11]

Ellet made no attempt to obtain new orders from Porter, and on April 28 he moved his brigade down to Fort Henry. While awaiting word from Stanton, he sent patrols into the interior. A week elapsed and no orders came from either the secretary or the admiral, so he dropped down to Cairo to make repairs. Once again he refrained from advising Porter of his whereabouts and instead wrote Stanton that he could not ascend the Tennessee above Duck River and could not communicate with Porter "without great delay." Porter had always been specific in his orders that when he could not be reached, Ellet should confer with the commander in charge of the district division. Fleet Captain Pennock maintained his headquarters at Cairo, but Ellet only wanted to hear from Stanton. "Will you advise me what course to pursue?" he asked.[12]

The secretary had resolved to not meddle in the affairs of the navy, but he soon learned that Porter had passed the batteries at Grand Gulf and taken Grant's transports down to Bruinsburg. Knowing Ellet would do nothing without orders, he authorized Halleck to send the Mississippi Marine Brigade to Vicksburg "with such of your boats as may be available and not required on the Cumberland and Tennessee." Ellet had already decided that none of his boats were required on the Tennessee or Cumberland because, in his estimation, both rivers were too low to navigate. Halleck's message reached Cairo on May 20, but Ellet had already departed for Memphis and on the 23rd dropped down to Helena.[13]

On the trip downriver, *E. H. Fairchild,* the brigade's supply vessel, fell behind the rest of the fleet, and as it passed an academy located a short distance above Austin, Mississippi, the enemy opened with two shore batteries. That same day another boat, the packet steamer *Bostonia,* had stopped at Austin and been robbed by guerrillas, who burned the boat and took its crew as prisoners. General Ellet learned of the attacks during the middle of the night. He climbed out of bed, put on his uniform, and issued orders to retaliate. He detached *Baltic,*

11. Fitch's Report, April 28, Ellet's Report, [May 29], 1863, *ORN,* XXIV, 85, 530.

12. Ellet to Stanton, May 7, 1863, *ORA,* XXIII, Pt. 2, p. 314.

13. Halleck to Ellet, May 20, 1863, *ibid.,* XXIV, Pt. 3, p. 333; Ellet's Report, [May 29, 1863], *ORN,* XXIV, 85.

Fairchild, Raine, Lioness, and *Fulton* to the mouth of the White River and at 2 A.M. on Sunday, May 24, started upriver for Austin with *Autocrat, Diana,* and *B. J. Adams.*[14]

At sunrise the boats touched shore at Austin, which Lieutenant Colonel Currie of the *B. J. Adams* described as "a clean neat snugly built little town" of about one hundred persons, mostly women and children. Dressed in their Sunday clothes, the villagers were just beginning to spill into the street when Major Hubbard's cavalry—about two hundred strong—came galloping down the gangway. Intent on surprising the band who had fired on *Fairchild,* the riders dashed through town on a reconnaissance and soon disappeared out of sight. The infantry came ashore next, and buglers brought them into line while officers pranced about on their horses. Following the route taken by the cavalry, the soldiers marched through town and vanished down a country road which led through a forest of immense trees. The townsfolk watched them go, and when the dust finally settled, birds began to sing and the soft, balmy air once again became filled with the fragrance of spring flowers.[15]

Finding no signs of the enemy at the academy, Hubbard learned that the guerrillas had moved inland. Believing that the infantry protected his rear, he neglected to post a guard as he advanced down the road. Coming to a fork, he looked for signs of recent use and decided to take the road to the right. Without bothering to leave a picket on the main road or near either fork, he sent his entire command galloping pell-mell into unfamiliar countryside.

The grayclads, commanded by Colonel W. F. Slemons, included eight hundred mounted men of the 2nd Arkansas Cavalry and 2nd Mississippi Partisans, and carried two 10-pounder Parrotts of the Quitman Light Artillery. Slemons had camped during the night at a landing about three miles above Austin. When pickets reported that Union cavalry had landed at the village, he retired along the main road, which carried his force about three miles due east of Austin. His pickets, however, did not remain in Austin long enough to observe the infantry disembark. When Major Hubbard's horse marines took the right fork of the road, Confederate scouts reported the movement. Slemons hurried

14. Ellet's Report, [May 29, 1863], *ORN,* XXIV, 85; Log of *Diana,* May 24, 1863, CMU; Francisco V. De Coster, "Battle on Coldwater River, Austin, Mississippi," Civil War Collection, MHS; Goodman to Slemons, May 21, 1863, *ORA,* XXIV, Pt. 3, p. 905.

15. Ellet to Stanton, May 25, 1863, *ORA,* XXIV, Pt. 2, p. 431; Clarke, ed., *Warfare along the Mississippi,* 77–79.

back down the main road, turned up the fork, and pushed his command forward with expectations of capturing all the horse marines.

When Hubbard reached the upper end of Beaver Dam Lake, eight miles east of Austin, he found no sign of the enemy. As he began a countermarch back to the main road, the Confederate column opened an unexpected fire on his doubled-up and disordered rear. Captain Crandall compared the unexpected attack to a volley of "shotgun fire into a bunched flock of quails." The firing erupted so suddenly that it threw the battalion into confusion. The horse marines leaped from their mounts and sprinted for cover in a ravine at a bend in the bayou at the upper end of Beaver Dam Lake. They sheltered their horses under the overhanging bank and fanned out along the muddy rim. Hubbard came face-to-face with a dire predicament. He could not escape without charging through a superior force, and because he held the outer arc of a narrow bend, he could see the enemy gradually overlapping his flanks. Colonel Slemons, who knew he had the advantage of roughly four men to Hubbard's one, sent in a demand for surrender. Hubbard, "furious as a desert lion stirred up in his lair," used a few expletives to reply that he "never would surrender," and the fight was on.[16]

For two hours a skirmish raged between the canebrakes occupied by the Confederates and the ravine held by the horse marines. The Quitman Light Artillery failed to depress their guns, and shot after shot whizzed over the heads of the marine battalion. Grayclads creeping through the canebrake approached so close to the ravine that the marines could distinctly hear Confederate officers urging the men forward. After spurts of wild firing, Hubbard discovered that his battalion had consumed most of their ammunition. Walking the lines with his sword drawn, he admonished the men to make their shots count. Seeing desperation on the major's face, one of the marines offered to exchange his uniform with that of a prisoner and, dressed in butternut, attempt to swim the bayou and bring up the infantry.[17]

General Ellet, riding with his infantry on the main road, had lost all touch with Hubbard's battalion until he heard the distant report of the enemy's artillery. He turned the infantry up the fork and double-quicked the regiment, convalescents and all, toward the sound. Riding

16. Chalmers to Johnston, May 26, 1863, *ORA*, XXIV, Pt. 2, p. 431; De Coster, "Battle on Coldwater River," Civil War Collection, MHS; Clarke, ed., *Warfare along the Mississippi*, 79–80, 82.

17. Crandall and Newell, *Ram Fleet*, 287.

ahead with his staff, Ellet came upon Slemons's rear guard and drew a heavy volley that disabled several horses. Slemons, surprised by the unexpected firing in his rear, broke off the engagement, mounted his troopers, and withdrew to the east. Hubbard's messenger then appeared beside the road and reported that the horse marines had exhausted their ammunition and needed immediate help. By the time the jaded infantry reached the scene of battle, Slemons's brigade had taken to the road, and Hubbard's men, being much cut up, were too winded and disorganized to pursue.

After two hours of fighting during which more than a thousand men participated, the Confederates reported only three men killed, twelve wounded, and three missing. Ellet tallied two killed and nineteen wounded. The most remarkable survivor among the Cavalry Battalion's wounded was Henry Couden of Company D, who received a shot in the face, lost his sight, took a ball in his left arm, another in his side, one in his foot, and survived to become, in later years, the chaplain of the House of Representatives.[18]

Leaving the Confederate dead and wounded where they fell, Ellet marched his weary command back to Austin. Women and children turned out to watch the marines file onto the boats, evidently relieved that the intruders were leaving. When word circulated that Ellet had sent aides ashore to warn the inhabitants that at 4 P.M. the town would be burned, many of the marines objected. "In vain the women besought the Commander to spare their little homes," Colonel Currie recalled, "telling of the great suffering he would impose upon their helpless children, the old, the feeble, the indigent," and pleading that they were not responsible for the war or the acts of the partisans who fired on passing riverboats. Ellet rejected their pleas, and many of the women returned to their homes to sit and wait for the arrival of the incendiaries. A tap on the bell of *Autocrat* signaled the firebrands to their work. From the decks of the boats, the horse marines watched with mixed feelings. Currie called the act "fiendish," condemning his fellow officers "who had gone in the service for protection of home and country" for "subduing a handful of women and children by that most barbarous crime of arson."[19]

18. Chalmers to Johnston, May 26, Ellet to Stanton, May 29, 1863, *ORA*, Pt. 2, p. 431; Couden to Crandall, January 24, August 10, 1903, and *Port Huron Daily Times*, February 14, 1895, Crandall Collection, ISHL.

19. Clarke, ed., *Warfare along the Mississippi*, 82–83.

At the designated hour, Austin burst into one fierce red sheet of fire. With their scant belongings, the inhabitants started up the road to take shelter in the nearby academy. Not satisfied with merely punishing the women, Ellet sent the torchbearers ahead to burn the school, where books still lay open, and where problems in arithmetic, scratched upon blackboards, still waited to be solved. As the boats shoved off from the smoldering town, the academy burst into flames, belching smoke from every door and window. Four miles downriver the marines could still observe a pillar of black smoke rising skyward. "It was an unmilitary act," declared Colonel Currie, adding that he "would never forget that sad scene of women and children left alone with their burning houses slowly eating away all hope."[20]

The general, however, considered the burning of Austin a necessary act of war. To justify the act, he embellished his reasons to Stanton, reporting that a search of the homes disclosed a "lively trade" in contraband—whiskey, salt, molasses, and dry goods—and large quantities of medicine in unbroken packages. He also reported two loud explosions during the fire, implying that the guerrillas cached their ammunition and supplies in village dwellings.[21]

Captain Isaac D. Newell had drawn the distasteful assignment of setting Austin on fire. His company had been detailed to guard the boats while the general led the reconnaissance with the horse marines. Newell sent a detail into Austin to search it, and numerous men came back to the boats drunk. Gathering together a second detail, he renewed the search himself. In one instance a member of the party reported being spit upon, but aside from that, the captain found "nothing of importance, and no considerable capture of contraband stores was made." When Ellet returned to Austin, he ordered Newell to burn it. "With a sad heart," the captain recalled, "but with a loyal soldier's spirit of obedience, I executed this order to the very letter. The memory of this incident is one of the most unpleasant of all my war experiences." He recalled one loud explosion that came from the basement of a large building and concluded that the Rebels had stashed a small quantity of ammunition there.[22]

On the evening of May 25, Ellet returned to Helena with *Autocrat,*

20. *Ibid.,* 84; De Coster, "Battle on Coldwater River," Civil War Collection, MHS.
21. Ellet to Stanton, May 25, 1863, *ORA,* XXIV, Pt. 2, p. 431; Ellet to Porter, [May 29, 1863], *ORN,* XXIV, 531.
22. Crandall and Newell, *Ram Fleet,* 289–90.

Diana, and *B. J. Adams* and penned a message to Stanton. His horse marines had been roughly handled at Beaver Dam Lake, and his infantry had not been particularly effective in bloodying Slemons's brigade. Though adept at burning southern villages, Ellet could not report a single military accomplishment. Nonetheless, he asked the secretary to reinforce him with Colonel Charles E. Lippincott's 33rd Illinois, adding that if the request was approved, "no additional boats would be required." Stanton could not understand why Ellet kept corresponding with the War Department instead of with Porter, so he ignored the request.[23]

Finding nothing at Helena to require his presence, Ellet decided to go down to White River, pick up the rest of his boats, and take the brigade back to Young's Point. Eight weeks had elapsed since he last communicated with Porter, who on May 15 had returned from Red River to the mouth of the Yazoo. The admiral had received no reports from the general, and because of his disinterest in the Marine Brigade, the lack of communication evoked no curiosity. Porter expected Ellet to be on the Tennessee River and in close communication with Captain Pennock. When the sun rose at Young's Point on May 29, he discovered that Ellet had returned. Porter had all but forgotten the brigade, but finding the boats within reach again, he immediately sought ways for the brigade to support General Grant.[24]

During the day, news of Ellet's presence at Young's Point filtered into Confederate headquarters at Vicksburg. General Pemberton immediately issued a directive alerting his officers to watch for an amphibious attack on the Water Battery. Had Ellet made the attack, his inexperienced brigade would have been chewed up by the defenders and his boats captured or sunk. But Grant needed transports and convoy vessels, and attacking the Water Battery never entered his thoughts. He wisely asked Porter to lend him the Marine Brigade, and Porter, having no other use for the boats, consented. Ellet disliked the assignment, almost as much as he disliked Porter.[25]

23. Ellet to Stanton, May 25, 1863, *ORA,* XXIV, Pt. 3, p. 349.
24. Porter to Welles, May 8, 15, 1863, *ORN,* XXIV, 658, 664.
25. Tupper to Bowen, May 29, Grant to Porter, May 31, Hurlbut to Halleck, June 3, 1863, *ORA,* XXIV, Pt. 3, pp. 930, 368, 381.

CHAPTER 12

OPERATIONS AT VICKSBURG

O n May 29, when the Marine Brigade returned to Young's Point, much had changed. Grant had landed at Bruinsburg, marched his army to Jackson, Mississippi, brought his entire force to the rear of Vicksburg, and commenced a siege. From Young's Point the Marine Brigade could hear the distinct roar of heavy artillery fire behind the city. General Sherman's corps formed the right wing of Grant's army and had taken a position on the bluffs fronting Mint Spring Bayou. While Grant pounded Vicksburg's entrenchments and looked for ways to penetrate the Confederate lines, he also wanted outposts established because he expected another force under General Joseph E. Johnston to attempt to relieve Vicksburg by attacking the Union rear. To cover Sherman's hotly engaged corps, he asked Porter to send the Marine Brigade, which he called "a floating non-descript force," to Snyder's Bluff to occupy it until relieved by regular troops.[1]

1. Crandall's Logbook, May 29, 1863, Crandall Collection, ISHL; Grant to Porter, May 29, 1863, *ORA,* XXIV, Pt. 3, p. 361; Grant, *Memoirs,* I, 544.

Ellet reached Snyder's Bluff on the morning of May 30 and sent a detachment up to establish an outpost. The arrival of the Mississippi Marine Brigade at the mouth of the Yazoo rattled General Pemberton, who ordered Brigadier General John S. Bowen to send a brigade to defend the Water Battery (Sterling's) threatened by Ellet's appearance. Later, he ordered Major General Martin L. Smith to place a regiment in reserve to protect another battery (Hoadley's). Pemberton could not have formed a very accurate impression of the diminutive nature of Ellet's brigade because he erroneously compared it with Sherman's, McPherson's, and McClernand's corps.[2]

Grant needed reinforcements worse than he needed Ellet's boats at Snyder's Bluff. As soon as the marines disembarked, he asked Porter to detach the brigade's boats and send them to Memphis to bring down fresh troops. Ellet received Porter's orders at 3 A.M. on June 1 and five hours later started six boats for Memphis. *Autocrat* and *Diana* reached the city at noon on June 3, the others arriving later. Ellet walked to General Hurlbut's headquarters and reported his boats ready to receive Grant's reinforcements. Hurlbut replied that there were no troops awaiting transportation and wrote Halleck for instructions. Hurlbut then heard from Grant and advised Ellet that troops would not be ready for embarkation for several days.[3]

Ellet had landed his infantry at Snyder's Bluff but not his cavalry, so he disembarked his horse marines at Marion, a small town on the Arkansas shore opposite Memphis, to give the men a little exercise. Major Hubbard led the battalion inland on what Ellet described as a "scout for the enemy and in search of smuggled goods." Hubbard interpreted any order to search for smuggled goods as authorization to raid private property, and though he caught several Confederates during the cross-country sweep, the loot consisted of dry goods, household items, and a flour barrel containing 200,000 percussion caps. Returning to the boats with fifteen prisoners and three large wagons loaded with "smuggled goods," Hubbard convinced Ellet that a "very large contraband business" flourished across the river from Hurlbut's headquarters.[4]

2. Porter to Grant, May 29, 1863, *ORN,* XXV, 50; Pemberton to Johnston, Tupper to Bowen, Memminger to Smith, May 29, 1863, *ORA,* XXIV, Pt. 3, pp. 929–30.

3. Grant to Porter, May 31, Hurlbut to Halleck, June 3, 1863, *ORA,* XXIV, Pt. 3, pp. 368, 381; Ellet's Report, June 15, 1863, *ORN,* XXV, 149; Log of *Diana,* June 3, 1863, CMU.

4. Ellet to Porter, June 15, 1863, *ORN,* XXV, 149–50; Crandall's Logbook, June 5, 1863, Crandall Collection, ISHL.

Grant's reinforcements embarked at Memphis on June 8, and the following afternoon the boats shoved off for Vicksburg. At 9 A.M. on the 11th the fleet reached Young's Point, where Ellet learned that the troops were to be conveyed to Snyder's Bluff. He sent the boats ahead and stopped in the rear of Vicksburg to confer with Grant. There he learned that a Rebel force under Major General John G. Walker had attacked Milliken's Bend but was repulsed by the garrison's black and white troops. Though the Confederates retired inland, they were thought to be 4,000 strong and a constant threat. Grant believed Pemberton might try to use this force to help the Vicksburg defenders escape across the river, so he decided to disperse the raiders before they caused more trouble. He authorized Ellet to bring Brigadier General Joseph A. Mower's Eagle Brigade back to Young's Point and disembark them there. For the first time in many weeks, Ellet had his command unassigned to any specific duty, so on June 13 he sent Major Hubbard's horse marines on a reconnaissance toward Richmond, Louisiana.[5]

While waiting for Hubbard to return, Ellet set in motion a plan to harass the enemy from a point on the peninsula directly across from Vicksburg. Captain Newell's Company A obtained Spencer repeating rifles from Porter, and Ellet wanted to see whether the bullets would reach across the river. The admiral agreed to the trial but warned that the experiment would be hotly contested by the enemy.

Early on the morning of June 14, Ellet and Newell crossed the peninsula with two squads of infantry and a half-dozen deckhands carrying picks and shovels. The blacks began digging a square rifle pit under the crest of the levee, but the enemy's Water Battery across the river "frightened [them] nearly out of their wits." Ellet sent the hands back to the boats and decided that as long as his men could take cover behind the levee, they could do with the one rifle pit.

Every morning, General Pemberton sent a train of wagons down to the river to have casks filled with water for the men fighting in the trenches. The heavy vehicles always made the trip at daylight, and on the morning of June 14 they began their slow descent oblivious to any new danger. Just as the teamsters backed into the river to begin filling, Ellet gave the signal and both squads opened with their Spencers. The

<hr />

5. Ellet to Porter, June 15, 1863, *ORN*, XXV, 150; Dennis to Rawlins, June 12, Porter to Grant, June 16, 1863, *ORA*, XXIV, Pt. 2, pp. 447–48, 454–55; Crandall and Newell, *Ram Fleet*, 298; George W. Driggs, *Opening of the Mississippi* (Madison, 1864), 26.

rapid staccato of rifle fire produced an immediate effect. The terrified drivers gathered up their lines, lashed their horses, and retired in haste up the embankment.

Pemberton could not afford to have his water supply endangered, and immediately ordered the Vicksburg batteries to fix their guns on the sharpshooters and force them to take cover while the water wagons filled. From his side of the river Ellet could hear the long roll beaten all along the Vicksburg waterfront as gunners filed into the batteries. Newell's marines jumped into their solitary rifle pit moments before every gun facing the river opened on the levee. For thirty minutes shot and shell plunged into the ground, jarring Newell's shooters who lay nestled in their holes and speculating on the final outcome. Off and on during the day the teamsters returned to the river to fill their casks, and when Newell observed them coming down the hill, the company would disperse along the levee and pepper the drivers with a rapid fire, causing the whole affair to be repeated again.[6]

On June 14 Porter learned that Major Hubbard had located the Rebels responsible for attacking the garrison at Milliken's Bend, so he asked Ellet to join him for a conference. The general left Newell at the levee and departed across the peninsula to join the admiral on *Black Hawk*. Earlier in the day, Grant and Porter had put their heads together and decided upon a joint operation involving Ellet's command. From Duckport, Mower's Eagle Brigade would march the 2nd Brigade, 3rd Division, XV Army Corps, toward Richmond, Louisiana, and on the morning of the 15th unite his force with the Marine Brigade, coming by road from Milliken's Bend.

At 10 A.M. on June 15, Mower and Ellet met at the junction of the two roads and paused for a consultation. Confederate pickets stationed at the crossroad observed the movement and retired to warn General Walker of approaching trouble. By the time Mower and Ellet put their forces back on the road, Walker had posted a heavy line of skirmishers along a wide ditch fringed by willows about two miles outside Richmond. Ellet's command, supported by the 5th Minnesota, meandered down the road and was greeted by a volley from grayclads hidden in the brush. The blueclads took cover and dispatched a courier asking Mower to bring up his artillery. Walker knew his small force faced twice

---

6. Crandall and Newell, *Ram Fleet,* 299–300.

his numbers, and rather than wait until Mower's brigade arrived, he sent the 18th Texas Infantry against Ellet's marines and the Minnesotans and drove the blueclads back upon Mower's main column. Stopped by artillery, the Texans fell back on Walker's line, taking refuge behind trees and in gullies on the opposite side of the ditch. Walker then opened with his batteries, and Ellet brought up his artillery. For an hour the batteries played upon each other without effect.

Mower and Ellet worked their infantry around the left flank of the enemy, dislodged the defenders, and chased them across the Richmond bridge. The Confederates burned the structure, and while Mower's men rebuilt it, the Marine Brigade amused themselves by setting fire to the town. Ellet finally got two hundred men across the bridge and found the road to Delhi littered with furniture, pianos, paintings, and all sorts of booty abandoned by the enemy. Being unfamiliar with the area, he recalled the marines and returned to the bridge. Walker retreated to Delhi to reunite his force with Brigadier General Henry E. McCollough's command, and this discouraged both Mower and Ellet from continuing the pursuit. Mower reported one killed and eight wounded—Ellet three wounded, one seriously. Thus ended another foray into Louisiana that failed to break up Confederate attacks.[7]

Ellet returned to Young's Point on June 16 to find that Captain Newell's experiment with the Spencer repeating rifles had attracted the curiosity of Lieutenant Colonel Currie. Accompanied by Captain Thomas C. Groshon, an experienced artilleryman, Currie had crossed the peninsula and walked under the brow of the levee until he found a washout. The two men crawled to the ridge and, with field glasses, looked directly into the city. Currie scanned the buildings carefully and discovered a foundry working full blast near the river where scavenged shot and shell from Union guns were being melted and recast into Confederate projectiles. Ellet had not yet returned from the Richmond expedition, so Currie asked Porter's permission to emplace a 20-pounder Parrott behind the levee for the purpose of putting the foundry out of business. Porter, always seeking new ways to harass the enemy,

---

7. Porter's Report, June 18, Ellet's Report, June 17, 1863, *ORN*, XXV, 175–76; Mower's Report, June 17, Porter's Report, June 16, 1863, *ORA*, XXIV, Pt. 2, pp. 451–52, 454; newsclip dated July 15, 1863, Crandall Collection, ISHL; J. P. Blessington, *The Campaigns of Walker's Texas Division* (New York, 1875), 110–12.

consented, but he doubted the feasibility of the plan and warned Currie not to be surprised if the effort failed. When Ellet returned on the evening of the 16th, he learned of Currie's project and endorsed it.[8]

On the night of June 19 Currie's crew removed the Parrott from *B. J. Adams,* and with help from Captain Oscar F. Brown's cavalry company and four companies of infantry, man-hauled the gun onto a tug and transported it up to the far side of the peninsula. At nightfall they lugged the gun ashore, lashed it to plank, and using brute force slid it to the other side. Fifty black deckhands with picks and shovels hurried forward and began work on the levee, digging an angular excavation with its apex pointed at Vicksburg. At 2 A.M. the gun arrived with the infantry, and Currie divided the force into work crews of fifty, allowing two hours' rest for each. While one crew worked on the emplacement for the gun, another crew dug a tunnel twenty feet long and widened it into a cave to store ammunition.[9]

Currie recalled that when daylight came, "We were like miners, working away, hidden from view, in the depths of the levee and so sheltered . . . to [be able to] continue the excavation." By sunset the work parties had cut halfway through the levee, and after nightfall another detail pulled the Parrott's gun carriage and one hundred rounds of ammunition across the peninsula.

Currie wanted the gun casemated, but his only source of iron was rails of the Vicksburg, Shreveport and Texas Railroad, which ran in front of the levee and terminated at De Soto. Knowing the noise of removing rails would draw the attention of the enemy, Currie waited until dark and sent twenty men along the tracks to find a handcar. They filled it with railroad iron farther up the line and quietly wheeled it back. While waiting for the iron, workers embedded crossties in the levee to provide a structure for mounting the rails. For two nights details worked on enclosing the casemate by reversing every other rail to make them interlock. One night a gang mishandled a rail and dropped it on top of another. It clanged and clattered so loudly, Private Amos W. Bellows recalled, that he "never heard as loud a noise, before nor since." Moments later a probing shell from Vicksburg's batteries

8. Ellet's Report, July 9, 1863, *ORN,* XXV, 77; Clarke, ed., *Warfare along the Mississippi,* 86–87.

9. Clarke, ed., *Warfare along the Mississippi,* 87; Groshon to Ellet, July 5, 1863, *ORN,* XXV, 78; Anonymous, "A Michigan Comrade's Account of the 'Gun Planting' and Surrender of Vicksburg," Civil War Collection, MHS.

whipped across the river and landed near the excavation, but the firing stopped after a few minutes and the men went back to work. A small amount of noise could be tolerated, since the steady thump of Porter's mortars lobbing shells into the town smothered much of the racket made by the men building the casemate.[10]

Working in the dark had its drawback. When details finally cut through the levee, they discovered that the tracks had been elevated above the ground and formed a four-foot embankment directly in front of the Parrott. At dark Currie detailed men to ditch through the railroad bed, and while one crew dug, Mark Root and Eli Morse of *Diana* went down to the river to hack down some willows obstructing the view of the city. To see what to cut, Root carried a lantern under an overcoat while Groshon stood by the gun in the casemate and gave directions from the fort. After felling the first tree, Root heard the Water Battery fire "when—zip! came a shell," he recalled, "burying itself in the ground about ten feet from us." Groshon shouted for the men to douse the light, but "just then came another shell, a little closer than the other." Rattled by the shelling, Root could not find the valve to shut off the burner, so he chucked the lantern under his overcoat and ran for the casemate. Both men stumbled into the tree just cut, became entangled in the limbs, and fell down. The lantern spilled to the ground, shining brightly, and three guns on the hillside opened on the point of light. Shells began dropping near the casemate, and Groshon, out of patience, "used language at least not appropriate for Sunday school occasions," Root recalled, "but we finally got out of the brush, and made our way back to the casemate, carrying our lantern, still burning."[11]

That night Currie assigned a detail to pull weeds by their roots and transplant them around the hole in the levee. At noon Currie made a "sly peep" outside to view his creative camouflage from the other side. "Imagine my feelings," he declared. "The hot sun had withered all the transplanted bushes, and every moment the gap hedged in by the vivid

10. Clarke, ed., *Warfare along the Mississippi*, 87–88; Anonymous, "A Michigan Comrade's Account of the 'Gun Planting' and Surrender of Vicksburg," Civil War Collection, MHS; Bellows Diary, June 21, 1863, and Adam Decker to Crandall, n.d., Adam Decker Letters, Crandall Collection, ISHL.

11. Mark Root Diary, June 22, 1863, in Crandall and Newell, *Ram Fleet*, 305; C. G. Fisher to Crandall, June 1, 1907, Fisher Letters, Crandall Collection, ISHL; Clarke, ed., *Warfare along the Mississippi*, 88.

green of growing plants . . . grew more startling." Currie ducked back inside, certain that a hail of shells would follow, but none came and work continued. Being nearly exhausted, he put the earthwork, now named Fort Adams, under the command of Captain Groshon and on the night of June 22 returned to his boat for some badly needed rest.[12]

At 9 A.M. on June 23 Groshon opened on Vicksburg and fired five rounds. The first two shots cleared the uncut willows away and splashed into the river, but the final three shots landed in the city. The enemy replied with seventeen rounds from their 32-, 64-, and 128-pounders. Fort Adams sustained no damage, but at nightfall the men added another layer of protective railroad iron to the casemate.[13]

On June 24 Groshon fired seven more shots and received eighteen back. One struck the casemate but did no damage. By then the men were beginning to feel more secure, and on the 25th Groshon fired twenty rounds at Paxton's foundry and machine shop, smashing boilers and putting both facilities out of business.

Annoyed by their inability to silence the Parrott, the Confederates attempted to "play a sharp trick" on the marines and sent a yawl across the river under a flag of truce. The boat contained eight wounded Union soldiers. Groshon suspected that the enemy intended to search for the location of the gun, so he sent a lieutenant with a squad of marines down to the water's edge to meet the party and keep them from landing. While relinquishing their prisoners, the grayclads scanned the levee but departed no wiser than when they came.[14]

On June 26 Lieutenant E. H. Nichols of the Light Artillery brought a 12-pounder howitzer across the peninsula, and soon both pieces played upon the city. The enemy began to realize that only a lucky shot would quiet the pestiferous battery embedded in the levee and held their fire. On the 27th the two guns sent twenty-eight shots into the city, hitting the Warren County Courthouse and blowing up a magazine. Ellet began moving more guns into Fort Adams, and the firing caused so much annoyance among the Vicksburg defenders that they replied on the 28th with sixty-four rounds and on July 3 with

12. Clarke, ed., *Warfare along the Mississippi*, 88–89; Log of *Diana*, June 22, 1863, CMU.

13. Groshon to Ellet, July 5, 1863, *ORN*, XXV, 78; Crandall and Newell, *Ram Fleet*, 306; Clarke, ed., *Warfare along the Mississippi*, 90.

14. Groshon's Report, July 5, 1863, *ORN*, XXV, 78; Crandall and Newell, *Ram Fleet*, 306; Clarke, ed., *Warfare along the Mississippi*, 96.

ninety. The enemy found the range and hurled dozens of projectiles against the casemate, cutting railroad iron into pieces and tearing up the ground, but not a shot penetrated to the battery. Porter expressed satisfaction on hearing that the enemy was wasting its shot and shell and said, "If we succeeded in doing no other harm, 20 shots for one was such a good return that the rebels would soon exhaust their ammunition."[15]

Fort Adams harassed Vicksburg until the afternoon of July 3, when word came that Pemberton was meeting with Grant to discuss terms for Vicksburg's possible surrender. Later, the men learned that Pemberton would capitulate in the morning. After the surrender on July 4, Colonel Edward Higgins, commanding Vicksburg's river batteries, approached Ellet and asked for permission to go across the river to "see what kind of contrivance" had been built for protecting the battery. Higgins stated that after firing each shot, the Confederate gunners time and time again believed that the Parrott had been demolished along with everything around it, only to see that curious pillar of smoke that curled up through a hole after every discharge of the 20-pounder. When Ellet escorted Higgins into the casemate, the colonel shook his head and said, "Well, that's one of the best 'Yankee tricks' I have ever seen."[16]

For a change, Porter had something complimentary to say about the antics of the Marine Brigade. Ellet sent the admiral a glowing letter about Currie's success in destroying Vicksburg's foundry, and for once Porter believed what Ellet told him. "I think I can approve all that General Ellet has said in relation to the officer [Colonel Currie] in charge of it. . . . [He] annoyed the enemy very much . . . [and] it certainly stopped the work in the foundry and prevented rebels from casting cannon balls, at which they were busily engaged." As a reward, Currie received a sixty-day leave.[17]

During the days before the surrender of Vicksburg, military activity had escalated along the west bank of the Mississippi River. From the 17th to the 26th of June, Ellet had kept his cavalry busy scouting the interior. When an informant warned that the enemy planned to attack

15. Groshon's Report, July 5, Ellet's Report, June 24, 1863, *ORN,* XXV, 78–79, 80; Anonymous, "A Michigan Comrade's Account of the 'Gun Planting' and Surrender of Vicksburg," Civil War Collection, MHS; Clarke, ed., *Warfare along the Mississippi,* 91.

16. Clarke, ed., *Warfare along the Mississippi,* 91–92.

17. Ellet's Report, July 9, June 24, Porter to Welles, July 20, 1863, *ORN,* XXV, 77, 79; Clarke, ed., *Warfare along the Mississippi,* 93.

Milliken's Bend again, Porter sent reinforcements from the Marine Brigade. The cavalry landed at sunrise on the 27th and found the enemy in full retreat. Two days later the grayclads struck at Goodrich's Landing, Louisiana, about ten miles above Milliken's Bend, and captured two black companies of the 1st Arkansas Volunteers at an Indian mound. Responding once more to Porter's orders, Ellet got under way on the night of the 29th and reached the landing in the morning.[18]

The garrison at Goodrich's Landing consisted of two black regiments—the 1st Arkansas and the 10th Louisiana—under the command of Colonel William F. Wood, who, according to one marine, occupied a "very good little fort." Two companies had been captured on the preceding day because they had taken shelter in a smaller fort perched on a mound about fifty feet high. After tearing up the grounds around the fort, the grayclads, part of Colonel William H. Parsons's cavalry, moved toward Lake Providence, burning cotton gins, farmhouses, and slave shanties along the route. Brigadier General Hugh T. Reid dispatched the 1st Kansas Mounted Regiment to coax Parsons's riders back to the town, where he laid a trap to bag them. The ruse worked until Major Hubbard arrived from Greenville on *John Raine,* overshot the landing, and "fired one of its pop-guns at the rebels." The shot frightened off the enemy and annoyed Reid because it scuttled his carefully laid trap.[19]

When Ellet learned that *Raine* had been fired upon near Goodrich's Landing, he ordered up his infantry, cavalry, and artillery. At daybreak on June 30, he united his force with Colonel Wood's two black regiments and marched to the Mounds in search of Parsons's raiders. The general expected to make quick work of the task and neglected to give his men time to eat breakfast. Five miles back from the river he discovered that he had taken the wrong road. A countermarch brought the force to the road leading to Tensas Bayou, and with the command clamoring for food, Ellet allowed the men to stack arms, rest, and pick blackberries. The cavalry missed the berry festival because Ellet sent them ahead to reconnoiter.

18. Crandall and Newell, *Ram Fleet,* 309; Log of *Diana,* June 26, 27, 29, 30, 1863, CMU; Porter to Welles, July 2, Ellet's Report, July 3, 1863, *ORN,* XXV, 212–13, 215; Reid to Clark, July 6, Walker to Surgent, July 10, 1863, *ORA,* XXIV, Pt. 2, pp. 450, 466.

19. Reid to Clark, July 6, 1863, *ORA,* XXIV, Pt. 2, p. 450; Ellet to Porter, July 3, 1863, *ORN,* XXV, 216; Crandall and Newell, *Ram Fleet,* 309–10; Blessington, *The Campaigns of Walker's Texas Division,* 112–13.

At noon a courier from Major Hubbard reported that a strong body of cavalry with several pieces of artillery had been located and checked. He urged Ellet to bring up the infantry and artillery as quickly as possible. The general recalled his command, but the men who fell into line were all black. By the time the berry pickers finished filling their bellies and returned to their units, Colonel Parsons's cavalry had crossed Tensas Bayou and burned the bridge behind them. Ellet arrived at the bridge and posted his men along the bank just in time to watch the enemy retire. In his report he proudly claimed that he dislodged them, but because he had deprived his brigade of breakfast and water, only 150 of his 800 marines were present for the fight. He could not have known that General Richard Taylor had ordered Walker's division to Berwick Bay, and that because of the order, Parsons withdrew his force without pausing to fight.[20]

After it became apparent that Parsons had withdrawn, Ellet crossed portions of three companies over the charred sleepers and sent the men in pursuit. They found the road strewn with abandoned booty stolen from more than twenty burning plantation houses. Scattered about smoldering slave shanties Ellet discovered the charred remains of human bodies and concluded that Parsons had indiscriminately burned the blacks along with their bungalows. Later, Lieutenant S. F. Cole of the horse marines came across the bodies of several white officers who had commanded black companies. They had been nailed to trees, crucified, and set on fire. Other men had been nailed to slabs and roasted alive. Ellet may have been fortunate that none of his men fell into Rebel hands. During the brief fight he lost only one man, cavalry captain William H. Wright of Company D, but more than one hundred men fell from heat prostration after marching twenty-five miles without food or water. By the time the command returned to their boats, the survivors could barely stand.[21]

Had Porter looked into the omitted details of Ellet's report, he would not have been so quick to give praise when he wrote, "General

20. Ellet to Porter, July 3, 1863, *ORN*, XXV, 215; Walker to Surgent, July 10, 1863, *ORA*, XXIV, Pt. 2, p. 466; Crandall and Newell, *Ram Fleet*, 310; Blessington, *The Campaigns of Walker's Texas Division*, 133–14; John Q. Anderson, *Campaigning with Parsons' Texas Cavalry, C.S.A.* (Hillsboro, Tex., 1967), 112–13; Bellows Diary, June 30, 1863, Crandall Collection, ISHL.

21. Ellet to Porter, July 3, 1863, *ORN*, XXV, 215; Extract from the *St. Louis Missouri Democrat*, n.d., *ORA*, XXIV, Pt. 3, pp. 589–90.

Ellet gave the party at Goodrich's Landing a lesson which they did not soon forget, and having completely routed the enemy, returned to the mouth of the Yazoo." If Ellet learned nothing else from the Goodrich's Landing affair, he absorbed one harsh lesson—never take men on long marches in hot weather without providing them with ample food and water.[22]

During this period Lieutenant Colonel Samuel J. Nasmith, commanding the 25th Wisconsin, had an opportunity to observe the horse marines in action. On one occasion he employed the brigade's boats to transport his regiment to Greenville, where a battery from Colonel John B. Clark's Confederate artillery had cut embrasures in the levee and fired upon passing supply vessels. Nasmith's report characterized the brigade as "entirely worthless. At no time were my orders obeyed willingly, and the officer in command [Major Hubbard] was disposed to find fault and cavil when any real service was required of them. They failed me altogether when most wanted, and, instead of being of any assistance to me, they were, to use no harsher language, a positive injury to the expedition." Ellet never read Nasmith's report, and being very protective of his command, he would probably have done nothing.[23]

On July 1 Ellet ordered all the boats down to Young's Point to give the men an opportunity to recover from their fatigue. The brigade remained there until the 3rd, when negotiations between Grant and Pemberton brought a cessation to the fighting. That evening the boats moved to De Soto Point to await the expected surrender in the morning. Ellet held his vessels in readiness, and at 11 A.M. on the 4th he signaled them to follow *Black Hawk,* Porter's flagship, to the Vicksburg levee.

Autocrat, bearing Ellet and his staff, became the second boat to touch the city wharf after the surrender. The brigade bounded ashore and soon joined in animated discussion with the tattered butternuts who had just stacked arms. "They were a hungry lot of soldiers," Captain De Coster observed, and "had been living on mules, dogs, etc., for weeks. They came down to our ships and the boys robbed themselves to feed them." The grayclads expressed special interest in the bothersome battery Colonel Currie had planted near the point opposite the city. They all

22. Porter, *Naval History,* 336.
23. Anderson, *Campaigning with Parsons' Texas Cavalry,* 109; Nasmith to Rawlins, July 1, 1863, *ORA,* XXIV, Pt. 2, pp. 517–18.

agreed that the "Marine guns had given them great annoyance, and had done them no small amount of damage."[24]

With the surrender of Vicksburg, Admiral Porter became quite generous in his praise of the horse marines. His only source of information was Ellet's reports—none of which contained truly accurate accounts of the brigade's operations in the field. But on July 4, 1863, the euphoric admiral charitably informed Welles that "While the Army have had a troublesome enemy in front and behind them, the gunboats, Marine Brigade under General Ellet, and a small force under Generals Elias S. Dennis and Mower, have kept at bay a large force of rebels, over twelve thousand strong, accompanied by a large quantity of artillery." Welles could be excused for wondering why, as recently as April, Porter had stated that he had no use for the brigade and asked that it be transferred to Grant.[25]

On Independence Day, Ellet's relationship with Porter had never been better, but the general's skill in retaining the admiral's support and admiration was about to be tested.

24. Crandall and Newell, *Ram Fleet,* 312; De Coster, untitled article, Adam De Coster Letters, Crandall Collection, ISHL.

25. Porter to Welles, July 4, 1863, *ORN,* XXV, 104; Porter to Welles, April 2, 1863, *ibid.,* XXIV, 523–24.

CHAPTER 13

GRANT TAKES
COMMAND

After the fall of Vicksburg, Ellet found it difficult to keep the Mississippi Marine Brigade actively employed. Since the Goodrich's Landing affair, midsummer diseases had filled the hospital boat *Woodford* with the sick, and by mid-July thirteen men had died. Porter sent the brigade to Lake Providence on July 5 and to the mouth of White River four days later, but in both instances he recalled the command because of false alarms.[1] In the meantime, Port Hudson surrendered on the 9th to General Banks, and for the first time since the beginning of the war, President Lincoln noted that the "Father of the Waters again goes unvexed to the sea."[2]

On July 10, having no new orders from the admiral, Ellet made a stop at Goodrich's Landing and sent the cavalry to Tensas Bayou on a

---

1. Crandall's Logbook, July 18, 1863, Crandall Collection, ISHL; Ellet to Porter, July 5, 9, *ORN*, XXV, 236, 260.

2. Lincoln to Conkling, August 26, 1863, Basler, ed., *Collected Works of Lincoln*, VI, 409.

reconnaissance. The enemy had abandoned the area, so the cavalry returned to Vicksburg to the cheerful news that the paymaster had arrived. The morale of the brigade temporarily improved once they had crisp greenbacks in their pockets. Ellet granted numerous leaves to both officers and men, but what to do with those on duty became an irksome problem.[3]

When left on his own recognizance, Ellet had a penchant for getting into mischief. Bored with inactivity, he took the fleet down to Ashwood Landing, near the mouth of Big Black River, and on July 21 landed on the Louisiana shore. A detachment of cavalry under Captain James R. Crandall trotted down the gangway and departed on a scout toward Lake St. Joseph. Several hours later they returned with one Confederate lieutenant, Andrew S. Routh, two enlisted men, several "disloyal citizens," and a large assortment of confiscated goods. Ellet considered the scout a success, but he neglected to report the action to Porter.[4]

On August 4, A. T. Bowie, a citizen of Natchez, sent a complaint to Union brigadier general Thomas E. G. Ransom, in charge of the troops who had landed and occupied the city on July 13. Bowie described depredations on the property of Routh's father by a company of cavalry "styling themselves" as "Ellet's marines." According to Bowie's account, the horse marines burst into Routh's home demanding arms while claiming to be "a corps of cavalry independent of the authority of the United States, and whose pay was their booty." They broke open a barrel of whiskey, got the slaves drunk, and in that manner learned where Routh had hidden his valuables. After confiscating silverware and household goods worth $25,000, the horse marines arrested Andrew Routh, who had not served in the Confederate army since April, and incarcerated him in a Vicksburg jail.[5]

General Grant learned of the incident ten days later and admitted that "this is but one of numerous complaints made of the conduct of the Marine Brigade under General Ellet." He wrote Adjutant General Lorenzo Thomas that while the charges were probably exaggerated, the brigade's conduct was "bad, and their services but very slight in comparison to the great expense they are to the Government and the injury they do." He believed the boats should be transferred to the

3. Crandall and Newell, *Ram Fleet,* 314–15.
4. J. R. Crandall to Ellet, January 25, 1864, *ORN,* XXV, 729.
5. A. T. Bowie to Ransom, August 4, 1863, *ORA,* XXX, Pt. 3, p. 25.

army quartermaster to transport soldiers, and that the marines should be compelled to serve on land as a conventional unit of infantry and cavalry under a qualified commander. If the brigade could not be transferred, Grant suggested, the men should "be mustered out of the service and the boats taken for general use." Since Stanton had formed and financed the brigade, General Thomas referred Grant's recommendation to the secretary, who took it under advisement.[6]

Six months passed before Grant found time to question Ellet on the alleged depredations. By then the incident had been mostly forgotten, but Captain Crandall, who led the horse marines on the raid, dutifully reported that while two barrels of whiskey had been opened "by a large number of negroes belonging to Mr. Routh's plantation," the only contraband destroyed or removed consisted of gunpowder, ball, bacon, lard, sugar, and several boxes of silverware and dry goods stored together with the ammunition. Crandall blamed the pillaging on "two or three hundred . . . ungovernable" slaves, claiming that they "broke into rooms and destroyed or carried off large amounts of goods." Ellet picked up on Crandall's theme and claimed that Routh had already recovered most of his property from his slaves and that any missing silverware must be "in possession of the negroes in the vicinity of [Routh's] residence."[7]

On July 13, a few days before Ellet's unauthorized raid on Routh's plantation, Porter made another attempt to shed the Marine Brigade and wrote Welles recommending that the men and its vessels be turned over to Grant. Porter must have colluded with Grant on the details of the transfer because the recommendations going to their respective superiors read identically. Both Porter and Grant agreed that the brigade had become so reduced in size as to become ineffectual but that the boats could be used to transport as many as 10,000 men. Porter, however, stated that the remnants of the Ram Fleet should be turned over to the navy as transports, though they were "mostly worn out and . . . run at great expense."[8]

Welles concurred, but Stanton did not want his creation to be given to Grant, nor the men of the Ram Fleet absorbed by the navy, so

6. Grant to Thomas, Thomas to Stanton, August 14, 1863, *ibid.*, 24.

7. J. R. Crandall to Ellet, January 25, Ellet to McPherson, January 31, 1863, *ORN*, XXV, 729–30, 727.

8. Porter to Welles, July 13, Thomas to Stanton, August 14, 1863, *ibid.*, 293–94, 298; Grant to Thomas, August 14, 1863, *ORA*, XXX, Pt. 3, p. 24.

on August 4 he authorized Halleck to reject the proposal. The issue remained unresolved. Porter wanted no responsibility for the brigade because of Ellet's embarrassing independent operations, and Grant wanted the brigade's boats but to dispossess its members. Under the existing arrangement, Grant could only obtain use of the boats by applying through Porter, and the admiral never fully affiliated the brigade with his own command because he considered it mainly an army enterprise. From the days of the formation of the Ram Fleet, Welles never wanted anything to do with the brigade, but Stanton still wished to exercise some control of it. While discussions on the subject continued in Washington, Ellet obtained no orders from either Porter or Grant and, for the moment, continued to act on his own.[9]

On July 22 Grant began looking for boats to move reinforcements to Helena. He considered the transfer urgent because of threats from Major General Sterling Price's Confederate army. The fastest way to move one of Major General Cadwallader C. Washburn's units was on the Marine Brigade's boats, but Ellet insisted upon carrying his whole command, horses and all, thereby limiting the number of men Grant could embark. Vexed by Ellet's demands, Grant grumbled to Washburn, "They are not subject to my command, or it would be different." Ellet might have bought Grant's favor had he given more thought to the commanding general's needs.[10]

Discussions concerning the disposition of the Marine Brigade continued without Ellet's knowledge. General Thomas acted as intermediary between Grant and Porter at Vicksburg and between Halleck and Stanton at Washington. He even suggested that once the brigade's boats were assimilated into Grant's command, General Ellet, when on shore, could be given "a command more suitable to his rank."[11]

By August 24 Stanton began to bend by having Halleck authorize Grant "to use any of General Ellet's brigade for temporary shore duty, and any of his boats for temporary transports," but because the brigade had been enlisted for "special service" as an amphibious force and contained "river-men," it should not be converted exclusively for land op-

9. Welles to Porter, August 10, Stanton to Welles, August 5, 1863, *ORN*, XXV, 294, 295.

10. Grant to Washburn, July 20, 23, 1863, *ORA*, XXX, Pt. 3, p. 536, 546. See also Grant to Schofield, July 21, 1863, *ibid.*, XXII, Pt. 2, p. 385.

11. Thomas to Stanton, August 14, 1863, *ORN*, XXV, 298.

erations. Several years passed before members of the Marine Brigade learned of these discussions. Warren Crandall, historian of the Marine Brigade, discovered the correspondence at the turn of the century, writing, "it appeared that General Thomas lent his good offices to please and accommodate both [Grant and Porter], utterly ignoring the rights and feelings of both General Ellet and his men."[12]

By then, more problems concerning the operations of the Marine Brigade filtered into Washington, and on August 27 Stanton authorized Halleck to officially turn the Marine Brigade over to Grant. "He directs that you . . . reduce it to discipline, trying and punishing the guilty parties," declared Halleck, adding, however, that the brigade should not be dismantled, though portions of it could be detached and put on shore if deemed "necessary for the good of the service." To add to command confusion, Stanton failed to advise Welles of the decision, and not until October 24 did Porter learn that Ellet and the Marine Brigade no longer reported to the navy.[13]

Because of loose discipline in Ellet's command, the marines received blame for more than their share of raiding and looting. Other uniformed boatmen took advantage of the brigade's reputation and staged their own raids. On three occasions between May 23 and July 13, 1863, a force identifying itself as Ellet's marines stopped at McGehee's Landing in Arkansas and stripped Miles H. McGehee of $15,000 in livestock and provisions and tore up his garden and orchard. Deponents claimed that the men served on the boat *Lady Pike* and came dressed in Marine Brigade uniforms. Ellet denied the charge on the premise that he never commanded a boat named *Lady Pike,* but he admitted having sent the hospital boat *Woodford* to McGehee's Landing on the "12th or 13th of July" to procure fruit, vegetables, and poultry to feed three hundred sick. "If Mr. McGehee was not paid at that time," Ellet retorted, "it was because he made no claim." On May 23 Ellet could not have been at McGehee's Landing because he with three of his boats were at Austin, and the other boats had been sent to the mouth of White River. With the general gone, however, one of his

---

12. Halleck to Grant, August 24, 1863, *ORA,* XXX, Pt. 3, 144; Crandall and Newell, *Ram Fleet,* 316.

13. Halleck to Grant, August 27, 1863, *ORA,* XXX, Pt. 3, p. 183; Porter to Welles, September 20, Welles to Porter, September 29, Welles to Porter, October 24, 1863, *ORN,* XXV, 295, 300.

venturesome captains may have slipped down to McGehee's Landing on an unofficial raid, but not with a boat named *Lady Pike,* unless they first borrowed or captured it.[14]

To these and other allegations, Warren Crandall replied that "charges of marauding and robbery, whenever brought to Ellet's attention, were always promptly and vigorously investigated, for he was intolerant of any sort of lawlessness." Because Ellet often detached his boats for special assignments, he could not keep an eye on what men did with their time. During the weeks following the surrender of Vicksburg, neither Porter nor Grant paid much attention to the brigade except to call it into service as transports. Neither branch of the service kept the boats supplied with coal, forcing Ellet's skippers to stop at plantations for fence rails. If marines felt inclined to loot, there was nothing to stop them.[15]

On August 18, after running troops to New Orleans, the boats were met by musket fire from a squad of drunken grayclads at Bayou Sara. Ellet stopped to round up the male citizens for questioning, and when nobody felt inclined to name the bushwhackers, the general burned the local saloon. He returned to the squadron and headed for Vicksburg, reaching there out of fuel and without new orders.[16]

Sickness, rather than battle casualties, had reduced the brigade in numbers, and inattention from Porter and Stanton only made matters worse. Even Charlie Ellet, who had been so active with both the Ram Fleet and the Marine Brigade, resigned and went home, accompanied by Lieutenant H. G. Curtis, his adjutant. Because the brigade acted as a national organization belonging to neither the army nor the navy, General Ellet could not get replacements because men recruited into the brigade would not be credited to the levies imposed upon the states in which they lived. Stanton had the authority to issue a general order enabling states to receive credit for Marine Brigade enlistments, but he chose not to. Instead, on August 29, he advised Ellet that the brigade had been placed under General Grant and that all applications "for authority to recruit, or for other purposes, must be made through him." Since Halleck had already instructed Grant to retain the unit as an auxiliary force for "special service" and to not "break up this brigade,"

14. Ellet's Report June 5, Deposition of V. T. Warren, November 7, 1863, Ellet to McPherson, January 31, 1864, *ORN,* XXV, 128, 727–28, 726–27.

15. Crandall and Newell, *Ram Fleet,* 317–18, 320.

16. *Ibid.,* 320.

Grant had no alternative but to repair the boats and recruit replacements. So in late August, Ellet took *Autocrat* to Cairo to lay the groundwork for filling his vacancies and departed on leave for Philadelphia.[17]

Grant's interpretation of "special service" involved one of the most curious expeditions of the war. He sent the Marine Brigade to Port Gibson, Mississippi, via Rodney, under sealed orders and instructed Ellet not to open them until the men had landed. "Imagine our surprise on reading the orders," wrote cavalryman Almon J. Pierce, "that we were expected to capture and carry back to Vicksburg as prisoners fifty of the most aristocratic Confederate young women in the city." After establishing headquarters at the home of a local judge, the marines dispersed to carry out their mission, ordering the town's beauties to report to headquarters in two hours or suffer the penalty of having their homes burned. "There was great weeping, wailing and gnashing of teeth from tender mothers, loving sisters and irate fathers and brothers," Pierce recalled. "The result was that before the hour was up, the last fair prisoner had put in an appearance, though in a very defiant mood."

To transfer the ladies to Rodney, Ellet commandeered all the dilapidated vehicles and broken-down horses found in the vicinity and hitched them together with plow harnesses and bits of rope. After packing the prisoners on board, the marines hauled the ladies over war-devastated roads to the boats, where a large crowd gathered to hoot at Ellet's kidnappers and wave farewell to their friends. Not until reaching Vicksburg did the marines discover the reason for their unexplained and unpleasant mission. A number of northern schoolteachers had been captured by Confederates and taken into camp to "wash and mend for the soldiers and perform other menial services." In retaliation, the Port Gibson ladies would remain hostages until exchanged for the captured teachers. The transaction took thirty days. "They were, however, very gay delightful days," Pierce recalled, and "more than one romantic marriage . . . was the direct outcome of our raid upon Port Gibson."[18]

On August 27 Lieutenant Colonel Currie returned to Vicksburg

17. Stanton to Ellet, August 29, Halleck to Grant, August 24, 27, 1863, *ORA,* XXX, Pt. 3, pp. 212, 144, 183; Log of *Diana,* August 21, 1863, CMU; Clarke, ed., *Warfare along the Mississippi,* 93.

18. A. J. Pierce, "The Raid upon Port Gibson and What Caused It," Almon J. Pierce Letters, Crandall Collection, ISHL.

from a sixty-day leave and found the general had departed, leaving Major Hubbard of the cavalry in charge of *B. J. Adams, Baltic, Diana, Raine, Fairchild,* and *Woodford.* Hubbard had no plans aside from waiting for *Lioness* to barge down a load of coal. Currie read Hubbard's orders and noted that Ellet wanted boats to cruise the river between Greenville, Mississippi, and Napoleon, Arkansas, and to watch for guerrillas. Being fresh from leave and eager for a little action, Currie decided that instead of "sailing up and down the river," he would disobey the general's orders, land the brigade, and "seek a fight" in the guerrillas' "own haunts." Instead of waiting for *Lioness,* he made an equal distribution of the available coal and issued orders for the five boats to be ready to get under way in the morning.[19]

Currie wasted no time. On August 31 he landed the cavalry on the Louisiana shore across from Griffith's Landing, captured seven prisoners, and returned with a large quantity of beef. During his absence deckhands had gone ashore and, as a precaution against depleting their coal, obtained a large supply of wood. Having but two companies of cavalry, Currie decided to mount the infantry and spent the next seven days scouting both sides of the river for mules. Each day scores of unbroken animals joined the brigade. To accommodate the rapidly expanding herd, Currie set details to work adding stables to the transports and improvising saddles and bridles for the volunteer mule marines.

Under way again, the boats reached the mouth of White River, and on the morning of September 9 Currie landed two cavalry companies and two of his mule-mounted infantry companies at Beulah Landing on the Mississippi shore. He planned to lead them on a reconnaissance, and instructed the boats to meet him at Bolivar Landing.[20]

Currie detached his command one company at a time, sending each ahead of the other, all with orders to search every plantation along the way for guerrillas, arms, and contraband. At a junction about fifteen miles inland, he dispatched Captain Ed. G. Hughes's mounted infantry company down a side road with orders to reconnoiter, and in less than half an hour he observed the mules returning with an "old fashioned [U.S.] stage coach" containing four men, a driver, and the

19. Log of *Diana,* August 27, 1863, CMU; Clarke, ed., *Warfare along the Mississippi,* 94–95. Napoleon was at the mouth of the White River.

20. Crandall and Newell, *Ram Fleet,* 321–22; Log of *Diana,* August 31, September 8, 9, 1863, CMU; Clarke, ed., *Warfare along the Mississippi,* 97–98.

coach's escort—three officers and fifteen men—all heavily armed. As time had lapsed into late afternoon, Currie made no search of the vehicle but attached it to the column and conveyed it to the boats waiting at Bolivar Landing.

Reaching the landing at nightfall, he herded the tight-lipped prisoners on board and formed a detail to search the coach. Minutes later the party returned to *Diana* and presented Currie with a black carpetbag containing $1,200,000 in Confederate money and a draft payable at Alexandria, Louisiana, for $1,000,000 more. The search also uncovered a package of official dispatches to Lieutenant General E. Kirby Smith's Trans-Mississippi Department and a large collection of private mail. The captured Confederate couriers admitted having intended to cross the Mississippi River at Bolivar Landing in small boats during the night and carry the money to Little Rock to meet the department's payrolls and buy war matériel.

On September 12 Currie sent *Raine* to Cairo with the money, mail, and prisoners. Ellet, who was on leave in Philadelphia, learned of the capture and wrote Stanton, asking for instructions. The secretary, knowing that Confederate bills were worth about fifteen cents on the dollar to the holder, nervously replied that all the money and dispatches were to be immediately brought to the War Department. The general's son, Lieutenant Edward C. Ellet, drew the assignment and personally carried the mail and the money to the secretary's office.[21]

Having disposed of the captured cash, Currie returned to the work of scouting and campaigned without instructions from anyone. He added more injury to the morale of Kirby Smith's unpaid Trans-Mississippi grayclads when in mid-September the horse marines captured another paymaster carrying a draft for $1,000,000 and cash in the amount of $52,340. When on September 24 General Hurlbut ordered Currie to Vicksburg, the brigade had captured a total of $3,252,340 in Confederate currency and drafts. As soon as Currie reached the city, Hurlbut ordered the marines ashore so the boats could be used as transports. The brigade despised garrison duty but enjoyed the rest.[22]

21. Clarke, ed., *Warfare along the Mississippi*, 98–100; Crandall and Newell, *Ram Fleet*, 322–24; Ellet to Stanton, Stanton to Ellet, September 21, 1863, *ORA*, XXX, Pt. 3, p. 757.

22. Crandall and Newell, *Ram Fleet*, 324–25; Log of *Diana*, September 24, 1863, CMU.

On the afternoon of October 18 idleness came to an end. From Goodrich's Landing, Brigadier General John P. Hawkins, commanding the District of Northeastern Louisiana, reported a Confederate strike force of four thousand men advancing from Delhi to attack his black regiments. Major General James B. McPherson happened to stop at Goodrich's Landing, and when Hawkins pleaded for reinforcements and a battery of artillery, McPherson sent the Marine Brigade.[23]

The horse marines consumed a day getting their animals and gear back onto *B. J. Adams, Baltic, Fairchild,* and *Horner,* the only available boats. They shoved off on the morning of October 19 and, carrying only two days' rations, splashed ashore that evening at Goodrich's Landing. Currie detached a company of cavalry and one piece of artillery with orders to feel for the enemy. The horse marines clashed with a band of guerrillas led by John Jarrette and dispersed in every direction. When the company failed to return in the morning, Currie sent the entire battalion. The reconnaissance lasted five days and ended in a useless chase covering 150 miles, but the marines eventually located the lost company, whose members told lurid stories of Jarrette's plundering of the government's leased plantations. During the scout, General Ellet returned from leave on the ram *Fulton,* spent one night with his command, and then departed for Vicksburg. Having no new orders from either Ellet or McPherson, Colonel Currie packed up the brigade and steamed up to Griffith's Landing in Washington County, Mississippi.[24]

Currie's independent incursions into Mississippi and Louisiana lasted until early December. Aside from capturing a few prisoners and another $12,000 in Confederate money, he collected horses, mules, and provisions, and lived mainly off the land. The cavalry trotted about the countryside pursuing false rumors planted by prisoners and informants. On November 4 Currie finally made contact with a small Confederate force at Deer Creek. The grayclads skedaddled across a bridge, and Currie attempted to hold them in place while a courier galloped to the rear in search of the artillery and a company of mule-mounted infantry. The southerners became wary and began to fall back. Currie, fearing the enemy would slip away, charged across the bridge. After a two-mile chase,

---

23. McPherson to Grant, October 20, 1863, *ORA,* XXX, Pt. 2, p. 805.

24. McPherson to Sherman, October 29, 1863, *ibid.,* 807; Currie's Report, November 19, 1863, *ibid.,* XXXI, Pt. 1, pp. 33–34; Crandall and Newell, *Ram Fleet,* 325–26; John N. Edwards, *Noted Guerrillas, Or the Warfare on the Border* (St. Louis, 1880), 221–25.

the Rebels vanished into the canebrake. For his efforts, Currie captured a wagon and loaded it with "25 fat hogs."[25]

During the next six days Currie made raids along both banks of the Mississippi, bagging prisoners, livestock, and a Confederate mail carrier with a sack of official correspondence. When learning on November 10 that guerrillas, commanded by a man called Captain Montgomery, had recently burned the steamboat *Allen Collier,* Currie led a small cavalry force to the partisan leader's plantation in Bolivar County. On November 10 the horse marines emptied Montgomery's home and set it on fire. Mrs. Montgomery lamented, "This is no more than I expected when I heard what my husband had done." As tendrils of fire consumed the home, Currie put his force back on the road and began a thirty-five-mile march through the countryside, destroying yawls and flatboats hidden in the canebrake. The jaded column returned to the boats the following day with an enormous load of provisions, supplies, and plunder.[26]

Currie continued his raids until the evening of November 18, when General McPherson sent the brigade back to Goodrich's Landing. General Hawkins had succumbed to another series of rumors and believed that the enemy had massed 16,000 troops against his garrison. Currie hurriedly dropped down to the landing and sent a company of cavalry on a scout. Finding no sign of the enemy, the Marine Brigade lingered in the area for a week. Currie gave the cavalry a run ashore, and for two weeks the brigade raided the area while waiting for orders.[27]

None of Currie's reports ever intimated that the Marine Brigade, operating on its own, ever behaved badly, but the unauthorized raids bothered Admiral Porter, who had developed an entirely different impression of the brigade's so-called scouting sorties. He expressed great relief when on October 24 he learned that the brigade had been turned over to Grant. By then the admiral's differences with the Marine Brigade—principally its independent actions and General Ellet's scurrilous comments regarding the navy—had mushroomed into a relationship of bitter adversity.

Admiral Porter and General Sherman had bonded during the Vicksburg campaign. And now, because the brigade currently operated in Sherman's department, Porter wrote the general suggesting that the

25. Currie's Report, November 19, 1863, *ORA,* XXXI, Pt. 1, pp. 34–35.
26. *Ibid.,* 34–36.
27. McPherson to Grant, November 22, 1863, *ibid.,* Pt. 3, pp. 227, 229.

unit be "broken up, the vessels used as transports, and the officers and men put on shore. I cannot tell you," he added, "of all the reports made to me against the brigade. Its robberies and house-burnings are shameful; and though I felt it to be my duty to report all the matters that came to my notice, yet a feeling of delicacy toward a branch of another corps prevented my doing so."[28]

On March 25, 1863, after Charlie Ellet had run the Vicksburg batteries during daylight and lost *Lancaster*, Porter had attempted to arrest the general and his nephew. This permanently strained the relations between the admiral and the general. Ellet never forgave Porter, and surreptitiously published what the admiral described as a few "contemptible articles"—news clips that Porter never read until General Hurlbut presented him with copies. "In these transactions," Porter declared, "the Ellets were guilty of gross falsehoods in making malicious statements, and lied deliberately in afterward denying them." Though admitting he never questioned the general on the matter, Porter advised Sherman that he had "lost respect for the whole party, and was glad to get rid of the command." Sherman explicitly trusted Porter's opinion, but Grant had orders from Stanton to sustain the brigade, and Sherman could do nothing about it.[29]

On October 30, a day after writing to Sherman, Porter suppressed his contempt for General Ellet and in an act of dignified protocol wrote, "As our official relations are at an end, permit me to express my appreciation of the zeal you have always manifested in regard to the public service." He did not bother to ask why, during the latter part of August, Ellet had not informed him of the command change. For the admiral, it was simply a matter of "good riddance." Sad news, however, explained Porter's reluctance to say anything unkind to Ellet. That day he had learned of the sudden and unexpected death of the general's nephew, twenty-year-old Colonel Charles Rivers Ellet, who had fallen ill soon after tendering his resignation. Porter always admired the young man's courage, once commenting to Welles that he wished he had more young officers like him.[30]

For the moment, however, General McPherson had found ways to

28. Welles to Porter, October 24, 1863, *ORN*, XXV, 300; Porter to Sherman, October 29, 1863, *ORA*, XXXI, Pt. 1, p. 783.

29. Porter to Sherman, October 29, 1863, *ORA*, XXXI, Pt. 3, p. 783.

30. Porter to Ellet, October 30, 1863, *ORN*, XXV, 301; *Washington, D.C., Evening Star*, March 12, 1892.

keep the Marine Brigade employed. General Ellet had been on leave or at Cairo since the transfer of the brigade to the army, and McPherson found Colonel Currie quite responsive to orders. On December 2, when Confederates threatened the garrison at Natchez, McPherson looked for General Ellet but could not find him, so he sent Colonel Currie on the mission to seek and destroy one of the wiliest Confederate cavalry brigades operating in Mississippi.[31]

31. McPherson to Sherman, December 2, 1863, *ORA,* XXXI, Pt. 3, p. 309.

CSS Arkansas, *after embarrassing the Union squadrons under Farragut and Davis, was disabled by the ram* Queen of the West *off the levee at Vicksburg.*

Courtesy of the U.S. Naval Historical Center, Washington, D.C.

USS Essex, *commanded by William "Dirty Bill" Porter, failed to destroy the CSS* Arkansas *and left the work to the Ram Fleet.*

Courtesy of the U.S. Naval Historical Center, Washington, D.C.

Queen of the West *attacks the transport* City of Vicksburg *moored at Vicksburg's landing.*

Reprinted from *Harper's Weekly,* February 28, 1863.
Courtesy of Louisiana State University Libraries.

The capture of Queen of the West *by Confederate forces at Fort Taylor (later Fort De Russy) on February 14, 1863.*

Reprinted from *Harper's Weekly,* March 21, 1863.
Courtesy of the U.S. Naval Historical Center, Washington, D.C.

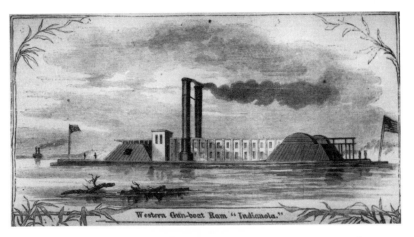

Western Gun-boat Ram "Indianola."

The ironclad gunboat USS Indianola, *surrendered by its commander after being attacked by the Confederate rams* William H. Webb *and* Queen of the West

Reprinted from *Harper's Weekly,* February 7, 1863.
Courtesy of Louisiana State University Libraries

Rear Admiral David Dixon Porter, who encouraged the formation of the Mississippi Marine Brigade, became disillusioned by the unit's lack of discipline and encouraged its transfer to the army
Reprinted from *Battles and Leaders of the Civil War*

*Lieutenant Colonel John A. Ellet commanded the Ram Fleet
after the formation of the Mississippi Marine Brigade.*
Courtesy of the U.S. Army Military History Institute

*Captain Warren D. Crandall, the Mississippi Marine Brigade's
assistant adjutant general and unit historian*
Courtesy of the U.S. Army Military History Institute

Lieutenant Edward C. Ellet, son of Brigadier General Alfred W. Ellet
Courtesy of the U.S. Army Military History Institute

Lieutenant Richard S. Ellet, son of Brigadier General Alfred W. Ellet
Courtesy of the U.S. Army Military History Institute

*Captain Isaac D. Newell helped to recover the lost records
of the Mississippi Marine Brigade.*
Courtesy of the U.S. Army Military History Institute

*Lieutenant Colonel George E. Currie commanded and led the Mississippi
Marine Brigade on many of its expeditions.*
Courtesy of the U.S. Army Military History Institute

Rear Admiral David Glasgow Farragut encouraged General Ellet to send two rams below the Vicksburg batteries, resulting in the loss of the ram Lancaster.
Reprinted from *Battles and Leaders of the Civil War*

CHAPTER 14

CHASING WIRT
ADAMS

On the evening of December 3, General McPherson received word that Confederate forces under the command of Brigadier General William Wirt Adams were back in the area and had fired upon three transports thirty miles above Natchez. Adams had deceptively spread his cavalry, moving them in companies and squadrons but never en masse. Believing that Adams intended to strike Natchez, McPherson ordered Brigadier General Walter Q. Gresham to embark two regiments of infantry, two of cavalry, and a section of artillery on transports and get them down to Natchez as quickly as possible. The Marine Brigade had just returned to Vicksburg from Goodrich's Landing, so McPherson called upon Colonel Currie to transport Gresham's cavalry and support the operation.[1]

Currie shoved off from Vicksburg on the morning of December 5 and reached Natchez at 5 P.M. Adams, with 1,059 men, had begun to consolidate his cavalry six miles south of Natchez and intended to

1. McPherson to Grant, December 9, 1863, *ORA,* XXXI, Pt. 1, pp. 594–95.

*The Mississippi and Red Rivers below Vicksburg, where the Mississippi Marine
Brigade often operated after the surrender of Vicksburg*
Reprinted from Coffin, *Marching to Victory*

strike the city in the morning. When Currie went ashore, he found the
garrison fully prepared to meet the attack. In the meantime, Adams
reached the same conclusion, and when the marines arrived with reinforcements, he decided to move down to Ellis's Cliffs and resume harassing river traffic with his artillery.[2]

2. Adams's Report, December 7, 1863, *ibid.*, 599.

On the night of December 5, and unaware of Adams's intentions, General Gresham made preparations to attack the Confederates in the morning. Union cavalry would take the Washington Road and the horse marines the Pine Ridge Road. Five miles out they would meet at the town of Washington and proceed together to Fayette. During the middle of the night, Currie aroused the Marine Brigade and ordered the animals fed and two days' rations prepared. At daybreak the horse marines trotted ashore with four pieces of artillery and began their reconnaissance. Six miles out of Natchez, Currie struck the Fayette road junction and found no sign of either Gresham or Adams. Puzzled by the unfamiliar roads, he paused to discuss the situation with his officers and dispatched scouts to look for Gresham.

The delay gave General Ellet just enough time to catch up with his command. *Autocrat* had brought the general to Vicksburg about twelve hours after Currie departed for Natchez. When Ellet reached Natchez on the morning of December 6, Currie had already gone ashore and taken the horse marines inland. Gresham, however, had not yet put his command on the road, and he told Ellet where to look for the marines. With his staff mounted and ready to ride, Ellet departed in haste and located the brigade where Currie had stopped to wait for Gresham's command.[3]

Having spoken with Gresham earlier, Ellet thought he knew where to find the general, but Gresham had taken a different road, and Ellet spent the day searching for him. After roaming across twenty-seven miles of unmarked country roads, finding neither friend nor foe, Ellet returned to Natchez at dusk and went to bed.[4]

The brigade had just settled in their quarters when two of Gresham's staff came on board *Autocrat* and informed Ellet of new plans. The enemy had gone in the direction of Ellis's Cliffs, and Gresham wanted the Marine Brigade to take the boats downriver and at 10 A.M. disembark below the cliffs. Gresham planned to assault the Confederate rear while Ellet attacked from the river, and with a little luck, bag Adams's entire force.

Ellet reached Ellis's Cliffs at the appointed hour, only to learn that while Gresham had cut off one escape route, Adams had taken another, going by way of the Woodville road toward Natchez. Once Gresham

3. Ellet's Report, December 8, 1863, *ibid.,* 598.
4. Crandall and Newell, *Ram Fleet,* 338.

discovered that he had been outmaneuvered, he dispatched a courier to Ellet urging the Marine Brigade to return to Natchez, saddle up, and trap Adams on the Woodville road. Ellet complied and steamed back to Natchez. At 2 P.M., while marching south from Natchez to shut the door on Adams's escape, the brigade encountered not one grayclad but collided with the advance of Gresham's command. Adams had simply started down the Woodville road expecting to be followed, and when he reached the Kingston road he turned east and vanished. Ellet admitted that nothing much had been accomplished, aside from giving "Mr. Adams something of a bad scare." General Adams, however, was not at all scared, and as soon as Gresham returned to Natchez, he resumed his raids along the Mississippi, seizing livestock, burning buildings, and removing slaves from the plantations "of certain traitors."[5]

Ellet scouted along the Mississippi for three weeks collecting a prisoner here and there, but he never encountered Adams's roving cavalry. On December 21 Gresham believed he had located the wily Confederate and once again summoned the Marine Brigade, which was posted near St. Joseph, Louisiana. "I will start today at 2 o'clock with three regiments of infantry, four pieces of artillery, and 200 cavalry for Fayette," Gresham wrote, adding that he would be there by "7 or 8 to-morrow morning to attack Wirt Adams. Would be glad to have your co-operation from Rodney."[6]

At 5 A.M. on December 22, Colonel Currie dropped down to Rodney and put six companies of mounted infantry ashore with two howitzers and the cavalry battalion. With the command as battle-ready as it could get, the marines started down the road to join Gresham at Fayette. A few miles from the rendezvous point, an unknown force of Rebels "impetuously attacked" the rear guard. Part of the so-called rear guard consisted of six mule marines and a Union recruiting officer who planned to stop at plantations along the road to enlist blacks for the army. When entering through a large gate to one plantation, the recruiting party recoiled when attacked by dozens of grayclads who came running out of a barn and a nearby woods and, as Amos W. Bellows of Company F reported, "began shooting at us." Before Currie could come to the rescue, the Rebels captured Corporal McCoy and Sergeant Carr,

5. *Ibid.*, 339; Ellet's Report, December 8, Adams's Report, December 7, 1863, *ORA*, XXXI, Pt. 1, pp. 598–99, 599–600.

6. Gresham to Ellet, December 21, 1863, *ORA*, XXXI, Pt. 3, p. 466.

who were riding mules. The rest of the men, on horses, jumped a ditch and made off across a meadow. McCoy and Carr were taken to Grand Gulf and thrown in jail. When the Confederates discovered papers on Carr authorizing him to recruit slaves, they hanged him. They then sent McCoy to Andersonville prison, where he died a few months later.[7]

Once again Adams's brigade eluded Gresham, and Currie returned with the marines to the boats. Having learned the importance of vigilance, Ellet detailed men from the infantry and posted pickets east of Rodney. Confederate scouts noticed that only one man stood watch while others slept, so at 2 A.M. on December 24 a squad of Adams's cavalry swooped through the camp and captured all the pickets but the marine on guard, who escaped in the dark.[8]

According to some members of the crew, Christmas passed with "a good dinner [of pickled pork], and some splendid egg nog," and for the next few days the men found little to do but run the cavalry ashore and scavenge for food. The boats remained off Grand Gulf from lack of fuel, so Ellet performed a muster and distributed pay. He made one organizational change, placing Major David Tallerday in charge of the infantry. Colonel Currie remained in command of the Marine Brigade, Major Hubbard continued to command the cavalry, and Captain Daniel P. Walling the artillery. Lieutenant Colonel John A. Ellet remained in charge of the Ram Fleet, which had been assigned to carrying out menial tasks for the army. *Lioness* and *Monarch* remained at times with the Marine Brigade, but they no longer carried a large number of infantry. No record exists of the number of men still assigned to the Ram Fleet, but on December 31, 1863, Ellet's returns for the Marine Brigade showed 41 officers and 719 men present for duty—about half the number originally recruited.[9]

General McPherson struggled to find ways to keep the Marine Brigade usefully employed. When in early January 1864 guerrillas raided plantations near Milliken's Bend and Goodrich's Landing, he issued orders for Ellet to take his command upriver to protect the

---

7. Bellows Diary, December 22, 24, 1863, Crandall Collection, ISHL; Crandall and Newell, *Ram Fleet*, 347–48.

8. McPherson to Grant, December 22, 1863, *ORA*, XXXI, Pt. 3, p. 472; Log of *Diana*, December 23, 24, 1863, CMU; Edwin Moon to Crandall, February 17, 1889, Edwin Moon Letters, Crandall Collection, ISHL.

9. Crandall and Newell, *Ram Fleet*, 348, 349; Returns of the XVII Army Corps, December 31, 1863, *ORA*, XXXI, Pt. 3, pp. 564, 571.

farms growing cotton for the U.S. Treasury Department. At the time, the brigade had gone ashore at Waterproof Landing, Louisiana, exchanged a few shots with a squad of grayclads, and confiscated a large quantity of corn for the horses. If Ellet received McPherson's orders, he never responded to them and remained with his command below Vicksburg. He had no coal to go anywhere, and kept the fleet moderately operational by having the fireboxes fed with freshly cut wood.

On January 5 Ellet dropped down to Natchez and at 1 P.M. sent a detachment ashore to seek and destroy Adams's cavalry. The grayclads had once again vanished, and after two days of scouting between Hamburg and Fayette, Ellet returned to *Autocrat* with seven prisoners who seemed incapable of shedding any light on Adams's whereabouts.[10]

On January 10, *Horner*, towing a barge of coal, found Ellet at Bruinsburg and the long process of filling the boats' bunkers began. The general, still looking for Adams's cavalry, sent part of Major Tallerday's mounted infantry on a scout to Oakland College with instructions to return by way of Rodney. Major Hubbard's cavalry took a different route with orders to join Tallerday at Rodney. The two detachments pounded the backcountry and collected a few prisoners, but they found no sign of Adams. Had Ellet stopped at Natchez to confer with General Gresham, he would have learned that Adams had last been seen at Liberty, Mississippi, about fifty miles southeast of Rodney, but Ellet seldom communicated with army officers unless ordered to do so. By chasing after Adams with widely scattered companies from the Marine Brigade, Ellet flirted with disaster, but by dumb luck or good fortune, he always managed to avoid it.[11]

If McPherson wondered why Ellet ignored his orders, he never pursued the matter, and the Marine Brigade remained in the vicinity of Rodney. Ellet sent daily scouts into country barren of the enemy. If he needed corn to feed the horses, he obtained it without resistance. If his men needed something to eat, they stopped at farmhouses and bought it. Adam Decker of Company K Infantry admitted paying for a meal composed of cornbread and milk with "two hundred dollars" in Rebel money taken from a Confederate paymaster—strong evidence that some captured currency never reached the War Department. Jesse B. Gordon of Company A Cavalry enjoyed the independence of operating

10. McPherson to Ellet, January 3, 1864, *ORA,* XXXII, Pt. 2, p. 20; Crandall and Newell, *Ram Fleet,* 350.

11. Gresham to Clark, January 9, 1864, *ORA,* XXXII, Pt. 2, p. 57.

without army supervision. He wrote of having great fun searching "buggies," capturing mail, pilfering cash, collecting contraband, and on rare occasions chasing enemy scouts.[12]

Ellet burned the coal brought by *Horner* so rapidly that by January 15 the crews of *Baltic* and *Diana* once again resorted to supplying themselves with green wood. Ellet planned to go to Vicksburg to confer with General McPherson, but as he prepared to depart, teamsters hauling wood came rushing to the banks shouting that the cutting party had been fired upon by "skulking enemies, up in the hills." The general dispatched four squads of cavalry to drive off the grayclads, and an hour later three men came dashing back to report that one squad had been ambushed and Lieutenant John B. Kirk mortally wounded. Ellet called out the entire command, only to learn that the squadron had been attacked not by Adams—who was still at Liberty—but by a Captain McGruder and a few Rebels from Bayou Pierre who had been flushed by one of the other patrols. The partisans had fired one volley and, without waiting to see its effect, fled into the woods. Kirk died nine days later, but two others wounded in the ambush survived.[13]

Ellet departed for Vicksburg on the evening of January 16, leaving the command with Colonel Currie. Having no use for idleness, Currie detached two companies of cavalry and sent them to Grand Gulf to arrest a Confederate conscript known to be at a certain house. One mile inland they encountered Confederate cavalry and sent back for reinforcements. Currie, suspecting that Adams had returned, dispatched every marine who had a mount.

The brigade had not been in enough skirmishes to understand Confederate tactics. In their exuberance to catch the enemy, Company C took the bait, cut loose from the brigade, and galloped after a few slowly retreating Rebels. Fifteen horse marines rushed headlong into an ambush and lost four men. Augustus Ralston paused with the rest of the company to wait for the brigade to come up, but the Confederates remounted and rode off. Company C resumed the chase for two or three miles before the Rebels dismounted to make another stand. Just then, Currie recalled the company. The Confederates heard the order

12. Adam Decker to Crandall, n.d., Decker Letters, Jesse B. Gordon to Crandall, n.d., Jesse B. Gordon Letters, Crandall Collection, ISHL.

13. Log of *Diana*, January 16, 1864, CMU; Crandall's Logbook, January 15, 16, Bellows Diary, January 16, and Dwight B. Mason Diary, January 16, 1864, Crandall Collection, ISHL; Force to Douglas, January 15, 1864, *ORA*, XXXII, Pt. 2, p. 107.

and attacked. Ralston's boots had become so slick with "a sticky red clay" that he could not remount his horse. Pitching his carbine aside and shedding every article that would slow him down, he legged it into the woods. "The rebels called out for me to surrender," Ralston declared, "and called me a name that was not very complimentary to my mother, but I did not stop to quarrel with them." Running "as fast as my legs would carry me," Ralston sprinted over a hill, leaped across a ravine, and dropped into a sinkhole in the middle of a canebrake. Finding his revolver gone and having no means of defense, he hunkered in the hole for two hours, barely stirring. Confronted with four to five miles of backtracking, Ralston came out of the canebrake and knew he was lost. With luck, he made his way back to the river and at dark hailed the boats. His horse had returned, no doubt following a much shorter route. The brigade "thought I was captured [with the others]," Ralston recalled, and "seeing me, cheered me lustily." Such were the campaigns of the Marine Brigade.[14]

Ellet returned to Grand Gulf on January 19, and during the day a rumor circulated that Mrs. Whitney, who lived on a plantation three miles inland and claimed to be a Unionist, planned to invite the general and his son Edward to "a big dinner." The general doubted Mrs. Whitney's fidelity because her husband, while leading a band of guerrillas, had been recently captured by Colonel Currie. Confederates planned to attack the house during the dinner and carry off the Ellets, no doubt intending to trade them for Whitney. Ellet never mentioned receiving the invitation, but on the designated day and hour, a mounted force of Rebels did surround the Whitney home in expectation of finding the Ellets there. A few days later, Captain James A. Crandall of Company A Cavalry visited Mrs. Whitney to ask if she had tried to trap the general. Mrs. Whitney denied the charge as absurd and promised to bake the general "a real nice cake . . . and bring it together with a bottle of wine." Crandall thought that would "be a great treat for the general," and two days later she arrived with cake and wine. The general's "gallantry was equal to the occasion," Crandall noted, but being a "total abstainer [and] almost a fanatical temperance man," he sent the cake to the cookhouse and gave the wine away. Ellet believed the whole incident had been a joke orchestrated by Crandall. He did not know that Adams, who

14. Augustus Ralston, "Sketch of a Skirmish at Grand Gulf, January 18, 1864," Augustus Ralston Letters, Crandall Collection, ISHL.

was thought to be near Port Hudson, had posted two strong detachments near Natchez and moved the rest of his force to Rodney to "catch foraging and marauding parties" of the Marine Brigade. Adams never mentioned a specific plan to kidnap Ellet, but he had placed his troops in position to do it.[15]

On January 20 rumors circulated that Adams had moved a force up to Port Gibson—inland from Rodney and Grand Gulf—so Ellet sent three companies of mounted infantry on a thirty-three-mile reconnaissance to locate him. The scout returned empty-handed, and Ellet gave up the hunt. Every boat had depleted its coal, so he took the fleet downriver to cut wood along the Louisiana shore, where Adams could not bother them. While the crews labored in the woods, a cavalry patrol circulated through the countryside confiscating thirty head of cattle and sundry other items.[16]

For ten days Ellet roamed the river between Grand Gulf and Natchez, and the men amused themselves by scouting both banks of the river. There seemed to be little reason to remain in the area. Adams could not be found, and Ellet's one-day patrols often consumed more time collecting provisions than looking for the enemy. Had Adams been nearby, he would probably have trapped and captured a large part of Ellet's divided command. The brigade's scouting parties frequently became social frolics. The men enjoyed "having a good time bantering [with] the girls."[17]

While details cut wood, General Ellet added a chapter to the sport of hunting. Thousands of ducks and geese gathered on the river to winter, and the birds grouped along the bars to feed. Ellet used two cannon loaded with canister and opened on the feeding flocks. Birds fell, and the yawls retrieved them. "Such a slaughter of game was never, before or since, seen on the river," wrote Crandall. "Roast goose was on the Brigade menu for many days."[18]

By February 1 the brigade had gathered enough wood to make the

15. Crandall and Newell, *Ram Fleet,* 358–59; Bellows Diary, January 18, 1864, Crandall Collection, ISHL; Sherman to Grant, January 19, Adams to Jack, January 23, 1864, *ORA,* XXXII, Pt. 2, pp. 146–47, 607.

16. Log of *Diana,* January 20, 1864, CMU; Crandall and Newell, *Ram Fleet,* 358–59.

17. "The Yawl Expedition," quoted in Crandall and Newell, *Ram Fleet,* 360.

18. Crandall's Logbook, January 27, 1864, Crandall Collection, ISHL.

trip to Vicksburg. Leaving *Diana* at St. Joseph with several cases of smallpox and *Switzerland* to cruise off Waterproof, Ellet put the fleet under way and reached Vicksburg the following evening. *Fulton* lay at the wharf with several barges of coal. Had Ellet left word where he could be found during his last visit to Vicksburg, *Fulton*'s skipper would have brought the barges down to Natchez.[19]

The Marine Brigade may have been fortunate that Adams had more important business than chasing an outfit posing no military threat. The cagey Confederate commanded more men—all of them tough, battle-hardened veterans—and none of them rode mules. General McPherson, who had also been busy with important military matters, eventually recalled that he had ordered the brigade to go to Milliken's Bend and summoned the marines back to Vicksburg.

In March, McPherson departed from Vicksburg to resume command of the Army of the Tennessee, one of three armies that were to constitute General Sherman's force in the forthcoming Atlanta campaign. He placed Brigadier General John McArthur in charge of the post and the defenses of Vicksburg. McArthur showed little interest in using the brigade for military missions, and by April 25 Ellet no longer felt restricted by McPherson's orders and detached *Raine* and *Fairchild*. He placed them under the command of Major James R. Crandall and sent them on an unauthorized raid to Grand Gulf.[20]

At Bayou Pierre, near Grand Gulf, the horse marines brushed against pickets from two battalions of Adams's cavalry and hastily withdrew to the boats. Crandall reembarked his small command and on April 28 dropped down to St. Joseph, where the men could safely spend the day collecting food and forage from local plantations. After refilling the larder, Crandall decided to try his luck at Rodney, but he found the area well picketed by Lieutenant Colonel Thomas R. Stockdale's regiment from Adams's command. Stockdale secreted a few pickets in Rodney and on May 1 lured Sergeant James W. Ellis and Charles F. Russell, two members of Company D Cavalry, into town to socialize. Watching from the boats, Captain De Coster saw the men captured and quickly landed his company. He galloped through town to rescue

19. *Ibid.*, February 1, 2, 1864; Log of *Diana*, January 28, 1864, CMU.

20. General Orders No. 98, March 12, General Orders No. 1, March 26, McPherson to Hurlbut, March 30, 1864, *ORA*, XXXII, Pt. 3, pp. 58, 162, 197; Ellet to Crandall, April 25, 1864, Crandall's Copybook, Crandall Collection, ISHL.

his friends, but Stockdale's scouts took their two prisoners and skedaddled. To his surprise, General McArthur discovered that Ellet had sent *Raine* and *Fairchild* below Vicksburg and ordered them back.[21]

Adams had moved his main force to the Yazoo River, and McArthur wanted the Marine Brigade's help in locating the elusive Confederates. Ellet also had a special interest in the expedition. He had been chasing Adams for many months without success, so he detailed *Autocrat, Raine, Baltic,* and *Fairchild,* along with two rams to carry black troops, and on the morning of May 5 departed up the Yazoo. At nightfall they tied up at Sartaria, twenty miles below Yazoo City, to await orders from McArthur, whose command was camped four miles inland. At McArthur's request, Ellet detached his cavalry to reconnoiter for the army. For the next three days the combined force crawled toward Yazoo City, Ellet by water, McArthur by land. When they eventually reached the town on the afternoon of May 8, they found the streets deserted.[22]

McArthur experienced no better luck than Ellet in catching Adams, and for four days he and the general muddled about Yazoo City while the horse marines scouted and plundered the country. On May 12, four miles up the river road, the battalion came upon a woman riding a mule. She refused to stop until confronted by Lieutenant Doane, who commanded the advance scouting party. The woman denied having seen mounted Confederates, but a short distance from her home a battalion from Adams's command fired on the rear of Doane's company and charged with a yell. The horse marines dismounted and opened with their carbines, checking the attack. Doane could not determine the size of the force in his rear and suspected that Adams had prepared another ambush up the road, so he ordered the marines to remount and led them into an open cotton field. The grayclads double-quicked back to their horses and attempted to keep the marines from reaching the main road. Doane led the command across the field, jumping fences and ditches in a headlong dash to safety. He came out on the road just ahead of the enemy and galloped back to Yazoo City, proud that "the Marines could run when they had to." Doane had stumbled into a

---

21. Crandall and Newell, *Ram Fleet,* 407–8; Ellet to Crandall, April 25, 1864, Crandall's Copybook, Crandall Collection, ISHL.

22. McArthur's Report, May 25, 1864, *ORA,* XXXIX, Pt. 1, p. 7; Crandall's Logbook, May 5–8, 1864, Crandall Collection, ISHL.

scouting party from Adams's command—one he should have been able to bloody had he stood and fought—but he returned to the boats with only one man slightly injured and a horse shot in the leg.[23]

On May 13 a tug arrived from Vicksburg with dispatches for General McArthur, and Ellet detailed Major Crandall's cavalry battalion to deliver the messages. Crandall expected to find McArthur at Benton, ten miles east of Yazoo City, but the general, after a running fight with Adams's brigade, had moved his force toward Pickens on Big Black River. After finding no trace of McArthur at Benton but evidence of skirmishing, Crandall concluded that the general "had the Johnnies on the run" and pushed on west.

At 10 P.M. the column came in sight of hundreds of campfires. Contemplating the prospect of hot coffee, the battalion trotted toward the encampment. "Who comes there?" demanded the picket. "The Marine Brigade," Crandall replied proudly. The pickets fired a round and ran. Thinking the pickets had misunderstood his answer, Crandall ordered the battalion to advance, "which we did at a brisk trot," reported Private J. H. Stevens, "and swinging around a point of timber, we found ourselves in the midst of Wirt Adams' camp." The grayclads, Stevens recalled, "were more surprised than we were [and] we promptly responded to the command 'Right about' and moved back at a lively pace, closely followed by the Confederate cavalry." Crandall never delivered the messages. He took the battalion back to Yazoo City, having covered forty miles without dismounting.[24]

On May 15 General McArthur returned to Yazoo City, closely followed by a regiment from Adams's command, and collected his undelivered messages. He decided to give the men a few days' rest while Ellet's cavalry continued to search for Adams's base of operations. During the reprieve, two men of the 11th Illinois turned up missing and were found hanging from a tree. McArthur's men blamed it on the townsfolk, all of whom had become destitute and mean and routinely insulted the local garrison.[25]

---

23. Lee's Report, May 11, Adams's Reports, May 9, 14, 1864, *ORA,* XXXIX, Pt. 1, pp. 10, 11; Crandall's Logbook, May 12, 1864, Crandall Collection, ISHL; Crandall and Newell, *Ram Fleet,* 408–9.

24. Crandall's Logbook, May 13, 1864, Crandall Collection, ISHL; Adams's Report, May 14, 1863, *ORA,* XXXIX, Pt. 1, p. 11; J. H. Stevens, "How the Cavalry Found Wirt Adams' Camp," in Crandall and Newell, *Ram Fleet,* 409–10.

25. Adams to Lee, May 15, 1864, *ORA,* XXXIX, Pt. 1, p. 11.

On the night of May 17, Private A. C. Byerly of Company D Cavalry observed three men from McArthur's command coming out of an alley and ordered them to halt. They fled down another alley, and moments later Byerly noticed smoke and flame spilling from the rear of a building. He gave the alarm, and as the fire quickly spread, he rushed to the aid of the people asleep in their homes. When the townsfolk brought up a small fire engine, members of the brigade helped to run out the hose and feed it with water. Other soldiers, mingling among the crowd, opened their pocket knives and sliced holes in the hose. The fire spread to the other side of the street and burned out of control. By morning the courthouse and all the stores on the town's main street lay in ashes. On this occasion, the Marine Brigade had no hand in starting the fire.[26]

On May 18 the horse marines started back to Vicksburg, having accomplished one of their goals. They had finally found Adams's brigade and wisely decided to leave it alone. "This terminated what was palpably an unsuccessful expedition," Captain Warren D. Crandall surmised, but General McArthur reported the mission a success. In an effusion of compliments, he recognized Ellet "for his kindness and assistance in doing everything he could to make the expedition successful." Ellet appreciated the rare praise because his relations with McArthur had been no better than those with McPherson or Porter.[27]

When Ellet returned to Vicksburg, he became immersed in an old problem and a new one—both involving Porter. "The Ram Fleet," grumbled Lieutenant Commander Phelps, "has failed, after repeated applications, to furnish prize lists in cases where entitled to share with the [Mississippi S]quadron." As a matter of record, Ellet had referred his claims to Stanton and felt required to do no more. The other problem, however, concerned claims of another character. "The Marine Brigade," Porter informed Welles, "took a great deal of cotton for which they gave no receipts, and represented themselves, I am informed, as gunboats." The accusation carried the smell of conversion and corruption within the Marine Brigade, but for Ellet, collecting cotton had been a much safer occupation than chasing Adams.[28]

26. Crandall and Newell, *Ram Fleet*, 410–11.

27. Crandall's Logbook, May 18, 1864, Crandall Collection, ISHL; McArthur's Report, May 25, 1864, *ORA*, XXXIX, Pt. 1, pp. 7–8.

28. Phelps to Welles, May 20, Porter to Welles, June 6, 1864, *ORN*, XXVI, 318–19, 363.

CHAPTER 15

THE QUEST
FOR COTTON

In conjunction with the Meridian Expedition scheduled to depart
from Vicksburg on February 3, 1864, General Sherman, on January
30, decided to send a combined force up the Yazoo River for the purpose of destroying boats and appropriating cotton, corn, and horses
"abandoned or held by disloyal citizens." The U.S. government now
actively sought cotton, and the Treasury Department distributed
agents throughout the lower Mississippi Valley to collect it. Sherman
dedicated two regiments to the task and informed Admiral Porter that
Lieutenant Elias K. Owen had volunteered to join the expedition with
his gunboats. To compensate for the use of Owen's squadron, Sherman
promised Porter that he would send up the Marine Brigade to patrol
the river between Milliken's Bend and Goodrich's Landing.[1]

1. Sherman to McPherson, Sherman to Porter, Sherman to Owen, January 30,
1864, *ORA*, XXXII, Pt. 2, pp. 183–84, 184–85.

Ellet coaled the fleet at Vicksburg and on February 4 shoved off for Milliken's Bend, leaving instructions for *Fairchild* to join the command "wherever it might be" in five days. He detached the boats at different points along the river, leaving the command scattered over sixty miles of river. On the west bank of the Mississippi, partisans from William C. Quantrill's Missourians had been raiding plantations, so when Ellet landed a force at Lake Providence, Louisiana, he naturally expected contact with the troublesome guerrillas.[2]

Before leaving Vicksburg, Ellet learned from General McPherson that the principal purpose of Owen's Yazoo River expedition was to obtain cotton. Ellet reasoned that if the navy had been empowered to collect cotton, then why not his brigade, so on February 5 he added a new initiative to the irregular duties of the horse marines. As soon as *Autocrat* touched shore at Lake Providence, he detached a force under Major Tallerday with instructions to circulate through the backcountry in search of cotton and Quantrill. At one plantation Tallerday asked the owner if he would recognize any of Quantrill's men should they happen upon his farm. When the planter replied "no," the major confided to the gentleman that the Rangers wore Yankee uniforms, that he was actually Quantrill and had come there "under proper orders to look after [your] cotton." The planter expressed relief, thinking he was among friends, and told Tallerday where he had stashed his crop. He also admitted removing the marking "C.S.A." from the bales to keep them from being confiscated by Union agents. Tallerday appropriated a few wagons, threw on the bales, and returned to *Autocrat* "made richer by a fine haul of cotton." Emulating Ellet's operations between Grand Gulf and Natchez, the marines spent most of their time searching for cotton and booty and an incidental amount of time hunting for the enemy.[3]

On February 11 Tallerday moved toward Lake Village, Arkansas, to investigate reports of guerrilla raids. An armed party of citizens bearing a flag of truce met the major and suggested joining forces to hunt down Quantrill's raiders. They denounced the renegade colonel as an "outlaw who was committing depredations without distinction between friend

2. Crandall's Logbook, February 4, 5, 1864, Crandall Collection, ISHL. Quantrill's band practiced the worst kind of guerrilla warfare, and on August 21, 1863, had burned and plundered Lawrence, Kansas, killing about 150 men and boys.

3. Mason Diary, February 5, Bellows Diary, February 7, 1864, Crandall Collection, ISHL; Crandall and Newell, *Ram Fleet*, 364–65.

or foe, or discriminating as to age or sex." Tallerday suspected a trap and declined, and for three days his force cautiously roamed the area collecting livestock without encountering one hostile Rebel. Quantrill never made an appearance. By February 13 the fleet had exhausted its coal, and Ellet sent some of the vessels back to Vicksburg for fuel.[4]

Finding *Fairchild*'s barges empty at Vicksburg, Ellet took *Autocrat* and *Raine* on an unauthorized trip downriver to cut wood. Instead of returning to Lake Village after filling his bunkers, he tied up at dark about six miles below Grand Gulf and dispatched Lieutenants Tobias S. Benson and Edward Ellet with thirty men and three yawls on a night scout. The detachment intended to land at Bruinsburg but got lost on the river and landed below the village. Their objective was Windsor, a two-story brick mansion with a "Captain's walk," all built on a commanding eminence five miles from the river and owned by the Widow Smith Coffee Daniels. The mansion had long been suspected of being both a lookout and a headquarters for Confederate operations in the area. The marines had stopped there on many past occasions but never found any evidence to implicate the owner.

As the scouting party approached the mansion, they saw lights burning inside and heard the sound of singing. The marines surrounded the house while Edward Ellet and Benson stepped ahead and rapped on the front entrance. A servant opened the door and, thinking the two men were friends, invited them inside. Ellet observed two uniformed officers having a marvelous time singing with the ladies. He tapped one on the shoulder and asked if they were Confederate officers. When the man acknowledged they were, Ellet replied, "Well, then, you are our prisoners." "The women fussed, cried, and called us all kinds of names," Ellet recalled, "but after a short tarry we took our prisoners and returned to the yawls." Thus ended another sortie of the Mississippi Marine Brigade.[5]

On February 14 Major James R. Crandall took one hundred cavalry ashore near Port Gibson for another night scout. From three prisoners captured along the road he learned that a company of Confederate scouts under Captain Lewis was quartered in slave huts about forty miles east of Rodney. Using a local slave as guide, Crandall located the road leading back to the huts and had the good fortune of arriving at 8 A.M.,

4. Bellows Diary, February 7, 1864, Crandall Collection, ISHL; Crandall and Newell, *Ram Fleet*, 365–66.

5. Crandall and Newell, *Ram Fleet*, 367–68.

the very moment when Lewis's pickets had retired for breakfast. With revolvers drawn, the horse marines charged the camp, killed three men, and captured Lewis, a lieutenant, a surgeon, and twenty-eight enlisted men. They also recaptured four men belonging to the 32nd Iowa. Fearing retaliation from Major Calvit Roberts, one of Wirt Adams's subordinates, the marines hurriedly burned the plantation house and about $25,000 in quartermaster and commissary stores before hightailing it back to the boats.[6]

Crandall's probe deep into the interior of Mississippi became one of the brigade's more successful outings. Up to this time Ellet had never operated more than a few miles from his boats, being content to raid along the river with a supporting force nearby. If Ellet truly wanted the brigade to succeed in its primary mission—to disrupt guerrilla activity along the river—Crandall's scout demonstrated that the Marine Brigade would have to expand its operations deeper into the interior. Searching for guerrillas, however, presented unavoidable risks, and the sudden willingness to imperil the command had more to do with seizing cotton than locating the enemy.

On February 14 Ellet unexpectedly received a new assignment—one involving an officially sanctioned search for Confederate cotton. General McArthur ordered the 12th Louisiana Colored Infantry, commanded by Colonel Charles A. Gilchrist, from Vicksburg to Grand Gulf for the purpose of establishing a recruiting station and assisting the Treasury Department in collecting cotton. Knowing the Marine Brigade was already in the area, McArthur put the African-American regiment under Ellet's command.

Gilchrist found Ellet off Rodney and explained his orders. A number of Treasury agents and speculators accompanied the colonel, and Ellet, not wanting observers in his midst, sent Gilchrist back to Grand Gulf and the agents back to Vicksburg, assuring both parties that much cotton could be extracted from the interior. Ellet formed an obscure arrangement with Gilchrist after the latter expressed concern over how money should be handled when paid to him by the speculators. Gilchrist admitted that he would be afraid to receive any cash himself because he had "read of officers getting into a great deal of trouble handling cotton." Ellet brushed off the colonel's concerns, asked him

6. Mason Diary, February 14, 1864, Crandall Collection, ISHL; James R. Crandall, "Capture of Capt. Lewis and His Company of Rebel Scouts," Civil War Collection, MHS.

to "impress" whatever transportation he needed to haul the captured cotton, and if money came into his hands, to not worry but to keep a ledger and "pay it over to the post quartermaster at Vicksburg."[7]

On February 20 Colonel Gilchrist began scavenging the countryside and collected 214 bales. Ellet came up to Grand Gulf that night and reported that the marines had located 900 bales marked "C.S.A." at Bruinsburg. Some of the cotton identified by Ellet appeared to be privately owned, and when Gilchrist raised the question, the general replied that "It made no difference." An argument ensued between the Treasury agents and the speculators over 516 bales of the questionable cotton, but Ellet authorized it to be loaded on the steamer *Welcome* and taken to New Orleans.

A day or two later the marines seized 350 bales from a plantation on Bayou Pierre owned by Mrs. Crane, who insisted the cotton belonged to her and not to the Confederate government. She claimed she had burned the Confederate bonds used to purchase it and now owned the cotton again, but Ellet took it anyway. In another raid the marines confiscated 282 bales and loaded it on a barge tied to the ram *Switzerland*. Gilchrist argued with Ellet over the ownership of the cotton, but the general said that it could not be condemned at Vicksburg and would have to be adjudicated by the courts. The colonel estimated that as many as 1,515 bales had been improperly acquired, and that "a lot of speculators, whose loyalty I very much suspect," had amassed quick fortunes. Gilchrist doubted whether his regiment had "assisted in putting one cent into the U.S. Treasury," but he refrained from accusing Ellet of attempting to secure a potful of prize money by coveting at least 632 bales for the Marine Brigade.[8]

On February 27 General Sherman learned that Ellet had moved his boats to Bruinsburg without permission from General McPherson. In an effort to keep Ellet from whimsically romping about the countryside, he ordered him to return his boats to the reaches of river between Vicksburg and Greenville exclusively for "the protection of the planting interest on the Mississippi River," and to not leave the area "without direct orders from the Department Commander." The following day *Diana* took Sherman and his staff down to New Orleans

7. Special Orders No. 42, February 14, Gilchrist's Report, March 9, 1864, *ORA*, XXXII, Pt. 1, pp. 395–96.

8. Gilchrist's Report, March 9, 1864, *ibid.*, 397–400; Mason Diary, February 25, 1864, Crandall Collection, ISHL.

for an important meeting with General Banks, but Ellet stayed at Bruinsburg. Only two possible explanations existed for Ellet's ignoring his orders—either he never received them, or the lure of cotton superseded any directives coming from the departing general.[9]

Ellet remained in the vicinity of Rodney and on March 4 dispatched Major Crandall to apprehend a large quantity of Confederate cotton located ten miles inland at Coleman's Cross Roads. An informant agreed to lead the battalion to the hiding place in exchange for a cash reward. From nearby plantations Ellet commandeered twenty-five wagons drawn by cattle and mules and turned them over to Crandall, whose force consisted of two companies of cavalry and a company of mounted infantry. The detachment reached the cotton's hiding place during the afternoon, found it marked C.S.A., loaded it on wagons, and started back toward the river.

As evening approached, Crandall made camp on a plantation near Red Lick Church and turned out three details to collect forage for the animals. The marines could never keep exclusively to their work and captured two fine horses from the nearby plantation. The owner came to camp a short time later to recover his animals, and in the course of conversation he warned Crandall that Major Calvit Roberts of Adams's brigade had been apprised of the cotton raid and was on the road with his entire command. The planter asked Crandall to move his camp a few miles away, because if a battle took place on his property, it "would be a severe shock to his wife and mother" and probably cause his home to be burned.[10]

Crandall summoned his officers for a meeting in Red Lick Church—not for prayer, but to determine whether they should unload the cotton, use it as a barricade, and fight it out on the plantation, or instead move immediately to Coleman's Cross Roads in the hope of eluding the enemy as night fell. The company commanders unanimously agreed to break camp, so Crandall put the unfed animals back on the road and posted Company D cavalry in front, Company C cavalry in the rear, and Company K infantry among the wagons. At dark a light rain began to fall, and the long train started through broken country where cuts fifteen to twenty feet deep flanked both sides of the narrow road. "We ran into

9. Special Orders No. 44, February 27, 1864, *ORA*, XXXII, Pt. 2, p. 488; Log of *Diana*, February 28, 1864, CMU.

10. James R. Crandall, "An Ambuscade," Civil War Collection, MHS.

as well planned and executed an ambush, as I think was made during the war," Crandall later recalled.[11]

Major Roberts had already worked his riders around Crandall's force, posted them atop the cuts, and set up two points of ambush. At the far ambush he blocked the road with fence rails. Roberts let Crandall's advance guard trot past the first point, drawing the wagon train into the trap. Then, as the head of the train passed the first ambush, Roberts opened fire from both sides of a cut twenty feet high. With the wagon train stretched out for about a mile on a narrow road so dark that nothing could be seen but the flashes of gunfire, Crandall became desperate. He sent one courier ahead to halt the advance and have them charge back upon the enemy. He then sent another courier to the end of the train to bring up the infantry. Company D cavalry mounted the cut to get a better position for firing on the enemy, but could not find them. The infantry, running to the rescue, tripped over fence rails the Rebels had thrown onto the road. As the horse marines galloped along the crest, the grayclads slid down the bank and took possession of the head of the train, shooting enough horses to barricade the road. Crandall saw the vise tightening on his men and attempted to gallop down the road, call up Company C, and put them on the enemy's flank. Crossing an old cotton field, he came to a ditch, and his horse, being slightly wounded, failed to make the leap and threw Crandall to the ground. The horse became wedged so tightly in the ditch that Crandall could not get the animal to its feet. Having lost his revolvers under the horse and being now on foot, he decided against returning to his command and walked back to the fleet at Rodney.

During the fight, the horse marines did not notice Crandall's absence. Company C cavalry entered the fray and provided enough covering fire to hold off the grayclads for about an hour. By then the brigade guide located another road and the marines slowly withdrew, reaching Rodney about the same time as Crandall. Only one man from Company D's advance guard survived the fight, while many others, captured during the clash, later escaped and rejoined the boats. Crandall took a strong detachment out at daylight to recover the recaptured cotton, but when they reached the site of the ambush, the enemy had knocked apart

11. *Ibid.*

the wagons and set everything on fire. Crandall's force salvaged a few undamaged bales and collected the wounded from the night attack. He then returned to the boats, reporting nineteen killed, wounded, or missing.[12]

At War Department headquarters in Washington, a new expedition was being planned. General Banks would move his army up the Red River to Shreveport, collecting Confederate cotton while taking military possession of northwestern Louisiana preparatory to carrying the war into East Texas. Admiral Porter would support the expedition with his ironclads and gunboats, collecting cotton up the tributaries of the Red River under the auspices of naval interests. Because Porter intended to commit much of his Mississippi Squadron to the operation, Grant ordered Sherman to make certain that the Marine Brigade remained between Vicksburg and Greenville to protect the government-leased plantations. At the time of Grant's order, neither he nor Sherman knew that Ellet had once again dropped below Vicksburg in an independent search for Confederate cotton. In relaying Grant's orders to McPherson at Vicksburg, Sherman added that "General Ellet's fleet can do all the ordinary patrolling" normally expected of Porter's squadron along the Mississippi.[13]

In the meantime, General Sherman agreed to detach three divisions under Brigadier General Andrew J. Smith to bolster Banks's army during the Red River Expedition. McPherson suddenly incurred the problem of finding transportation for Smith's 10,000 men, and some of the handiest boats available were those commanded by Ellet. For the Red River expedition, McPherson detached *Autocrat, Baltic, Diana, Raine,* and the hospital boat *Woodford.* He wanted to use all of Ellet's boats, but Sherman would not permit it.[14]

The flotilla shoved off from Vicksburg and on March 11 reached the mouth of Red River. By the time Smith stopped at Simmesport looking for Banks, smallpox had begun taking its toll among members of the Marine Brigade. Finding no sign of Banks, Smith landed his troops and on the 14th captured Fort De Russy. The horse marines participated in

12. *Ibid.;* "Marine Brigade," newsclip from *St. Louis Missouri Democrat,* n.d., Crandall Collection, ISHL; Crandall and Newell, *Ram Fleet,* 373–76.

13. Grant to Sherman, March 4, Sherman to McPherson, March 7, 1864, *ORA,* XXXII, Pt. 3, pp. 19, 35.

14. Sherman to Rawlins, March 8, 1864, *ibid.,* 40; General Orders No. 3, March 10, 1863, *ibid.,* XXIV, Pt. 2, p. 545; Log of *Diana,* March 10, 1864, CMU.

the march to Marksville and provided a bodyguard for Smith and his staff. Then, having received no word from Banks, Smith went up to Alexandria with Porter. The Marine Brigade remained behind to assist in the destruction of the fort. They took special pleasure in demolishing the earthwork because it was there, in 1863, that *Queen of the West* had been captured. With the fort reduced to rubble, the marines returned to their boats and on the afternoon of the 18th reached Alexandria.[15]

While waiting for Banks, Admiral Porter's gunboat crews began collecting tons of cotton and piling it on the landing at Alexandria. Having time on their hands, Ellet's marines decided to do a little hunting on their own. Their raids inland proved unproductive because Porter's sailors had picked the area clean, so they collected sugar, molasses, and other articles of value.

Knowing that Ellet would probably not come back to Vicksburg without prodding, McPherson sent him a reminder on March 16 to return to his post "as soon as the services of your brigade can be spared from the Red River expedition." Had Ellet departed a little sooner, he might have saved *Woodford*, which wrecked on the rapids during an attempt to get above the falls at Alexandria. Ellet used remarkably poor judgment in bringing *Woodford* up Red River. The boat contained dozens of men suffering from smallpox, and the crew had been in a perpetual state of mutiny. Ellet, however, blamed the loss of *Woodford* on Banks.[16]

McPherson's message ordering Ellet back to Vicksburg did not reach Alexandria until March 26. Knowing the looseness of Ellet's command and the general's penchant for unauthorized recruiting, Banks's adjutant instructed the general to not depart for Vicksburg with any "persons whomsoever [other] than those who came with your command to this department." The Marine Brigade weighed anchor off Alexandria on the morning of March 27, but before it reached the Mississippi, reports of looting began to filter back to Banks's headquarters. Brigadier General Charles P. Stone, Banks's chief of staff, dis-

15. Banks's Report, April 6, 1865, *ORA*, XXIV, Pt. 1, pp. 197, 203; Log of *Diana*, March 11, 12, 13, 14, 18, 1864, CMU.

16. McPherson to Ellet, March 16, 1863, *ORA*, XXXII, Pt. 3, p. 82; Banks's Report, April 6, 1865, *ibid.*, XXIV, Pt. 1, pp. 197, 203; *Report of the Joint Committee on the Conduct of the War*, 38th Cong., 2nd Sess. (Washington, D.C., 1864), II, "Red River Expedition," 7, 322; Haughey to Crandall, June 17, 1903, F. M. Haughey Letters, Civil War Collection, MHS; "Reminiscences of the Red River Expedition," James K. Periman Papers, Crandall Collection, ISHL.

patched a message to McPherson advising him that the "Marine Brigade is reported to these headquarters to have stopped at every landing thus far on its way out of Red River, solely for the purpose of pillaging and the destruction of private property." Banks, however, used the Marine Brigade's departure from Alexandria as one of many weak excuses for his poor performance, declaring that Ellet took with him 3,000 infantry. This exaggeration was never challenged, but the four boats returning to Vicksburg could not carry that many men.[17]

While Ellet dallied on Red River, the balance of his command—operating with *B. J. Adams, Monarch,* and *Fairchild*—raided along the Louisiana shore between St. Joseph and Waterproof. Using wagons salvaged from the disastrous setback at Coleman's Cross Roads, the marines swept inland collecting cotton and provisions while another detachment occupied a building ashore, using it as a trading post and filling it with powder, lead, groceries, cloth, medicines, and other goods they intended to trade for cotton. Having set up shop, they built a crude fort adjacent to their boats and began filling it with booty.

At 4 A.M. on March 21 a band of two hundred Missouri guerrillas under Captain Joseph C. Lea surprised the fort and drove the marines back to their boats with casualties. Lea, who had formerly been with Quantrill, had been sent by Lieutenant General Edmund Kirby Smith to stop Ellet's raids, and he intended to do so. Under constant fire from the popguns on the boats, Lea spent three days loading recaptured cotton and all the valuable trade goods on sleds, cotton carts, and seventy-five of the brigade's stolen wagons. He repulsed three feeble counterattacks by the marines and on March 24 withdrew with his heavily laden wagon train and put it on the road to Shreveport. General Ellet received news of the disaster several days later, but neither he nor the brigade's historian ever mentioned that the proud horse marines had been whipped and robbed by a band of determined guerrillas.[18]

The brigade's raids along the Mississippi alarmed Lieutenant General Leonidas Polk to such a degree that on March 21 he wrote

17. Field Orders No. 4, March 26, Crosby to Ellet, March 27, Stone to McPherson, March 29, 1864, *ORA,* XXIV, Pt. 2, pp. 735, 746, 768. Ellet never mentioned these raids, but Amos Bellows's Diary for March 25–29, 1864, mentions several stops to chase guerrillas and collect supplies, Crandall Collection, ISHL. See also *Report of the Joint Committee on the Conduct of the War,* 38th Cong., 2nd Sess., II, "Red River Expedition," 322.

18. Edwards, *Noted Guerrillas,* 272–75.

President Jefferson Davis suggesting a force of 3,000 to 6,000 cavalry be raised and supplied with thirty to sixty cannon to wipe out Ellet's "river fleet." Polk argued that small guerrilla bands could not deal with the Marine Brigade, nor could they discourage planters from returning to the cotton fields under contracts with the Union. Polk asked for approval to raise such a force and promised to "make navigation of the Mississippi impossible" and disrupt "Yankee schemes for cotton cultivation." For reasons Polk found difficult to understand, General Braxton Bragg, speaking for the president, rejected the proposal.[19]

Ellet returned to Vicksburg to learn that General McPherson had been ordered to Huntsville, Alabama, to take command of the Army of the Tennessee, leaving General McArthur in charge of affairs at Vicksburg. By April 2 Ellet had his boats back at the city coaling. *Raine* arrived late that afternoon, having been delayed first by a broken rudder and later by an effort to rescue a steamer torched by guerrillas. *Raine's* marines drove away the guerrillas, pursued them inland, and on departing arrested several local citizens and set their buildings on fire. For their efforts, the crew of *Raine* confiscated a few bales of cotton, loaded them on board, and returned to Vicksburg.[20]

McArthur deployed part of the brigade on the Yazoo River, but he retained *Autocrat, Baltic,* and *Raine* at Vicksburg for special assignment. On April 9 he sent the three boats to Goodrich's Landing to suppress guerrilla raids. Scouting parties turned up evidence of increased enemy activity during the Marine Brigade's absence. Ellet concluded that though "the country was full of Confederates, they seemed to keep out of the way of the Marines." While on a scout, Major Tallerday learned that the enemy had taken a cotton train to Grand Lake to make a deal with a trader. He immediately disembarked two companies from *Baltic* and struck the road leading to Grand Lake. Lieutenant R. S. Murphy, with a squad from Company H Infantry, reached the trader's boat first and captured a few pickets, but the train of wagons with its load of "white gold" had already vanished inland. For the Marine Brigade, searching for Confederate cotton above Vicksburg manifested signs of becoming a toilsome and unproductive enterprise.[21]

19. Polk to Davis, March 21, 1864, *ORA,* XXXIV, Pt. 2, p. 1065.

20. General Orders No. 1, March 26, McPherson to Hurlbut, March 30, 1864, *ORA,* XXXII, Pt. 3, pp. 163, 197; Crandall and Newell, *Ram Fleet,* 380–81.

21. "Lieutenant Murphy's Exploit at Grand Lake," in Crandall and Newell, *Ram Fleet,* 383–84.

With the Red River campaign distracting the attention of the Confederates, General Hurlbut believed that the Marine Brigade should be employed "not on regular or known beats, but suddenly and at unexpected times and places." To activate this scheme, Hurlbut needed permission from McPherson, whose instructions to Ellet remained explicit with regard to the brigade's cruising grounds. McPherson thought the idea worth trying, but he only authorized the use of the rams *Monarch* and *Lioness,* leaving Ellet's Marine Brigade unhappily employed between Vicksburg and Greenville.[22]

After detaching *Monarch* and *Lioness* for duty upriver, Ellet waited for a starlit night and on April 11 ordered *Diana* and *Adams* to shove off from Vicksburg and reconnoiter Milliken's Bend. *Adams* followed *Diana,* and Captain Isaac D. Newell, before going below for the night, left instructions with *Adams*'s sailing master to slack up because the vessels were running too close to each other. A few hours later, Newell recalled, "a terrific crash caused the old *Adams* to tremble from stem to stern," and he sprang from his bed and made for the hurricane roof. *Diana,* commanded by Colonel Currie, had grounded, and *Adams*'s pilot, being too close to change course, struck the vessel a staggering blow abeam. The impact cut fifteen feet off *Diana*'s stern guard, crushed in part of the hull above the waterline, demolished two animal stalls, and dropped a horse and a cow into the river. When *Adams* backed off, Newell asked for a damage report. The mate reported the vessel's jackstaff down and a stream of water rushing into the hold from a gaping hole in the bow. The crew dropped a tarpaulin over the gash and stopped the inflow of water. Currie backed off the bar, and both vessels limped back to Vicksburg for repairs.[23]

On April 20 Ellet felt an impulse to communicate with General McArthur and took *Autocrat* and *Raine* down to Vicksburg. There he learned of the collision and found the incident amusing enough to mirthfully suggest that Newell reassign *Adams* to the Ram Fleet. Newell felt more comfortable laughing about the accident than explaining it. McArthur took too little interest in the brigade to worry himself about the collision and merely asked Ellet to provide two boats

22. Hurlbut to McPherson, April 10, Hurlbut to McArthur, April 13, 1864, *ORA,* XXIV, Pt. 3, pp. 318, 348.

23. Log of *Diana,* April 12, 1864, CMU; Crandall and Newell, *Ram Fleet,* 384–85.

to convoy a supply vessel up the Yazoo. Rather than employ his flagship, *Autocrat,* in such a menial task, Ellet sent *Adams* and the injured *Diana.*[24]

At noon on April 22 *Diana* and *Adams* reached Liverpool and learned that the enemy had reoccupied Yazoo City. *Adams* continued a short distance up the river and discovered that the tinclad *Petrel* had been captured and torched by the enemy. Colonel Currie put the mounted infantry ashore for an overland reconnaissance to Snyder's Bluff while the other boats began evacuating the Liverpool garrison. Currie found no sign of the enemy or any reason to evacuate Liverpool. The garrison commander felt differently, so the boats hauled the troops down to the works at Snyder's Bluff. Disgusted with the affair, Currie took his boats back to Vicksburg.[25]

Meanwhile, General McArthur converted the brigade's flagship *Autocrat* into a quartermaster boat and transferred the troops to *Fairchild,* a change calculated to upset Ellet. Miffed at McArthur's act of intrusion, Ellet remained on *Autocrat* and used the order as an excuse to hatch a new mission. In this instance, he decided to remove all of his boats from Vicksburg. On April 25 he sent Major Crandall with *Raine* down to Rodney to scout for cotton and promised to send *Fairchild* as soon as the vessel could be refitted. He also ordered Colonel Currie to take *Diana* and *Adams* upriver, locate *Baltic,* and patrol the river, "arresting all trading boats, wherever found." Currie encountered *Baltic* ten miles upriver tucked in a bend with a captured trader loaded with cotton. On the 27th Currie's squadron captured two more trading boats loaded with cotton, and from one of the prisoners he learned that more cotton could be found at a plantation near Bayou Mason. These excursions had little military significance, but they enhanced the brigade's prospects for prize money.[26]

At 5 A.M. on April 28 Currie landed near Ashton, Louisiana, and pushed inland for Bayou Mason. The bridge across the stream had been destroyed, so Currie sent Captain Newell ahead with three companies of mounted infantry to look for a ford while the others re-

24. Crandall and Newell, *Ram Fleet,* 385; Log of *Diana,* April 21, 1864, CMU.

25. Chambers to Porter, April 23, Greer to Phelps, May 2, 1864, *ORN,* XXVI, 254–55, 258; Log of *Diana,* April 22, 23, CMU.

26. Crandall's Logbook, April 24, 25, Mason Diary, April 26, 27, 1864, Crandall Collection, ISHL; Log of *Diana,* April 25, 27, 1864, CMU.

mained behind to rebuild the bridge. The marines found no ford, but they did discover a pile of timbers on the opposite shore. A number of volunteers stripped off their clothes, swam across the bayou, and had just begun their work when a picket reported a small force of Rebels creeping toward them through a field. Newell's volunteers had thoughtfully brought their weapons, and "in nature's full dress started after the 'Johnnies.'" When the enemy showed fight, the marines remembered their nakedness and began to wonder how it would look if they were captured, so they fired a few random shots and hastily recrossed the bayou.

Newell returned to the main force and found that Currie had constructed a temporary bridge. The entire command crossed, only to observe a force of grayclads massing in the woods. Since Quantrill's guerrillas had been reported in the area, Currie recalled the troops and returned to the boats with four prisoners but no cotton. He sent the three prizes and their cargoes of cotton to Vicksburg, but remained at his post above the city and waited for the expected arrival of Ellet.[27]

On April 30, *Autocrat,* bearing General Ellet, joined Currie's detachment at Ashton and brought the news that Major General Henry W. Slocum had replaced General McArthur as commander of the District of Vicksburg. This gave Ellet some satisfaction because he never liked McArthur, or for that matter any senior officer of either the army or the navy. Ellet managed to get away from the city before Slocum had time to become acquainted with the irregular operations of the Marine Brigade or its general.[28]

Ellet spent the day mustering and inspecting the brigade, and on May 1 he transferred Company B Infantry from *Autocrat* to *Baltic.* When he learned of Currie's scrape with an unknown force of grayclads at Bayou Mason, he decided to take the entire brigade ashore and make another attempt to shove the enemy out of the way and search for the hidden cotton. He planned a pincer movement, sending half of his force downriver. They would land a few miles away, take the road leading back to Bayou Mason, and form a juncture with Currie's command at a designated point inland. The operation began on time, and in a swoop through the countryside, the only armed force the two detach-

27. Bellows Diary, April 27, 28, 1863, and Crandall's Logbook, April 28, 1863, Crandall Collection, ISHL; Log of *Diana,* April 28, 1864, CMU.

28. General Orders No. 3, April 12, 1864, *ORA,* XXXII, Pt. 3, p. 339; Crandall's Logbook, April 30, 1864, Crandall Collection, ISHL.

ments met was each other. Unable to find a single bale of cotton, the brigade rounded up a number of fat cattle and drove them back to the boats. On May 2 Ellet received orders to return to Vicksburg, but he left the boats of his command posted along the river and ordered them to resume patrols off their old stations.[29]

For four weeks, horse marines from *Diana, Baltic,* and *Adams* patrolled both banks of the Mississippi between Greenville and Lake Providence. Their daily jaunts inland netted a few prisoners, tons of provisions, and a little booty, but not much cotton. Many of the plantations had been leased to the government, and the cotton yield from prior years' crops had either been burned or taken out by agents who claimed to be operating under licenses from the Treasury Department. For Ellet and his men, campaigning deteriorated to frolics through the countryside, but a Confederate general named John S. Marmaduke had received so many complaints about the marines that he decided to send a brigade to pay them a visit.[30]

29. Crandall's Logbook, May 1, and Copybook, May 2, 1864, Crandall Collection, ISHL; Log of *Diana,* May 2, 1864, CMU.

30. Log of *Diana,* May 1–24, 1864, CMU; Crandall's Logbook, May 1–24, 1864, Crandall Collection, ISHL; Crandall and Newell, *Ram Fleet,* 389–96.

CHAPTER 16

GREETINGS FROM
COLONEL GREENE'S BRIGADE

Colonel Currie expressed the sentiments of the brigade when in early June he wrote his father, "I have both something and nothing to tell you and still may not make a letter of it. The 'nothing' has been the events of the past month." Currie went on to say:

> Daily sharp, short skirmishes with the roving bands of guerrillas, varied with the daily bickerings of those almost intangible enemies, the flies by day and the mosquitoes by night are fast telling upon the usual good nature of the fleet. So, to add to our discomforts the malarial water we are compelled to drink, and the excessive hot weather make us sigh for Peace. . . . This trying guerrilla war-fare, phoenix-like in its character, subdued, yet, day after day rising up out of the ashes of its defeat again to menace us, inflamed itself into alarming proportions, burst out on the sixth [of June] in a fierce struggle at Lake Village, the county seat of Chicot, Arkansas.[1]

1. Clarke, ed., *Warfare along the Mississippi,* 101–2.

The "something" concerned the unexpected appearance of Brigadier General John S. Marmaduke's cavalry brigade along the Arkansas side of the Mississippi River. Aside from small clashes with patrols from Wirt Adams's brigade, the horse marines had never been tested against a veteran force led by a determined cavalry commander who knew the territory and where to strike. Marmaduke, a thirty-one-year-old West Point graduate, had risen rapidly in the Confederate army. As colonel of the 3rd Confederate Infantry he received praise for his conduct at Shiloh, where he was wounded. Promoted to brigadier general on November 15, 1862, he added to his laurels during the battle of Prairie Grove. Elevated to the command of a cavalry division, Marmaduke twice accompanied General Price's raids into Missouri and later participated in the defense of Little Rock. His participation in repulsing Major General Frederick Steele's Camden expedition helped to prevent 14,000 blueclads from forming a juncture with General Banks near Shreveport, Louisiana, and helped bring to a close the Union's unsuccessful Red River campaign. Marmaduke boasted that with Banks out of the way, he could operate on the Mississippi and demolish the Marine Brigade, thereby enabling his force to capture and burn Union transports without interference. Marmaduke detached a brigade under Colonel Colton Greene and dispatched it to the area of Lake Village and Cypress Bend to make good his threat.[2]

Greene began moving his brigade toward the Mississippi in early May and found the "country filled with independent squads, deserters, skulkers . . . and speculators . . . the people much demoralized, and largely engaged in contraband trade." His orders were to put an end to Union raids and dispose of drifting bands of local partisans. While part of his cavalry circulated among the towns and villages, Greene moved the horse artillery to Cypress Bend, a bulging peninsula across from Greenville, Mississippi. He positioned his eight guns in such a way that he could limber up and move his artillery back and forth across the neck of the peninsula—Columbia being on the upper side of the bend and Leland Landing on the lower side—thereby enabling his gunners to engage the same vessel twice. A boat passing between the two points

2. Faust, *HTI*, 475–76; Marmaduke's Report, June 11, Greene's Report, May 26, 1864, *ORA*, XXXIV, Pt. 1, pp. 946–47; Crandall and Newell, *Ram Fleet*, 397. Marmaduke commanded two brigades—Colton Greene's, which operated along the Mississippi opposite Greenville, and Jo Shelby's, which was then to the north along the Arkansas River.

traveled eighteen miles by water, while Greene's artillery, operating near the base of the peninsula, had but three and a half miles to travel by horse. The attacks began on May 1 when Greene's horse artillery fired into the transport *Arthur* at Columbia, and since that time every passing steamboat became a target for the Confederates.[3]

On May 24, having received instructions from General Ellet to protect traffic on the river, Colonel Currie tied up at Greenville with *Diana, Adams,* and *Baltic*. Knowing his boats were weakly armed, he put the crews to work mounting more guns and strengthening the platforms. From Greenville he heard artillery fire at Columbia. Having seen the cotton boat *Delta* pass upriver, he supposed the firing had come from Greene's artillery. Sure enough, *Delta* came about and returned to Greenville so disabled that she required help from a towboat. In the meantime, the steamer *Longworth,* paddling downriver, received fire as it passed Columbia and reported being shot at "ten or twelve times." Colonel Greene, expecting *Longworth* to continue on its way, limbered up and moved his artillery to the lower side of the bend in the expectation of capturing the damaged vessel. *Longworth,* however, stopped at Greenville to ask assistance. Currie complied, ordered *Baltic* lashed to *Longworth,* and put them both under all the steam they could carry, while he, with *Diana,* prepared to engage the battery and absorb its fire.

Colonel Greene had no cover on the bend below Greenville, so he wisely spread his artillery along the shore. As soon as Currie spotted the grayclads, he opened with the 20-pounder Parrott. The Confederates paid no attention to the fire from *Diana* and simply waited for *Longworth* to come in range. To their surprise, they observed the steamer shielded by *Baltic* and opened on it. *Baltic* replied, and for a few minutes "shot, shell, and canister flew at a terrific rate." *Longworth* escaped unharmed, as did *Diana,* but *Baltic* lost one killed and two wounded when a shell burst in its wheelhouse.[4]

When Greene's artillery ignored the firing from *Diana* and calmly

3. Greene's Report, May 26, 30, 1864, *ORA,* XXXIV, Pt. 1, 947–48, 949; "From the Lower Mississippi," May 4, 1864, newsclip, Crandall Collection, ISHL. Amos Bellows described Columbia as "a little town of 15 houses, 3 stores, [and] 4 groceries—not a living person to be seen," Bellows Diary, March 21, 1864, Crandall Collection, ISHL.

4. Greene's Report, May 26, 1864, *ORA,* XXXIV, Pt. 1, p. 948; Log of *Diana,* May 24, 1864, CMU; Bellows Diary, May 24, 1864, Crandall Collection, ISHL; *St. Louis Missouri Democrat,* May 30, 1864.

concentrated their guns only on *Baltic* and *Longworth,* Currie quickly concluded that the grayclads posted on the beach were veterans. A band of guerrillas would have skedaddled after the first blast from *Diana*'s Parrott. *Baltic,* badly riddled from stem to stern, returned to Greenville for repairs, and Currie, aware of a new urgency, kept carpenters busy the balance of the day improving the boats' batteries.[5]

While Currie toiled, Greene's cavalry continued to move from point to point along the banks of the Mississippi. Aside from damaging *Delta* and battering *Baltic,* the Rebels disabled a transport, compelling the crew to burn it, and so badly damaged another steamer that it careened over and required a tow to the safety of the east bank. Not content to fire exclusively on commercial shipping, Greene also engaged the tinclad *Romeo,* struck it fifteen times, and sent it limping downstream. In a separate action farther downriver, Greene's scouts spied the steamer *Lebanon* anchored offshore. They stole a yawl, captured the vessel, and burned it.[6]

From Currie's perspective, Greene's horse artillery vanished just as quickly as it appeared. Four days passed and the Marine Brigade's reconnaissances ashore met with no resistance. Greene had merely exhausted his ammunition and returned to base to replenish it. On the night of May 29 he returned and posted his guns at Sunnyside. As the transport *Rocket* paddled into range, the grayclads opened fire and riddled the passenger decks. Currie heard the firing and ran *Diana* down to investigate, but by then Greene had limbered up his artillery and moved above Columbia to take a second crack at the steamer. When Currie came alongside *Rocket* to offer assistance, he found Adjutant General Lorenzo Thomas and his staff on board, along with General McArthur and his wife. He then ordered *Baltic* and *Adams* to convoy the transport past Columbia, but Greene greeted the trio with an artillery barrage that forced all three boats back to Greenville.[7]

On the morning of May 30 Currie again set out for Columbia using *Adams* to convoy *Rocket* while *Diana* and *Baltic* provided protective fire. Once again, Greene had moved down to Sunnyside, and while *Rocket* steamed past Columbia unmolested, the grayclads opened

5. Bellows Diary, May 24, 25, 1864, Crandall Collection, ISHL.

6. Greene's Report, May 26, June 8, 1864, *ORA,* XXXIV, Pt. 1, p. 948, 951.

7. Greene's Report, June 8, 1864, *ibid.,* 951; Log of *Diana,* May 29, 1864, CMU; Bellows Diary, May 29, 1864, Crandall Collection, ISHL.

on the transport *Clara Eames*, cut her steampipe, burst her boilers, and captured her cargo of cotton.

While Currie cruised back and forth around Cypress Bend, a band of guerrillas raided Greenville and sank the barge containing the brigade's coal. By May 31 the enemy seemed to be causing trouble everywhere along Currie's reach of the river. He could never pin down Greene's brigade, but then he never put the horse marines ashore to try to find it. To complicate matters, Currie learned that four more transports were steaming toward Greenville, but the welcome appearance of one of Porter's gunboats bought a few hours of silence from Greene's artillery.[8]

On May 31 *Autocrat* arrived from Vicksburg, and *Monarch*, which had been converted to a lightly armed gunboat, came down from Memphis. Their arrival proved timely because the following night Lieutenant Ed. H. Nichols stole downriver in a yawl and reported that the transport *Henry Ames*, which was bringing him to Greenville, and the tinclad *Exchange* had both turned back because of the presence of a Confederate battery at Columbia. *Exchange*'s engine had been disabled, and its captain, Acting Master James C. Gipson, had been severely wounded in the head. When General Ellet learned of the incident, he ordered *Adams* and *Monarch* up to Columbia to destroy the enemy's batteries. He put Captain Isaac D. Newell of *Adams* in charge of the operation, and subordinated both himself and Lieutenant Colonel John A. Ellet of *Monarch* to Newell's orders.[9]

As Newell prepared to shove off, two transports—*Missouri* and *James Watson*—came up the river. Hailing them into Greenville for protection, Ellet had *Missouri* lashed to the starboard beam of *Adams* and *James Watson* lashed to *Monarch*. Using his available flotilla, Ellet then moved upriver and engaged the Confederate battery, but the enemy held its fire until the boats bearing transports came in range. Greene's gunners concentrated their fire on *Adams*'s pilothouse, knowing that if they knocked it apart, both vessels would be crippled. For several minutes shot and shell rattled through *Adams*'s chimneys,

---

8. Greene's Report, May 30, June 8, 1864, *ORN*, XXVI, 804, 806; Bellows Diary, May 30, 1864, Crandall Collection, ISHL; Log of *Diana*, May 30, 1864, CMU; Crandall and Newell, *Ram Fleet*, 400–401.

9. Crandall and Newell, *Ram Fleet*, 401–2; Gipson to Owen, June 5, Owen's Report, June 2, 1864, *ORN*, XXVI, 354, 355.

smashed skylights, and severed escape pipes, but missed the pilothouse. Newell reached safety above Columbia, but *Adams* absorbed more than twenty shots from Greene's artillery.

After cutting *Missouri* loose, Newell spent a few hours making repairs and clearing the wreckage from his decks. Because of the condition of his vessel he conferred with Ellet, but the general insisted that *Adams* bring the transport *Henry Ames* down to Greenville while the other boats provided covering fire. Leaving *Exchange* above Columbia to continue with repairs, Newell lashed onto *Ames,* which was heavily laden with freight but whose passengers were "eager to run the battery with us." As Newell approached the Confederate battery, he could see "rebel guns and gunners . . . in plain sight on shore, the men with coats off and bare-headed." Newell stood by the Rodman gun on the forward starboard quarter and withheld fire until nearly abreast of the enemy. Greene's artillerists opened, and the first shot nipped off part of the Rodman gun's platform and sprayed Newell and the gun crew with splinters. "From this time, so long as we were within range of the battery," wrote Newell, "we heard music. The shells tore through the oaken barricades, and went crashing through the cabin, ranging aft and passing through the thin stateroom partitions as though they were egg shells. The chandeliers and the glass in the skylights jingled. The roar of our three pieces of artillery and those of the ram [*Monarch*] behind, together with the quickly repeated volleys of musketry, were deafening." The fight lasted about ten minutes, but *Adams* absorbed thirty-six shots and limped into Greenville riddled from stem to stern. During the engagement *Adams* lost two killed and two mortally wounded—one man's heart being shot from his body and onto the deck of *Ames*—but the transport got through safely and anchored off Greenville.[10]

Finding himself confronted by veteran Confederate artillery, Ellet began to rethink his role and grumbled that convoying should be relegated to the gunboats of the navy—not to his lightly armed, wooden-shelled riverboats. His efforts to place heavier guns on *Baltic* and *Diana* strained the decks and caused more damage than enemy fire, and at times the hastily improvised gun crews proved to be more of a menace to themselves than to the enemy. In late May, James K. Periman, a gunner on *Baltic,* accidentally shot off his arm during a duel

10. Owen to Porter, June 2, 4, 1864, *ORN,* XXVI, 355, 356; Greene to Ewing, June 8, 1864, *ORA,* XXXIV, Pt. 1, p. 952; Bellows Diary, June 2, 1864, Crandall Collection, ISHL; Crandall and Newell, *Ram Fleet,* 402–5.

with Greene's artillery. The boat had been so badly cut up that Ellet ordered it to St. Louis for repairs. Then, when *Baltic* started for St. Louis, it passed Columbia under the protection of *Monarch,* and enemy shore batteries punched more holes through both vessels.[11]

Ellet concluded that he had "played gunboat" long enough with his horse marines. While hatching a plan to shed the responsibility, he learned that Major General Edward R. S. Canby had been appointed commander of the Military Division of West Mississippi. Canby had arrived at Vicksburg on May 11 and soon afterwards became besieged by complaints of raids on transports and supply vessels. He did not know the strength or nature of the Confederate unit causing all the trouble at Cypress Bend, but he instructed Major General Andrew J. Smith to use the XXVI and XVII Army Corps to drive away the Rebels and urged him to employ the Marine Brigade in the expedition. He suggested that Smith confer with Ellet to determine the "character of the country . . . and the routes by which the rebels reach and retreat from the river." He also recommended "Colonel Currie, now of the *Diana* . . . as especially qualified for this purpose." Smith complied and dispatched a message to Currie informing him to "stay near Greenville so he could be found."[12]

Currie informed Ellet of the message from Smith, and the general seized the opportunity to go to Vicksburg and meet Canby. It was not Smith's intention for the Marine Brigade to abandon Greenville, but at 2 A.M. on June 3, Ellet got under way for Vicksburg with *Autocrat, Diana, Adams, Monarch,* and the transport *Henry Ames.* Ellet knew that General McClernand's wife was traveling on *Ames* to look after her ailing husband at New Orleans, but that alone could not justify withdrawing the entire squadron from the protection of transports rounding Cypress Bend.[13]

On the evening of June 3 Ellet reached Vicksburg, where he found *Raine* and *Fairchild.* For the first time in many weeks, he had most of his scattered brigade in one place. Colonel Currie reported to General Smith and informed him that the Confederate raids had been con-

11. Crandall's Logbook, June 2, 1864, Crandall Collection, ISHL; Periman to Crandall, September 23, 1910, Periman Papers, Crandall Collection, ISHL.

12. Canby to Smith, May 31, Melville to Currie, May 31, 1864, *ORA,* XXXIV, Pt. 4, pp. 137, 138. General Orders, No. 1, May 11, 1864, *ibid.,* Pt. 3, p. 543.

13. Crandall's Logbook, June 3, 1864, Crandall Collection, ISHL; Log of *Diana,* June 3, 1864, CMU; Crandall and Newell, *Ram Fleet,* 405.

ducted by Colton Greene's brigade from Marmaduke's division and not by guerrillas. In the morning Smith loaded most of his command on eighteen transports and put the remainder on *Adams, Diana, Fairchild,* and *Raine.* The flotilla, numbering twenty-eight vessels, departed from Vicksburg on June 4 and, with *Diana* in the lead, headed upriver for Lake Village, where Greene's cavalry had last been reported in force. *Diana,* injured during the fights at Greenville, lugged along with a damaged boiler that spewed steam and water into the firebox, and the column advanced at a crawl.[14]

Tiny Lake Village had once been located on a sweeping horseshoe bend of the Mississippi, but before the war the current had cut a more direct channel near the lower base of the peninsula and permanently separated the town from the river. Snugged on the west shore of its inland lake, the village had become important to the Confederates because a network of country roads passed through it and connected the interior to several landings on the Mississippi. Many of the roads west of town passed around swamps and through woods and hollows that Currie described as "bristl[ing] with shadows and dangerous retreats" that sheltered "desperate characters, guerrillas and other rebels." Currie had penetrated the area on several raids and considered it "as closed and impassable as the cave of the 'Forty Thieves.'" During his last reconnaissance, he had been chased back to *Diana* by Greene's cavalry but escaped before they could bring up their artillery.[15]

On a road eight miles downriver from Lake Village lay Sunnyside Landing, where on Currie's recommendation Smith decided to land 10,000 men and the Marine Brigade. At 5 P.M. on June 5 Currie pulled into the landing and disembarked his horse marines. With two squadrons of the 4th Iowa Cavalry and one 12-pounder mountain howitzer, he led a scout inland to locate the enemy but not bring on a fight. Currie must have forgotten his orders because one mile from the landing he encountered enemy pickets, drove them across a bridge spanning a small creek, and pursued them into a skirt of woods. Observing the grayclads forming a strong skirmish line, Currie dismounted his men, sent out Captain James P. Harper's Company H as flankers and,

14. Crandall's Logbook, June 3, 4, 1864, Crandall Collection, ISHL; Log of *Diana,* June 4, 1864, CMU; Clarke, ed., *Warfare along the Mississippi,* 103; Mower's Report, June 15, 1864, *ORA,* XXXIV, Pt. 1, p. 971.

15. Clarke, ed., *Warfare along the Mississippi,* 102–3. Lake Village was also known as Old River Lake and Lake Chicot.

in a coordinated assault, pushed the enemy deeper into the woods. Collecting his command for another assault, Currie pressed the Rebels through the woods, forcing them to spill out the opposite side and take refuge behind an old levee built along the lake. After a few minutes of quiet, Currie came out of the woods with his staff to look behind the levee and rode into a hail of fire. He galloped back to the woods, brought up the entire command, and drove the southerners off the levee. The firing had attracted the attention of Colonel Greene's cavalry, and as dusk fell, Currie could hear the approach of horse artillery on his left flank. He recalled his command and, with four casualties, returned to the boats.[16]

That night Currie spoke with General Smith, and together they formulated a hasty plan of attack. Neither officer had yet been able to assess the strength or weakness of the enemy, so Smith decided to let Currie take the lead, reconnoiter with horse marines, locate the Rebels, and keep them busy until relieved by the infantry.

At daybreak on June 6, Currie made an early start and in a drenching rain marched over the previous day's route and encountered the grayclads in exactly the same place. The enemy held a much stronger position and appeared to be posted under good cover. Currie dismounted the cavalry and sent Captain Newell's Company A ahead as skirmishers. At 8 A.M. he moved up the rest of his force and paused to wait for Smith's command, which had been detained by muddy roads made impassable by a torrential morning rain.

An hour passed, rain continued to fall, and skirmishers exchanged a few random shots. Colonel Greene had formed two regiments in a skirt of timber on the north side of a cotton field, resting his left on the foot of the levee. Currie, with the horse marines and two squadrons of the 4th Iowa Cavalry, deployed on a parallel line. After Newell's skirmishers nudged back the enemy skirmishers, Currie advanced his line and, at short range, stumbled into a blistering fire. The blueclads hunkered down in the mud, taking cover behind clumps of weeds, and returned the fire. Currie realized that his position had become perilous and began looking for Smith's 10,000 infantry and four batteries of field guns. "We could do nothing but show fight and wait," Currie recalled. "Any attempt to withdraw would bring on us an instant charge and capture."

When Newell sent word that he expected his skirmish line to collapse, Currie encouraged him to hold fast, assuring him that "the infantry was near." Smith's orders to Currie were to "meet the enemy, form line, and begin the contest," and to hold the line without bringing on a full engagement. "I had done so," Currie declared, "and now the serious part of the question was to hold them off until re-inforcements arrived."[17]

Fifteen minutes later General Smith came on the field with his staff, and Currie pointed out his battle line. Smith sent one of Brigadier General Joseph A. Mower's four-gun batteries and a brigade of infantry to the left to relieve Currie's line. Thinking a few shots from the battery would flush the enemy, Mower opened with a section of artillery. To Currie's astonishment—because the grayclads had kept their guns silent—Greene's masked batteries opened from one hundred yards and forced Mower to move his guns to the rear. Frustrated by the setback, Mower called up the infantry, and for several minutes the racket of musket fire became intense. Then, almost as suddenly, the firing trailed off to an occasional spurt.

Greene never intended to fight at the levee, only to draw out Smith's full force and lure it onto more favorable ground for battle. He quickly disengaged, drawing his force back to Lake Village. The grayclads withdrew across a sluggish stream known as Ditch Bayou, destroyed the bridge, and joined the rest of the brigade waiting on the opposite shore. Smith now realized that Currie had been contending with only a small force and that Greene's brigade occupied a position of strength. He could observe the enemy formed in dense woods on the other side of Ditch Bayou, a deeply cut and mucky stream forty yards wide and, for infantry, virtually impassable.[18]

Currie suggested that Smith confer with Captain Calvin G. Fisher of Company E, who had reconnoitered the area on past occasions and knew the topography. He also advised against advancing infantry across the bayou, where they would surely become bogged in deep mud and immobilized. "But the general thought he knew best," Currie recalled, "and a line of infantry at least a mile in length" advanced into the

---

17. Cockefair's Report, June 9, Greene's Report, June 9, 1862, *ORA*, XXXIV, Pt. 1, pp. 973, 984; Clarke, ed., *Warfare along the Mississippi*, 105–6; George E. Currie, "The Marines in the Smith Expedition Against Marmaduke," Currie Letters, Crandall Collection, ISHL.

18. Becht's Report, June 10, Van Beek's Report, June 7, Greene's Report, June 9, 1864, *ORA*, XXXIV, Pt. 1, pp. 975, 976–77, 985.

bayou and received volley after volley from Rebels "sheltered by the woods as securely as though they were out of range of our shot and shell. Not a man flinched," Currie noted, though every blueclad knew "some one had blundered." When Greene opened with his artillery, "cannons to the right . . . cannons to the left . . . [and] cannons in front, volleyed and thundered." In less than a half hour, more than a hundred Union dead and wounded lay in an old cotton gin that had been converted to a hospital a half mile in the rear.[19]

After Mower's artillery opened a hole in the Confederate right, Smith ordered Currie to take the cavalry across the bayou and flank the enemy. "The stream was not so deep," the colonel recalled, "but a thick muck at the bottom gave the horses no footing and they [crossed] as best they could." Currie reached the opposite shore first and for several minutes found himself alone. Had Smith's huge force not compelled Greene—whose men had depleted their ammunition—to fall back, Currie may not have had the luxury of waiting for his friends to join him.[20]

After a score of horse marines crossed, Currie galloped after the enemy but found not one. Coming to a fork in the road—one bearing to Lake Village and the other to a swamp—Currie noticed that Greene's command appeared to have split, so he sent an orderly back to General Smith for instructions. Smith opted to send the cavalry to Lake Village, but the message did not reach Currie until dusk. Rain continued to fall, and the horse marines hobbled into the village, dismounted, and tried to build fires. Flames sputtered, and the men spent an uncomfortable night eating cold rations and sleeping in wet clothes. They were the lucky ones, because every house and building in Lake Village became a hospital for Smith's wounded infantry.[21]

At 8 A.M. on June 7 Currie moved his command back to the boats, which had been sent up to Columbia Landing, while Smith took his corps to Luna Landing, another three miles upriver. Currie had just begun to relax on *Diana* when a staff officer came on board to report

---

19. Mower's Report, June 15, Hubbard's Report, June 11, 1864, *ibid.*, 971–72, 973–74; Clarke, ed., *Warfare along the Mississippi*, 106–7; Currie, "The Marines in the Smith Expedition Against Marmaduke," Currie Letters, Crandall Collection, ISHL.

20. Greene's Report, June 9, 1864, *ORA*, XXXIV, Pt. 1, p. 985; Currie, "The Marines in the Smith Expedition Against Marmaduke," Currie Letters, Crandall Collection, ISHL.

21. Bellows Diary, June 7, 1864, Crandall Collection, ISHL.

that General Smith wished to see him. The captain of the Marine Brigade's dispatch boat had shut down its boilers, so Currie, accompanied by his orderly, made the trip on his "pleasure" horse—his "work horse" being fatigued.

On reaching Luna Landing, Currie spent an hour with Smith, and as he prepared to leave, his dispatch vessel unexpectedly arrived from Columbia. Currie took the boat, and because his horse refused to go on board, he sent it back with his orderly. The colonel watched his "beautiful horse as he was led away," and then he shoved off to return to *Diana*. Currie never saw the horse again. As the orderly trotted leisurely down the road paralleling the river, thousands of soldiers watched from transports as a small group of Rebels sprang from the bushes and captured Currie's orderly and both horses. A few days later the marines took a prisoner who admitted to being one of the party who snatched the colonel's horse. "General Marmaduke took my horse for his own use," Currie later learned, "and was very proud of him, as he might be."[22]

Currie blamed Smith for a bungled campaign, claiming that the general should have been able to surround Greene's brigade and capture the whole lot in a sweeping pincer movement. Smith, however, knew nothing of the area's topography or the size of Greene's command, and Currie had the advantage of hindsight. Greene, however, anticipated that Smith would send a second column against his rear and had posted a strong guard at Lake Village. In many respects, the roving cavalry of Marmaduke's and Adams's commands practiced similar tactics. Currie explained it well when he wrote, "The guerrillas fought only when concealed. Theirs was the practice to shoot and run. They were hungry wolves that dogged our footsteps," never exposing themselves to a stand-up, knock-down fight. Currie should have counted himself lucky. Aside from the loss of his orderly, he listed only one other casualty, Sergeant Snell, seriously wounded during the Lake Village affair. Had the dispatch boat arrived at Luna Landing a few minutes later, Currie would have joined his horse and orderly as prisoners in Marmaduke's camp.[23]

22. Clarke, ed., *Warfare along the Mississippi*, 107–10; Currie, "The Marines in the Smith Expedition Against Marmaduke," Currie Letters, Crandall Collection, ISHL.

23. Greene's Report, June 9, 1864, *ORA*, XXXIV, Pt. I, p. 984; Currie, "The Marines in the Smith Expedition Against Marmaduke," Currie Letters, Crandall Collection, ISHL; Crandall and Newell, *Ram Fleet*, 418. During the fight at Old River Lake, Smith reported 161 casualties and Greene reported 4 killed and 33 wounded. See *ORA*, XXXIV, Pt. I, pp. 975–85 *passim*.

On the evening of June 7, General Ellet came up from Vicksburg with *Autocrat* and *Monarch*. He had missed all the excitement and arrived just as Smith, in response to orders from General Canby, embarked his corps for Memphis. On the passage up to Luna Landing, *Autocrat* and *Monarch* received musket fire as they passed Greenville, so on the morning of June 8 all five boats dropped down to investigate. Ellet landed and took a detachment into town. Several houses and Greenville's public buildings "mysteriously" burst into flame, but Amos Bellows blamed the fires on his comrades. The general then called a conference of his officers. Greene's brigade still operated across the river, but Ellet had a different mission in mind—and one less risky.[24]

24. Canby to Washburn, June 4, 1864, *ORA,* XXIX, Pt. 2, p. 78; Bellows Diary, June 8, and Crandall's Logbook, June 7, 8, 1864, Crandall Collection, ISHL.

CHAPTER 17

THE LAST CAMPAIGNS
OF THE HORSE MARINES

Greene's artillery continued to disrupt navigation on the Arkansas
shore opposite Greenville, but Ellet wanted no more trouble from
the feisty veterans. Instead of challenging them, he sent the marines
twenty-five miles in the opposite direction in hopes of capturing the
steamer *H. D. Mears,* a handsome prize rumored to be on the
Sunflower River.

At daylight on June 9 the horse marines departed from Greenville
with six companies of mounted infantry, the cavalry battalion, one howitzer, and four companies of the 2nd Wisconsin Cavalry, all carrying two
days' rations. The column made good progress until reaching Bayou
Phalia, a narrow but deep and miry stream that could not be crossed on
horseback. Scouts located a small ferry upstream, and the brigade consumed most of the day transporting their mounts to the opposite side—
twelve at a time. Ellet posted three companies and the howitzer at the
stream to guard the ferry and led the remainder of the brigade into unknown territory. Four miles later the horse marines came upon a large

plantation, so remote that it had never been visited by a hostile force. Finding it well stocked with chickens, hams, bacon, and meal, the brigade camped for the night and appropriated all the food the men could carry.[1]

That night a slave came into camp and reported two parties of Confederates socializing at nearby plantations. Ellet called for Captain Newell and said, "We want those fellows. You will take your company, or so much of it as you deem necessary, and go after them." Newell shook awake enough men to make up two squads and, with the slave acting as guide, trotted off in "one of the darkest nights I ever saw."

At the first house, he crept to the front door and heard shuffling that sounded like men rushing to load their weapons. Without waiting, he kicked in the door and found five Texans fixing for a fight. Newell ordered them to throw down their arms, and when the Confederates observed the number of carbines pointed at their bellies, they complied.

The second home, a mile away, stood like a brilliant candle flickering in a universe of darkness. Every window of the house was open, and the night seemed filled with dozens of voices all melded together as one. The dance had been interrupted because the fiddler had broken a string. Having made repairs, the caller shouted "all promenade" just as the horse marines "went pell mell over the fence." The Confederate officers heard the clatter and rushed to the hall where they had stacked arms. Newell ran to the door and shouted, "My men are all around this house; think of your women. If you fire a shot, you take the responsibility." Thirteen Texans threw down their arms and surrendered. On the way back to camp, Newell asked the guide how he happened to know that the marines were in the neighborhood but all the whites seemed ignorant of the fact. "I knowed when you uns crossed de fust hosses ovah de bayou," the slave replied, and "got 'er 'spatch ovah de grapevine telergraf." Puzzled, Newell asked, "How many of the darkeys around here knew we were coming?" Without hesitation, the guide replied, "All de darkeys . . . know it." Despite southern resistance, the slaves had already surmised how the war would end and had decided to give support to the Union.[2]

1. Crandall's Logbook, June 9, 1864, Crandall Collection, ISHL.

2. Evans's Report, June 13, 1864, *ORA*, XXXIX, Pt. 1, pp. 231–32; Bellows Diary, June 9, 1864, ISHL; Isaac D. Newell, "A Night Raid Stops a Dance," in Crandall and Newell, *Ram Fleet*, 419–21.

On the morning of June 10 Ellet led the column to the Sunflower River, and from there to Indian Bayou, where the marines found the steamer *H. D. Mears* snugged in among the willows. While a detachment burned the vessel, the main column circulated through this rich, isolated, and comparatively undisturbed section of Mississippi, collecting 150 horses and mules and large quantities of stores and provisions. At midday on the 11th the horse marines returned with their booty to Bayou Phalia and, "in a wearisome rain," crossed once again on the ferry. Dozens of blacks of both sexes followed the column back to the boats, "happy in the assurance of freedom" under the marines' protection. Ellet regarded the raid as successful, but he had lost the opportunity to capture 175 bales of cotton. Captain Perry Evans and scouts of the 9th Texas Cavalry got there first and, expecting a visit from the horse marines, set it afire.[3]

On the afternoon of June 12 Ellet ordered the boats back to Vicksburg for repairs. *Diana* still required a number of planks to replace those crushed in a collision with *Adams,* and a section of *Autocrat's* disabled boilers had to be sent to New Orleans to be refurbished. Other boats, perforated by shells from Greene's artillery, also needed patching, and on the 21st *Raine* went up the Yazoo in search of timber. During this period the heat remained insufferable, made worse by orders to keep 150 pounds of steam in the boilers in case of an emergency.[4]

On July 2, after nearly three weeks of inactivity, Ellet embarked his force, along with Mississippi's 52nd U.S. Colored Infantry. The squadron dropped down to Rodney, and at 6 A.M. on July 3 the troops splashed ashore with a single howitzer and took the road leading east. One mile inland the column began skirmishing with enemy scouts, and the fighting continued periodically throughout the day. The march progressed slowly because the African Americans had no mounts, and the day became intensely hot. At noon the advance reached Coleman's Cross Roads—the point where roads from Port Gibson, Natchez, and Fayette converged, and for the brigade, a place of unpleasant memories. By the time the infantry arrived, another three hours had elapsed. Having covered but twelve miles since leaving Rodney, Ellet established

3. Crandall's Logbook, June 10, 11, 1864, Crandall Collection, ISHL; Perry to Ellis, July 27, 1864, *ORA*, XXXIX, Pt. 2, p. 731.

4. Crandall's Logbook, June 17, 18, 21, 22, 23, 1864, Crandall Collection, ISHL; Log of *Diana*, June 14, 1864, CMU; Clarke, ed., *Warfare along the Mississippi*, 13–14.

his headquarters in the Coleman plantation house, detailed a strong picket, and ordered his men to make camp.[5]

Colonel Currie continued to be puzzled about the purpose of the expedition because General Ellet had not communicated the plan to his officers. Even more mystifying had been the order of marching—Major James R. Crandall's cavalry in front, followed by the African Americans, a train of thirty empty army wagons, and finally Currie's own mounted infantry. Currie could not comprehend the purpose of bringing so many wagons inland except to gather cotton, but he knew the area had been picked clean. Since only two days' rations had been cooked, everyone predicted a short expedition and the men contented themselves by happily going into camp.[6]

As darkness approached, Ellet called several of his officers together to explain the next day's orders. Soon after reveille, he wanted a reconnaissance made—Currie to place his mounted infantry on the road to Port Gibson, and Major Crandall to take the cavalry in the direction of Fayette. If either column met enemy resistance "too strong to handle," they were to send back for the howitzer and reinforcements from the black regiment.[7]

At 3:30 A.M. on July 4 the bugler brought the command to its feet, and after an early breakfast both columns filed onto the road and trailed off in opposite directions. Three miles down the road to Fayette—just as the sun rose—the cavalry stumbled into a nest of grayclads who fired at Charles Hubbard of Company B and killed him instantly. While Crandall charged the bushes where the enemy lay hidden, Captain De Coster searched about for a courier to ride back for reinforcements. Billie Corrie volunteered to carry the message, turned his horse out of ranks, and sped back toward camp. Ellet summoned the 52nd U.S. Colored Infantry and sent Corrie galloping down the road at "breakneck speed" to recall the detachment marching on the Port Gibson road. An hour later, Colonel Currie got the message, ordered "right about," and sent his mounted infantry racing up the road to rescue Crandall. As Currie approached Coleman's Cross Roads, he spotted the general standing nearby and stopped for orders. "Take your regiment," Ellet said, "and move on to [Crandall's] assistance . . . you are to assume

5. Crandall's Logbook, July 2, 3, 1864, Crandall Collection, ISHL; Log of *Diana,* July 2, 1864, CMU; Crandall and Newell, *Ram Fleet,* 424–25.

6. Clarke, ed., *Warfare along the Mississippi,* 114–15.

7. *Ibid.*.

command of all the forces in the field." Knowing a colonel commanded the 52nd U.S. Colored Infantry, Currie replied, "General, there is an officer already there who outranks me." "Tell that officer," Ellet said impatiently, "it is my orders that you take command."[8]

When Currie came upon the scene of the early fight, he found fences on both sides of the road thrown to the ground, dead horses lying about, and for a mile along the road, evidence of a running battle. The horse marines had driven the enemy down the road, but by the time Currie located Crandall, he found both men and horses fatigued by the struggle and lolling under the shade of trees. The enemy, still in sight, appeared to be enjoying the interregnum and doing the same. The colonel commanding the 52nd U.S. Colored Infantry regiments approached Currie and volunteered to step aside, confessing that he did not "understand this mode of warfare." Currie appreciated the gesture, as it spared him the embarrassment of delivering Ellet's order. He quickly formed a skirmish line from companies of the 52nd, placed the howitzer on a hill to protect them, and deployed Crandall's winded cavalry in reserve.

At Currie's signal, the skirmishers advanced, holding their fire until they reached the enemy position on a hill. Near the summit the grayclads opened with a volley. The skirmishers fired back, and while everyone reloaded, the African Americans charged, driving the enemy across an open field and into a distant belt of timber. Currie brought up the mounted infantry, but the enemy had so securely positioned themselves in the timber that the horse marines retired. Exhausted and weary from the heat, the command rested an hour before returning to Coleman's Cross Roads.

Unobserved, the grayclads followed the marines back to camp, and while the brigade unsaddled and fed their horses, a handful of Confederates crept up a nearby hill and fired a volley into the camp. The bugler trumpeted "boots and saddles," and "in a twinkling" Currie had the men mounted and riding in the direction of the firing. At the foot of the woods covering the hill, Ellet came up with his staff and conferred with Currie, who believed the enemy's sporadic firing was intended as a distraction and warned the general to post a heavy force in the rear and to watch the flanks. Ellet thought otherwise and ordered up the black

8. Crandall and Newell, *Ram Fleet*, 425–26; Clarke, ed., *Warfare along the Mississippi*, 116.

infantry. Then, as an afterthought, he decided to personally visit the outposts on the Port Gibson road and asked Currie to come along and look for himself. As they started down the road an old, weathered slave came running toward them, breathless and terrified, reporting that "forty thousand mounted rebels were passing around the picket line to get into our rear."[9]

Currie and Ellet reversed direction and galloped back to the Coleman house. The colonel recalled his horse marines, mounted them, and held them in readiness where with the African Americans at the foot of the hill. The general hailed Major Crandall and ordered the cavalry battalion to go onto the Rodney road—at best a narrow country lane—and make a reconnaissance. A half mile down the road the Confederates charged in force, routed Crandall's cavalry, and drove the marines back to Coleman's plantation in "terrible confusion."

Ellet had placed himself at the crossroads and remained a silent spectator until the melee on the Rodney road came surging back upon him and minié balls began whizzing about his ears. Spurring his horse, he crossed the field to Currie's command and shouted, "Colonel, in the name of God what shall we do?"

"Do?" Currie replied. "Let's fight."

The general appeared rattled by the unexpected attack, so Currie shouted, "Bring down the infantry from the hill [and] form them in that field west of the Rodney Road. I will dismount my regiment and whip them in my front in five minutes." The general still seemed confused, so Currie repeated the advice, suggesting that Ellet ride over to where the black troops were posted and form them in line of battle on the south side of the field with their right resting on the Rodney road. Instead of sending one of his aides, the general nodded and galloped off to give the orders himself.

Currie moved his infantry toward the scene of the fighting and found the narrow road "filled with men and horses in an inextricable mass. . . . Riderless horses came snorting and plunging into camp with fierce eyes and distented [*sic*] nostrils." Horse marines appeared on foot, some fleeing while others stood their ground and fought. As Currie formed a line to check the enemy, he caught sight of Coleman's daughter in a second-story window of a nearby house directing the grayclads' movements by signaling them with her handkerchief. In a loud voice she could hear, he called upon two men to shoot her if she

9. Clarke, ed., *Warfare along the Mississippi*, 116–18.

appeared in the window again, and Coleman's daughter was seen no more.[10]

The enemy formed in line along the north end of a cornfield, half facing the African Americans and the other half facing Currie's infantry. The tall corn shielded the southerners' approach, but Currie sheltered his men behind rail fences and Coleman's outbuildings and waited. He ordered the men not to fire "until the rebels were so close" that each man could pick a target and hit it. Currie then went into the Coleman house, took position at a second-story window, and attempted to direct the fight from there. He could see grayclads converging on both sections of the field. The 52nd U.S. Colored Infantry fired first, and the fight in the open field on the left became desperate. Moments later, Currie's command opened at short range and collapsed the Confederate attack. He ordered the enemy charged with fixed bayonets and "whipped them in our front in less than five minutes."

The retreating Rebels merely jogged across from the cornfield and joined in the battle against the African Americans. The fighting on the left grew intense, but the black columns held their ground, repulsing one attack after another. Currie, watching from the window, reflected that the men in the 52nd Infantry regiment "had learned to endure under the lash, and they now displayed such desperate courage and determined endurance, that it amounted to heroism; and after each attack drove their former masters from the field until they withdrew from the contest, leaving their dead and wounded behind."[11]

The enemy fell back on the Rodney road, barring the Marine Brigade's route back to the boats and leaving Ellet with the impression that they intended to renew the fight. The general consulted with his officers and decided to return to the boats that night, even if they had to fight their way through a cordon of Confederates. James D. McClain, Currie's young orderly, stood nearby and distinctly heard the general say none too calmly, "Boys, we must get out of here before night—or we never will."

At sunset the jaded procession started down the road, the cavalry in the lead, followed by the mounted infantry, the train of empty army wagons, and the general, who brought up the rear with the howitzer and the African Americans. Ellet never explained the purpose for car-

10. *Ibid.*, 118–20; Crandall and Newell, *Ram Fleet*, 428.

11. Clarke, ed., *Warfare along the Mississippi*, 120–21; Bellows Diary, July 4, 1864, Crandall Collection, ISHL.

rying so many wagons, but they became useful in hauling back the dead and wounded.[12]

The road to Rodney lay through narrow cuts twenty feet deep—so ideal for ambush that Currie scattered troops a half mile in advance of the main column to act as scouts. The entire command expected to be attacked, as had happened four months earlier in the same place—and not knowing how, where, or when the attack would come kept them constantly on edge. Currie fully expected the grayclads to lie along the bank and pick off the brigade as it filed down the dark, constraining corridor. Just as the rear of the last of the African Americans entered the second cut, the enemy attacked with such sudden violence that those in front believed the entire regiment had been killed or captured, but the firing ended almost as abruptly as it began. Until the brigade reached Rodney, the Confederates nibbled away at the rear of the column, causing more confusion and fear than damage or injury to its members. Captain De Coster, who had been cut off with five of his men during the fight, recalled "getting the bullets not only of the rebels but from our own infantry. I had my horse shot from under me and the matter looked very uncertain for a while." Thirty-nine years later De Coster still recalled the pangs in his stomach from having nothing to eat "from four in the morning until ten o'clock at night."[13]

Neither Ellet nor Currie ever officially reported the fight, and no Confederate record exists to identify the officer or unit involved in the clash at Coleman's Cross Roads. Ellet referred to the enemy as guerrillas, but they were probably a detachment from Wirt Adams's brigade and most likely under the command of Captain Thomas R. Stockdale. Three skirmishes occurred during what Currie called the "Glorious Fourth," and though casualties are not known on either side, the 52nd U.S. Colored Infantry suffered most heavily, having lost thirty-two men in the morning fight and thirty-eight or more by the time the command reached Rodney. Captain Crandall counted noses on the morning of July 5 and believed that only one man had been killed and fifteen wounded or missing, but other accounts indicate that the bri-

12. *Ibid.*, 121; James D. McClain to Marine Brigade, August 19, 1889, McClain Papers, Civil War Collection, MHS. McClain was still a lad, an orphan perhaps twelve or thirteen, who joined Currie at Benton Barracks at St. Louis. He called the colonel "old cock-eye," as did others of the brigade, but never to his face.

13. Clarke, ed., *Warfare along the Mississippi,* 121–22; De Coster, untitled article, De Coster Letters, Crandall Collection, ISHL.

gade's losses were greater. Crandall also claimed that nine prisoners had been captured, but he never identified their unit. For four days the Marine Brigade loitered between Grand Gulf and Rodney, skirmishing with enemy scouts. Whatever Ellet intended to accomplish went unrecorded, and after a few days of unsuccessful scouting he took his boats and the empty wagons back to Vicksburg.[14]

While the Marine Brigade skirmished at Rodney, General Adams had been annoying Union forces operating on Big Black River, so on July 10 General Slocum ran out of patience and mounted a force to bring on a decisive engagement with the pestiferous cavalry commander. Slocum had just returned to Vicksburg from an expedition which had resulted in the brief occupation of Jackson, but the effort had done nothing to disrupt Adams's operations. Now, with A. J. Smith's blue-clads operating near Tupelo, Mississippi, Slocum had a new initiative—to keep Adams occupied between the Big Black and Pearl Rivers to prevent him from rushing troops to reinforce Major Generals Stephen D. Lee and Nathan Bedford Forrest as they contended with Smith. To occupy Adams's attention, Slocum called upon the Marine Brigade and placed 2,000 cavalry and mounted infantry under Ellet's command. He added 4,000 infantry from Brigadier General John P. Hawkins's division and prepared to lead the expedition himself.[15]

Slocum took his force across a pontoon bridge spanning Big Black and led them down the road to Port Gibson. On July 12, when scouts reported the enemy at Utica, Slocum switched directions and turned east. Sporadic firing along the line of march kept Ellet's cavalry busy, but Adams's main force remained well concealed. Finding everything quiet at Utica on the 13th, Slocum countermarched, reached Port Gibson the following day, and for most of the afternoon skirmished with the enemy, but he could not draw them out.

On the morning of July 15 he decided that he no longer needed the infantry brigades of Hawkins and Colonel Frederick A. Starring, so he marched them to Grand Gulf and put them on boats to Vicksburg. Adams watched the departure of the troops, redeployed his cavalry, and attacked Ellet's outposts. The marines had just been relieved by a squad from Colonel Joseph Kargé's 2nd New Jersey Cavalry, armed

14. Clarke, ed., *Warfare along the Mississippi*, 122; Crandall's Logbook, July 5, 1864, Crandall Collection, ISHL; Crandall and Newell, *Ram Fleet*, 427–28.

15. Ferguson to Shepard, July 9, Lee to Bragg, July 7, 1864, *ORA,* XXXIX, Pt. 2, pp. 170, 690; Crandall's Logbook, July 5–10, 1864, Crandall Collection, ISHL.

with seven-shot Spencer repeating carbines, and as soon as the enemy charged, they stumbled into a hail of fire. The fight then became general, and Ellet moved the horse marines into line. Adams attacked with a fury, driving Ellet back, and the pursuit continued for several miles. As Ellet retreated, he established points of ambush, and Adams soon tired of the chase and recalled his men. Once again, Ellet failed to tally his losses. Crandall estimated them at "about seventy-five," but the 2nd New Jersey alone accounted for four killed, four wounded, and twenty-seven missing.[16]

On July 16 General Slocum decided to take the brigade's boats for another foray, leaving Ellet and his command at Grand Gulf. Adams, seeing another opportunity to dispose of the Marine Brigade, attacked in force. Ellet, having been left with two black infantry regiments, quickly posted them in Grand Gulf's old rifle pits, dug by the Confederates in 1863. Adams's force ran into unexpectedly stiff resistance, and some of his men attacked with such determination that they fell into the pits dead. Adams finally withdrew after finding Ellet's force too strong, and losing twenty-six dead, six wounded, and fifteen taken as prisoners.[17]

Currie had been ill at Vicksburg during Slocum's encounter with Adams's cavalry, and for the first time in several months General Ellet had led his force without the help of his reliable colonel. With the exception of the skirmish at Grand Gulf, where Ellet had his back to the river and no boats to support him, he had always been able to cut and run. The two African-American regiments fighting from the rifle pits saved the day, but for some reason Ellet no longer felt inclined to write battle reports.

On July 19 Ellet received orders to redeploy the brigade at Milliken's Bend, provide the men with ten days' rations, and send the boats down to Vicksburg for temporary use as transports. The marines found a pleasant wooded area to pitch their camp and looked forward to a few days of uninterrupted rest. Having appointed their campsite with many personal

16. Crandall's Logbook, July 11–15, and Bellows Diary, July 15, 1864, Crandall Collection, ISHL; Kargé to Morgan, July 24, Starring's Itinerary, n.d., 1864, *ORA*, XXXIX, Pt. 1, pp. 247, 355–56.

17. Bellows Diary, July 16, 17, and Crandall's Logbook, July 16, 17, 1864, Crandall Collection, ISHL; Kargé to Morgan, July 24, Starring's Itinerary, n.d., 1864, *ORA*, XXXIX, Pt. 1, pp. 247, 356.

comforts, they prepared to relax, but on the morning of the 21st Ellet received orders to move the brigade to Omega Landing, six miles upriver. Guerrillas had been reported operating beyond Bayou Mason, which meant scouting in some of the hottest weather the horse marines had yet experienced.

Monarch and *Switzerland* moved the command to their new campground—a spit of land between the levee and the river having no shade during the day and swarming with mosquitoes at night. To cover themselves from the blistering sun, the marines constructed she-bangs by spreading their blankets over poles. They had just settled in moderate comfort when rumors of Confederate activity put the brigade on alert.

On July 23 Captain Newell took the majority of the marines up to Goodrich's Landing on a reconnaissance. When he reached there, the guerrillas were reported operating near Lake Providence. Newell trotted over to Lake Providence, only to learn from other informants that the grayclads had gone back to Goodrich's Landing. Disgusted, he returned to camp. Rumors continued, but Newell ignored them. It was just too hot to go chasing after guerrillas. Besides, the boats would be back in a few days to take the brigade away from their torrid and unhealthy encampment at the landing.[18]

Two of the boats, however, experienced more difficulties than the sweltering horse marines. After landing troops at Memphis, *Adams* and *Fairchild* started back downriver. On July 27, as they approached Sunnyside Landing, Greene's artillery opened with eight guns. Twenty-seven shots ripped through *Fairchild,* cut the steam escape pipe, shot away part of the steering apparatus, and forced the captain to shut down the engine. A shell exploded in the deckhands' quarters and set the bedding ablaze. *Adams* turned back, and *Fairchild* drifted downriver until met by a gunboat and towed to safety. The gunboat returned to Sunnyside Landing and chased off the grayclads, enabling *Adams* to continue on to Omega Landing. The sun set as the encampment came in sight, and through an incident of exceptionally bad navigation, *Adams* crashed into *Fairchild,* damaging both vessels. On the 28th the two boats limped into Vicksburg, only to learn they had but

18. Crandall's Logbook, July 19, 21, 22, and Bellows Diary, July 19, 20, 21, 1864, Crandall Collection, ISHL; Crandall and Newell, *Ram Fleet,* 433–35.

one day to make repairs because General Canby wanted troops delivered to Morganza, Louisiana, by the 30th.[19]

Through the last days of July and the first days of August the Marine Brigade remained inactive at bug-infested Omega Landing while General Ellet and his staff enjoyed the comforts of Vicksburg. Captain Newell continued his policy of ignoring rumors and refused to do anything more than post pickets and perform a small amount of scouting. On August 4 most of the boats returned to the landing, and Newell anxiously awaited new orders. Ellet's instructions arrived the following day. He gave the brigade two days to prepare for military inspection. The camp must be put in perfect order, guns and accouterments overhauled until they sparkled, horses sleeked until they shined, and the boats thoroughly cleaned.[20]

Groans pervaded the encampment, and for two days the brigade speculated on the reason for the inspection. Answers to their questions were already in the works, but not even Ellet knew the cause.[21]

19. J. H. Stevens, "An Exciting Time at Sunnyside," in Crandall and Newell, *Ram Fleet,* 436; Crandall's Logbook, July 28, 29, 1864, Crandall Collection, ISHL; Log of *Diana,* July 30, 1864, CMU.

20. Special Orders No. 84, August 1, 1864, *ORA,* XLI, Pt. 2, p. 497; Crandall's Copybook, August 5, Crandall's Logbook, August 5, 1864, Crandall Collection, ISHL.

21. Special Orders No. 86, August 3, 1864, *ORA,* XLI, Pt. 2, pp. 535–36.

CHAPTER 18

DISSOLUTION

On August 7, Major General Napoleon J. T. Dana, the new commander for the District of Vicksburg, dropped down to Omega Landing to inspect the Mississippi Marine Brigade. The forty-two-year-old general had been wounded during the Battle of Antietam, and since returning from sick leave in July 1863 he had seen little fighting and served in areas requiring mostly administrative work. He came with Ellet on *Autocrat* and departed for Helena after a two-hour inspection. Upon leaving, he instructed Ellet to have his company commanders prepare "descriptive rolls" for all their men.[1]

In a report to General Canby, written eight days later, Dana made no recommendations for changes in the brigade but said, "It is now far below its original number, and its means of transportation are proportionately too great. . . . Indeed, the Marine Brigade is now so insufficient in number when all together that it is not sufficient of itself to compose any important expedition." Dana found it particularly curious

1. Boatner, *Civil War Dictionary,* 221; Crandall's Letter Book, August 7, Bellows Diary, August 7, 8, 1864, Crandall Collection, ISHL; Clarke, ed., *Warfare along the Mississippi,* 126.

that the artillery company no longer had cannon, arms, or horses, items which General McPherson had borrowed for an expedition and never returned. He noted that Ellet required a staff of eleven officers, and considered them entirely too many for an aggregate force of only 613 effectives. He seemed equally baffled as to why Ellet needed six large transports, three towboats, three tugs, two rams, and six barges for cavalry horses when his entire brigade could be accommodated by less than half that number. Charles A. Dana, one of Stanton's assistant secretaries, had never been an advocate of the brigade, having fourteen months earlier informed the secretary that "the Mississippi Marine Brigade, with its seven large steamers, and its varied apparatus of artillery, infantry and cavalry, is a very useless as well as costly institution."[2]

General Dana also mentioned an unresolved matter regarding the disposition of cotton transported by the Marine Brigade. Ellet had ordered *Fairchild* to carry 129 bales of cotton to New Orleans, for which the buyer paid Captain John R. Crandall a freight cost of $25 a bale. Crandall delivered the cotton but turned over only $5 a bale to the quartermaster. Dana sought an explanation but found Crandall conveniently absent from the inspection.[3]

The efficiency of the Marine Brigade sustained another blow on August 9 when Colonel Currie resigned. Ellet had pocketed Currie's discharge papers until after the inspection and then held them another two days while he went upriver with General Dana. The relations between Ellet and Currie had never been agreeable, mostly because the colonel considered the general an inept tactician. When word filtered through camp that Currie had resigned and planned to embark on the first transport to St. Louis, the news created a dispiriting influence within the command. Many came to express their regrets, intimating that perhaps the time had come for them to go home, also. During a banquet in Currie's honor on board *Diana,* the transport *Empress* hove into view and the colonel hailed it to come alongside. Without waiting for the ceremony to conclude, Currie picked up his bags, said his good-byes, and with the cheers and the shouts of his old command ringing in his ears, took the first step in resuming his life as a civilian.[4]

2. Napoleon Dana to Christenson, August 15, 1864, *ORA,* XLI, Pt. 2, p. 712; Charles Dana to Stanton, June 11, 1863, *ibid.,* XXIV, Pt. 1, p. 96.

3. Napoleon Dana to Christenson, August 15, 1864, *ibid.,* XLI, Pt. 2, p. 713.

4. Ellet to Currie, August 7, 1864, Crandall's Letter Book, Crandall Collection, ISHL; Clarke, ed., *Warfare along the Mississippi,* 126–30.

But not quite.

Crowded from stem to stern with four hundred passengers and freight, *Empress* paddled slowly toward St. Louis. One of the pilots came to Currie and said that two ladies wished to see him. Much to his surprise, the women lived back of Goodrich's Landing and had often seen him pass on scouting missions. One had once given him a glass of milk and thought his good conduct "entitled them to claim an acquaintance." Currie found his new lady friends delightful companions. Wherever he went, they followed, and all three enjoyed the cooler air of the ship's pilothouse, where only special passengers were permitted.

At Cypress Bend the captain conferred with Currie on the prospect of passing Columbia without encountering Greene's artillery. While discussing the subject, the pilot reported smoke rising above the levee at Columbia. Currie took one look and declared it a Rebel camp. Burning green cottonwood and heavily laden, *Empress* lumbered slowly upriver at four miles an hour. When they came opposite the landing, a masked battery of six guns uncovered near the water's edge and opened fire, perforating the boat's cabin and sweeping the decks. Down the levee tumbled a swarm of grayclads who stood alongshore and pelted the steamer with musket fire. "It was the most terrible and trying time in all my army experience," Currie recalled, because he found himself "pent up in the pilot house, a room not more than fifteen feet square," with fifteen people, half of whom were women.

Pandemonium erupted on the decks below. Women screamed, children wailed, and broken glass flew in every direction as shells ripped through the frail cabins. Currie attempted to shield a woman and her child by pulling them to the floor of the pilothouse and covering them with his body. Being but three hundred yards offshore, *Empress* absorbed about twenty-four shots a minute, and one finally sheared the steering cable to one of the side wheels. With one wheel out of commission, the vessel could barely stem the current, and the first mate, who was among those in the pilothouse, directed the pilot to blow the steam whistle as a gesture of surrender. The enemy paid no attention to the signal and continued firing.

Though officially a civilian, Currie still wore his uniform, and he resolved not to spend the balance of the war in some Confederate prison camp. Ignoring the protests of the mate—the captain had been decapitated by a projectile—Currie assumed command of the boat and ordered the pilot to stand toward the opposite shore and back downstream. About two miles above the upper bend, he observed a pillar of smoke coming from a steamer and told the pilot to blow the whistle of distress. A few minutes later the tinclad *Romeo* came around the bend, and Acting Master Thomas Baldwin opened with his two bow guns on the shore batteries. While *Romeo*'s guns occupied the attention on the enemy, Baldwin hawsered onto *Empress* and towed her upriver and out of range. With many passengers dead or wounded, Currie took over the burial detail while women cared for the wounded. Three days later the vessel reached Memphis and removed the wounded. At Cairo a large crowd rushed on board curious to witness the wreckage of the famous riverboat. Later, at St. Louis, hundreds of people jammed the landing, piling onto the decks before the vessel tied to the wharf. Currie picked up his bags and quietly departed. He had served his country faithfully, and the time had come to leave the last months of the war to his comrades.[5]

At Vicksburg, how much more of the war Currie's comrades were willing to fight became a contentious issue. On August 10 the marines returned to the city to learn that General Canby had dissolved the brigade. Enlisted men with unexpired terms of service would be sent back to their original regiments or be assigned to the Vicksburg garrison. Officers of the brigade would be mustered out of the service—the exception being General Ellet, who had orders to "report in person to the Secretary of War." The vessels would be turned over to the quartermaster for use as reserve transportation. And it now became clear to the marines why General Dana, during his inspection, had asked for "descriptive rolls" of all the enlisted men: it gave the general's staff insight as to where to reassign them.[6]

Ellet protested the order, reminding the general of the original conditions under which the brigade had been formed. The marines, he argued, could not be sent back to regiments from which they had been taken, since all the men had been mustered out before enlisting with the brigade. Canby then modified his order and directed that the brigade be consolidated into a single infantry regiment to serve on land. Ellet again protested, informing the general that most of the men had been convalescents who had joined the horse marines to ride and

5. Clarke, ed., *Warfare along the Mississippi*, 130–41; Owen to Pennock, August 14, Log of *Romeo*, August 10, 1864, *ORN*, XXVI, 503–4.

6. Special Orders No. 86, August 3, 1864, *ORA*, XLI, Pt. 2, pp. 535–36; Bellows Diary, August 10, 11, 1864, Crandall Collection, ISHL.

not to march. Ellet explained the promises made to induce the men to enlist, emphasizing that to force them to serve out unexpired terms as infantry would violate that agreement. Canby needed men, and Ellet lost the argument. On August 26 Canby issued orders placing the command temporarily under Lieutenant Colonel John A. Ellet and assigned it to General Dana.[7]

Dana renamed the unit the Marine Regiment and placed it under Colonel Frederick A. Starring, commander of the 1st Brigade, 1st Division, XVII Army Corps. By then the men had turned over all their arms, equipment, horses, and government property to the quartermaster's department, but they remained on the boats and waited for their discharges. When they learned that their brigade had been reduced to an infantry regiment, they became suspicious of their own officers, accusing the Ellets of attempting to retain their commissions at the expense of the enlisted men. One brigade diarist wrote, "There is a good deal of cursing and swearing, and some threats made among the boys." When Dana learned of unrest in the regiment, he believed that the Ellets had fomented insubordination among the men in order to secure discharges for the entire command. The marines demanded positive assurance from the Ellets that their discharges would be obtained, and Dana demanded "unqualified submission to his orders" before he would consider any claims of the men. He threatened to clap in irons "any officer making any concessions . . . or promises [to the marines], or who should even offer his resignation, or file any written protest or petition against the proposed change." In the meantime, Colonel Charles W. Sawtelle, Canby's quartermaster, waited at Natchez to receive the Marine Brigade's boats, but none came.[8]

General Ellet ignored Canby's orders to go to Washington, and his prolonged presence made him appear responsible for provoking the disturbances. The trouble started on his flagship, *Autocrat,* after the horse marines received orders to go ashore. John Ellet could not control his new command and asked for help, advising Colonel Starring that while some of the marines refused to obey his orders, he feared that the rest had become "equally mutinous." Starring, flanked by the

7. Special Orders No. 60, August 26, 1864, Crandall's Copybook, Crandall Collection, ISHL.

8. Starring to Rodgers, August 29, 1864, *ORA,* XXXIX, Pt. 2, pp. 318–19; Mason Diary, August 26, 1864, Crandall Collection, ISHL; Sawtelle to Christenson, [August 17, 1864], *ORA,* XLI, Pt. 2, pp. 742–43.

72nd Illinois Infantry and the 5th Illinois Cavalry, went to *Autocrat* and found the Ellets "very much excited" by the situation. General Ellet asked if Starring would fire upon the marines if they refused to go ashore. The colonel replied that he would, if necessary, but he would prefer to arrest the ringleaders. The marines blamed John Ellet for "selling them out" in exchange for command of the new regiment, thereby inducing him to step aside. Major Tallerday, being less objectionable to the men, told Starring that he could take the men ashore and promised no trouble. After Starring placed the regiment under the command of the major and withdrew his armed guard, Tallerday marched the marines to their new campsite. The guard then rounded up forty-eight mutineers and shuffled them off to prison, but on their promise of good behavior he sent them back to the regiment.[9]

Having surrendered all their equipment to the quartermaster, the men pitched pup tents near the river and continued to castigate the Ellets for deceiving them. Some marines became so hostile toward Alfred and John Ellet that Starring posted a protective guard on *Autocrat*. The men interpreted the precaution as an act of cowardice on the part of the Ellets, thereby forcing Starring to extend the guard to all the boats and eventually around the campsite as well. After observing the regiment for a number of days, Starring reported the marines "demoralized, insubordinate, undisciplined, and grossly ignorant." He also noticed that although the junior officers attempted to maintain order and obey orders, "they are dissatisfied [and] think themselves aggrieved and wronged." Looking into the antecedents of the Marine Brigade, Starring concluded that the present trouble originated from the men's being enlisted for "a particular branch of the service," and that, having come from "every State of the Union," they lacked the cohesiveness that binds the loyalty of volunteer soldiers to their home regiment. The colonel learned that the marines had been promised prize money but had not received any, and after further research, decided that "as a regiment, they will never be of any service or benefit whatever." He suggested mustering them out, allowing those who wished to reenlist.[10]

Starring failed in his efforts to dispose of the regiment. Left with the task of reorganizing the marines as a unit having neither mounts

9. John Ellet to Carter, August 27, Starring to Rodgers, August 29, 1864, *ORA,* XXXIX, Pt. 2, pp. 319–20.

10. Starring to Rodgers, August 29, 1864, *ibid.,* 320.

nor boats, he quickly dispelled all hopes of the men of returning to their comfortable quarters on the boats. He turned the vessels over to the quartermaster with instructions that they be dispersed. By mid-November, four old rams—*Monarch, Switzerland, Lioness,* and *Horner*—still operated out of Vicksburg, but the vessels of the Marine Brigade received assignments elsewhere. The boats came and went, but most of them were sent to repair yards and some of them stayed there.[11]

General Ellet prepared to go to Philadelphia to await orders, and Captain Warren D. Crandall closed his office as assistant adjutant general and turned over his records, books, and papers to the adjutant general of the District of Vicksburg for transmission to Washington. The last individual to see the documents considered them of so little importance that he lost or destroyed them. The only members of the Marine Brigade bidding Ellet farewell were the officers and men of *Monarch.* They had served under the general during the Memphis fight and during the months when *Monarch* performed duty as the Ram Fleet's flagship. Ellet praised the handful of men for their loyalty, service, and support. He promised to "gather them up again as his official family," but the separation would become final.[12]

On August 30 Colonel Starring began consolidating the old Marine Brigade into one regiment, using as the unit's foundation its own infantry regiment. By transferring officers and men from the Ram Fleet, Starring eventually brought the strength of the regiment to a thousand men. Finding a surplus of captains and noncommissioned officers, he reduced in grade a large number of men—an act that fostered more grievances. Starring spent considerable time in his newly acquired regiment's camp personally attending to the complaints of the men. "The Marines could not have fallen into better hands," Captain Crandall observed, but the enlisted men had already hired lawyers to litigate their complaints. When Starring issued the regiment a fresh supply of arms and camp equipment, the men adhered to the advice of their attorneys and accepted them "under protest." Starring ignored the complaints until one of Major Tallerday's morning reports, signed by the company commander's orderly, included below the signature the word "protest."

11. Sawtelle to Stanton, November 19, 1864, Miscellaneous Papers, Crandall Collection, ISHL; Meigs to Stanton, November 3, 1864, *ORA,* Ser. 3, IV, 891. See also Sawtelle to Stanton, November 19, 1864, *ibid.,* Ser. 1, XLI, Pt. 4, p. 609.

12. Crandall and Newell, *Ram Fleet,* 444–45.

Starring's face reddened. "Captain, what does this mean?" he growled. Because officers had taken no part in the legal action, the captain stormed back to his orderly sergeant and then learned that the men had been advised by their attorneys to protest everything.[13]

James H. Purdy, formerly a major in the 59th New York Infantry, and Clark Wright, formerly colonel of the 6th Missouri Cavalry, had established law offices in Vicksburg and took an interest in the marines' complaints. Intending to leave for Washington on other business, Purdy advised his clients that while he could not force General Canby to discharge members of the former brigade, he might be able to petition their case before President Lincoln. He asked for a $500 retainer, traveling expenses, and $15 in cash from each member if he secured their discharges. The marines agreed to the terms, paid Purdy his front money, and bid him good-bye. Disembarking at St. Louis, Purdy prepared a circular letter and sent it to the governors of the sixteen states represented by his clients. In it he explained the injustice conferred upon the members of the brigade and the irregular conditions under which the unit had been formed. He ended the letter by invoking the governors' cooperation in making a unified appeal to the president.

Being ignorant of the action of the enlisted men, the officers of the former brigade also composed a statement of the injustices done themselves. Starring endorsed it, as did General Dana, and it, too, eventually landed on Secretary Stanton's desk.[14]

Meanwhile, time passed and no word came from Washington. With colder weather approaching, the men dug caves in the hillside and fitted them with small fireplaces. When one dugout collapsed and killed a man, Starring issued orders for the men to obtain wood and build a winter barracks for each company. Since going into camp the regiment had been confined to garrison duty at Vicksburg, and they appreciated the opportunity of going once again up the Yazoo, this time to cut cypress for their buildings.

Major Purdy did not keep his clients very well informed, but he assiduously looked after their interests. Armed with favorable replies from the governors and a strong plea from General Ellet, who remained

13. *Ibid.*, 446–47; Crandall's Logbook, August 30, 1864, Crandall Collection, ISHL.

14. Purdy to Crandall, August 20, 1889, Purdy Letters, Civil War Collection, MHS; Crandall and Newell, *Ram Fleet*, 447–48.

unassigned at Philadelphia, Purdy traveled to Washington and presented himself at the White House. John Hay, one of Lincoln's secretaries, told Purdy he must be patient because the president had little time for visitors. The lawyer called each morning for three weeks before obtaining an audience. Depressed by General Grant's lack of progress in the Petersburg trenches, Lincoln hesitated to discharge a thousand soldiers and turned the problem over to Assistant Secretary of War Charles A. Dana, who had been acting as secretary during Stanton's illness. Purdy then spent another three weeks pestering Dana for a decision. On December 5 the assistant secretary greeted Purdy with an official letter ordering the discharge of the Marine Brigade. "Supremely happy," Purdy recalled, "I took the train that night for Cairo." A few days later Canby issued orders to discharge the marines. "The boys immediately boarded a steamer in waiting and were taken to Cairo," Purdy learned later, "from whence they scattered throughout the States, [and went] to their homes and families and sweethearts."[15]

Not all members of the brigade went home. Some lingered in the vicinity of Vicksburg, waiting as long as three weeks to be mustered out. Others, after finding garrison duty at Vicksburg unobjectionable, reenlisted. On January 21 Colonel Starring finally released the men from the last three companies—F, H, and I Infantry. Three officers and eighty-nine enlisted men drew one day's rations and said good-bye to the war. On January 22, 1865, the last vestiges of what was once the Mississippi Marine Brigade—ninety-two men—collected their pay, gave three cheers, and went home.[16]

The dissolution of the Mississippi Marine Brigade brought words of praise from the editor of the *New Albany Ledger:*

> Gen. Canby has done a good thing in mustering out of service the "Marine Brigade." . . . It has cost the Government immense sums, and so far as practical good is concerned, is not worth one cent. These *arks* made very comfortable summer resorts, and as such were largely in demand. They were generally where they were not wanted and seldom at hand when needed. Their removal will prove a great

---

15. Purdy to Crandall, August 26, 1889, Purdy Letters, Civil War Collection, MHS; James H. Purdy, "Major Purdy's Own Story of Securing Lincoln's Order," in Crandall and Newell, *Ram Fleet,* 452–54. See also Special Order No. 431, December 5, 1864, Ellet Papers, NA, and Special Order No. 2, January 2, 1865, *ORA,* Ser. 3, IV, 891.

16. Bellows Diary, January 21, 22, 1865, Crandall Collection, ISHL.

relief to the regular river boats. There is this about our regular army officer[s], they rarely tolerate anything useless, and a very great portion of the extravagant outlay of this war is attributable to the penchant of volunteer officers to introduce all sorts of experimental improvement . . . to help [that] officer lighten the Treasury.[17]

After reading the editorial, A. J. Pierce of Company I Infantry, Mississippi Marine Brigade, bubbled over with rage. Unable to constrain himself, he fanned the flames of controversy by composing a defensive diatribe accusing the editor of being "embittered by envy and jealousy." Pierce had been with the brigade since its formation, and he vociferously charged the paper with publishing scurrilous opinions in its "unprincipled, nondescript, Copperhead Journal." Pierce then undertook the "delicate task of exhonorating [*sic*] our character" by informing the "mendacious Editor and all others" of the many accomplishments of the brigade during the war. In his lengthy rebuttal Pierce failed to give any details of the brigade's campaigns and exhausted himself castigating the editor. Anybody reading the two articles side by side would conclude that the "mendacious Editor" had probably assessed the issue accurately.[18]

After the war, other observers from both sides offered their opinions. William F. Scott, who on several occasions campaigned with Ellet, referred to the horse marines as the most pampered unit in the service and one that "permitted their enemies to live in peace and die from natural causes. The soldiers ridiculed them on land and the sailors spoke of them disrespectfully on the water."[19] John N. Edwards, writing from the Confederate side, added that the tactics of the horse marines consisted of "making their appearance at unexpected points, capturing noncombatants, frightening women and children, [and] stealing cotton." With "an unlimited use of bravado, [they] had managed to impress the country people with an exaggerated idea of their prowess."[20]

Statements like this, coming from both sides, naturally irritated all members of the Ram Fleet and the Mississippi Marine Brigade. The men felt justified in their form of warfare, and like most good soldiers,

17. "Ellet's Marine Brigade," newsclips, *ibid*.

18. *Ibid*.

19. William Forse Scott, *The Story of a Cavalry Regiment: The Career of the Fourth Iowa Veteran Volunteers from Kansas to Georgia, 1861–1865* (New York, 1893), 175.

20. John N. Edwards, *Shelby and His Men* (Kansas City, 1897), 370.

they followed the orders of their general, and more often, their colonel.

Alfred Ellet eventually returned to his farm at Bunker Hill, Illinois, and spent more than a year pursuing the prize claims of the Ram Fleet and the Mississippi Marine Brigade. Because Charles Ellet, Jr., never lived to file the Ram Fleet's claims, and because Alfred never kept very good records, the claims for the prizes captured or destroyed at Memphis required the consent of Charles Davis, who was now a rear admiral and also attempting to collect prize money.[21]

Alfred Ellet eventually raised money and organized the Gregg Ornamental Brick Company in Eldorado, Kansas, where he became its president. The business never reached the retired general's expectations, and when he died there on January 9, 1895, he left a very small estate for his wife. Edward, his son and a member of his wartime staff, had to rewrite the Battle of Memphis and the operations of the Marine Brigade in order to convince the government that his mother was entitled to the general's pension.[22]

Pensions had become a problem for most members of the Mississippi Marine Brigade because the assistant adjutant general at Vicksburg—or someone who worked for him—discarded all the brigade's papers, deeming them worthless. As late as April 10, 1895, old soldiers like David S. Taylor were writing Warren Crandall for assistance in obtaining their pensions. F. M. Haughey had served on the hospital boat *Woodford* when it wrecked on the falls at Alexandria, Louisiana, and as late as June 17, 1903, no one had found his records. He had not collected one penny of pension money.[23]

Alfred Ellet's records—if he ever kept them—also disappeared for claims on prizes captured after the Battle of Memphis, which included several steamers and more than 3,000 bales of cotton. Whatever prize money was distributed never reached the hands of all the men. William F. Warren, who had been with the Ellets since the formation of the Ram Fleet, complained on January 25, 1898, that he had fallen upon

21. Tabor to Ellet, May 18, Davis to Ellet, May 22, Ellet to Davis, August 18, 1866, Ellet Papers, DUL.

22. Edward Ellet's Memorial, n.d., Ellet Papers, DUL; Alfred Ellet, "Charles Ellet, Jr., and His Steam Rams," Ellet Papers, DUL.

23. Taylor to Crandall, April 10, 1895, Taylor Letters, Haughey to Crandall, June 17, 1903, Haughey Letters, Civil War Collection, MHS.

hard times and asked Warren Crandall, who had become the brigade's historian, why it was taking so long to distribute prize money. Crandall was the logical person to ask, because as assistant adjutant general, he had kept the records.[24]

Eventually, the crews of *Queen of the West* and *Monarch* received prize money for the vessels destroyed at Memphis and elsewhere. All the rams at Memphis shared in the capture of *General Bragg* and *Sumter.* *Lioness, Sampson,* and *Switzerland* received prize money for the capture of *Fairplay.* Other enemy vessels had been destroyed by the Ram Fleet, but Ellet never claimed them. They included a ferryboat near Helena on June 21, 1862, and five days later the ram *General Van Dorn* and the transports *Polk* and *Livingston.* Before losing *Queen of the West,* Charles Rivers Ellet captured and destroyed the supply steamers *A. W. Baker, Moro, Berwick Bay,* and the steamer *Era No. 5,* which he brought to Biggs's landing. At the time, Porter admitted in a letter to Welles that *Queen* had destroyed more than $188,000 in Confederate property. *Queen* was also directly involved in disabling the ironclad ram *Arkansas* and the supply steamer *City of Vicksburg,* but at the time the circumstances of the destruction of those two vessels remained clouded.[25]

The Mississippi Marine Brigade also did its share of damage, destroying the *Thirty-Fifth Parallel* on March 10, 1863, and the steamer *H. D. Mears* on June 10, 1864. Between those dates, the brigade captured and burned at least fifteen flatboats and six trading vessels, but neither Ellet nor his adjutant bothered to report them.

Because of the loss of the Marine Brigade's records, none of the military officers or soldiers—with the above exceptions—ever received any reward or recognition for their service. Ellet had an opportunity to supply a prize list when reminded by the navy on May 20, 1864, but the circumstances under which the brigade acquired some of the cotton may have caused him to hesitate until after the war ended. By then, he had no records.

No one ever tabulated the cotton captured by the brigade, but by tracking through Crandall and Newell's *History of the Ram Fleet and the Mississippi Marine Brigade* and the thousands of documents produced by its members, a fair estimate would be a minimum of 3,000

24. Warren to Crandall, January 25, 1898, William F. Warren Letters, Crandall Collection, ISHL.

25. Ellet to Stanton, June 28, 1863, *ORA,* XV, 515; Porter to Welles, February 23, 1863, *ORN,* XXIV, 383.

bales. By then, there could be no claims for prize money because any proof had been destroyed along with the brigade's rosters, and Alfred Ellet failed to report many of the brigade's activities. One of Charles Ellet, Jr.'s, motivations in mobilizing the Ram Fleet had been to collect prize money. He died before officially presenting his claims, but in the end his records sufficed to support those claims. As far as Alfred Ellet's official records went, the Mississippi Marine Brigade became a military obscurity, and the men who served the general exited the war with one day's rations, muster-out pay, and nothing else.[26]

Were it not for the survivors and the pride of service they carried throughout their lives, the record of "the strangest outfit of all" could not have been written.

26. Crandall and Newell, *Ram Fleet,* 242, 444; Phelps to Welles, May 20, Porter to Welles, June 6, 1864, *ORN,* XXVI, 318–19, 363.

BIBLIOGRAPHY

PRIMARY SOURCES

Manuscripts and Documents

Central Michigan University, Mount Pleasant
  Clarke Historical Collection. Consisting of:
    Currie, George E. Letters.
    Log of the USS *Diana*.

Duke University Special Collections Library, Durham, N.C.
  Ellet, Alfred Washington. Papers.

Henry E. Huntington Library and Art Gallery, San Mateo, Calif.
  Farragut, David Glasgow. Papers.
  Fox, Gustavus Vasa. Papers.
  Porter, David Dixon. Papers in the Eldridge Collection.
  Welles, Gideon. Papers.

Illinois State Historical Library, Springfield
  Crandall, Warren Daniel. Collection. Consisting of:
    Bellows, Amos W. Diary.
    Bellows, Austin W. Letters.
    Brooks, James C. Papers.
    Byerly, A. C. Letters.
    Crandall, James R. Letters.
    Crandall, Warren D. Copybook, Papers, Logbook, and Newsclips.
    Currie, George E. Letters, including "The Marines in the Smith Expedition Against Marmaduke."
    Decker, Adam. Letters.
    De Coster, F. V. Letters.
    Ellet, Alfred W. Letters.
    Ellet, Charles. Letters.
    Ellet, John A. Letters.
    Falconer, Charles D. Letters.
    Fisher, C. G. Letters.
    Fulkerson, J. M. Letters.
    Gordon, Jesse B. Letters.
    Hooper, David E. Letters, Papers, and Diary.
    Lister, John W. Papers.

Mason, Dwight B. Letters and Diary.
McClain, James D. Papers.
Miscellaneous Papers.
Moon, Edwin. Letters.
Moriarty, J. D. Papers.
Morrin, T. D. Diary.
Murphy, Robert S. Letters.
Newell, Isaac D. Letters.
Periman, James K. Papers.
Pierce, Almon J. Letters and Diary.
Prouty, J. N. Letters.
Ralston, Augustus. Letters.
Reunion Record of Ram Fleet Survivors.
Root, Mark. Letters.
Sickal, James. Letters.
Sickal, Peter A. Letters.
Spilman, John J. Diary.
Stevens, J. H. Letters.
Taylor, David S. Letters.
Van Effs, George. Letters.
Warren, William F. Letters.
Wiseman, Levi. Letters and Memoir.

Library of Congress, Washington, D.C.
Porter, David Dixon. Collection, "Letter Book U.S.N.A."
Porter, David Dixon. Papers, 1842–1864. Includes his two-volume "Private Journal of Occurrences" and a volume labeled "Memorials of Rear Admiral David D. Porter, U.S.N."
Sherman, William T. Papers.
Stanton, Edwin M. Papers.
Welles, Gideon. Papers.

Missouri Historical Society, St. Louis
Civil War Collection—Ram Fleet and Mississippi Marine Brigade.
Anonymous, "A Michigan Comrade's Account of the 'Gun Planting' and Surrender of Vicksburg."
Biographical Data of Ram Fleet Members.
Couden, Henry N. Letters.
Crandall, James R. Manuscripts, "An Ambuscade" and "Capture of Capt. Lewis and His Company of Rebel Scouts."
Crandall, Warren D. "The Battle Before Memphis: The True Story of the Surrender and the Hoisting of the Flag."
Currie, George E. "Battle of Memphis."

De Coster, Francisco V. Letters, including "The Battle of Coldwater River, Austin, Mississippi," and "Capture of Capt. Lewis and His Company of Rebel Scouts" manuscripts.

Doss, Sylvester. Letters.

Haughey, F. M. Letters.

McClain, James D. Papers.

Moriarty, J. D. "No Time to Hold On" newsclip.

Purdy, James H. Letters.

Sanford, L. B. "Recollections of the Ram Fleet."

Sickal, Peter A. Letters.

Taylor, David S. Letters.

Warren, W. F. Letter and article, "The Ellet Ram Fleet."

Wyble, William F. Letters.

Phelps, S. Ledyard. Papers.

National Archives, Washington, D.C.—Record Group 45

Ellet Papers. Includes:

Bingham, J. B. Report.

Ellet, John A. Journal.

Farragut, David Glasgow. Papers.

Loose Papers, Mississippi River.

Mississippi Ram Fleet and Marine Brigade. Papers.

Mississippi Squadron Letters.

Navy Register.

Porter, David Dixon. Papers.

Stanton, Edwin M. Papers in Record Group 107.

Walke, Henry. Papers.

Welles, Gideon. Papers.

United States Naval Academy Museum, Annapolis, Md.

Farragut, David Glasgow. Papers.

Porter, David Dixon. Letter Books, Nos. 1 and 2.

University of Illinois Library, Urbana

Ellet, Charles, Jr. Papers (microfilm).

University of Michigan, Special Collections Library, Ann Arbor

Ellet, Charles, Jr. Papers.

University of Virginia, Alderman Library, Charlottesville, Special Collections Department

Cabell-Ellet Papers.

Official Records

Journal of the Congress of the Confederate States, 1861–1865. Reprinted in

Washington, D.C., in 1904 as *Senate Document No. 234, 58th Cong., 2nd Sess.*

Official Records of the Union and Confederate Navies in the War of the Rebellion. 30 vols. Washington, D.C., 1894–1922.

Official Report Relative to the Conduct of Federal Troops in Western Louisiana, during the Invasion of 1863 and 1864, Compiled from Sworn Testimony, under Direction of Governor Henry W. Allen. Shreveport, La., 1865.

Report of the Joint Committee on the Conduct of the War. 37th Cong., 3rd Sess. 3 vols. Washington, D.C., 1864.

Report of the Joint Committee on the Conduct of the War. 38th Cong., 2nd Sess. Vol. II. Washington, D.C., 1864.

U.S. Department of the Navy. *Annual Reports of the Secretary of the Navy.* Washington, D.C., 1821–1948.

The War of the Rebellion: A Compilation of the Official Records of the Union and Confederate Armies. 130 vols. Washington, D.C., 1880–1901.

Newspapers

Chicago Tribune
Cincinnati Daily Commercial
Grenada (Miss.) Appeal
Memphis Argus
Mobile Advertiser
New York Tribune
Port Huron (Mich.) Daily Times
Richmond Daily Dispatch
Richmond Examiner
St. Louis Daily Democrat
St. Louis Missouri Democrat
Vicksburg Whig
Washington, D.C., Evening Star

Books and Articles

Anderson, John Q. *Campaigning with Parsons' Texas Cavalry, C.S.A.* Hillsboro, Tex., 1967.

Basler, Roy P., ed. *The Collected Works of Abraham Lincoln.* 9 vols. New Brunswick, N.J., 1953.

Beale, Howard K., and Alan W. Brownsword, eds. *Diary of Gideon Welles, Secretary of the Navy Under Lincoln and Johnson.* 3 vols. New York, 1960.

Blessington, J. P. *The Campaigns of Walker's Texas Division* New York, 1875.

[Brent, J. L.] "Capture of the *Indianola.*" *Southern Historical Society Papers,* I, 91–99.

Brown, Isaac N. "The Confederate Gun-Boat *Arkansas.*" Johnson and Buel, eds., *Battles and Leaders of the Civil War,* III, 572–79.

Brown, James W. *Mississippi River Ram Fleet and Marine Brigade. Remarks of Hon. James W. Brown of Pennsylvania, in the House of Representatives, Friday, March 3, 1905.* Washington, D.C., 1905.

Butler, Benjamin F. *Autobiography and Personal Reminiscences of Major-General Benj. F. Butler: Butler's Book.* Boston, 1892.

Clarke, Norman E., Jr., ed. *Warfare along the Mississippi: The Letters of Lieutenant Colonel George E. Currie.* Mount Pleasant, Mich., 1961.

Coffin, Charles C. *Four Years of Fighting.* Boston, 1866.

———. *My Days and Nights on the Battlefield.* Boston, 1887.

Crandall, Warren D., and Isaac D. Newell. *History of the Ram Fleet and the Mississippi Marine Brigade.* St. Louis, 1907.

Dana, Charles A. *Recollections of the Civil War.* New York: 1898.

Davis, Charles H. *Life of Charles Henry Davis, Rear Admiral, 1807–1877.* Boston and New York, 1899.

Davis, Jefferson. *The Rise and Fall of the Confederate Government.* 2 vols. Richmond, 1938.

Driggs, George W. *Opening of the Mississippi.* Madison, 1864.

Edwards, John N. *Shelby and His Men.* Kansas City, 1897.

Ellet, Alfred W. "Ellet and His Steam-Rams at Memphis." Johnson and Buel, eds., *Battles and Leaders of the Civil War,* I, 453–59.

Ellet, Charles, Jr. *Coast and Harbour Defenses, or the Substitution of Steam Battering Rams for Ships of War.* Philadelphia, 1855.

———. *Military Incapacity and What It Costs the Country.* Philadelphia, 1862.

Farragut, Loyall. *The Life of David Glasgow Farragut, First Admiral of the U.S. Navy.* New York, 1879.

Foltz, C. S. *Surgeon of the Seas.* Indianapolis, 1931.

Gift, George W. "Story of the *Arkansas.*" *Southern Historical Society Papers,* XII (January–April 1884), 48–54, 115–19, 163–70, 205–12.

Grant, Ulysses S. *Personal Memoirs of U. S. Grant.* 2 vols. New York, 1885–86.

———. "The Vicksburg Campaign." Johnson and Buel, eds., *Battles and Leaders of the Civil War,* III, 493–539.

Hayes, John D., ed. *Samuel Francis Du Pont: A Selection from His Civil War Letters.* 3 vols. Ithaca, N.Y., 1969.

Herr, George W. *Episodes of the Civil War: Nine Campaigns in Nine States.* San Francisco, 1890.

Howe, M. A. DeWolfe, ed. *Home Letters of General Sherman.* New York, 1909.

Irwin, Richard B. "The Capture of Port Hudson." Johnson and Buel, eds., *Battles and Leaders of the Civil War,* III, 586–98.

———. "The Red River Campaign." Johnson and Buel, eds., *Battles and Leaders of the Civil War,* IV, 345–62.

Johnson, Robert U., and Clarence C. Buel, eds. *Battles and Leaders of the Civil War.* 4 vols. New York, 1884–87.

Jones, James P., and Edward F. Keuchel, eds. *Civil War Marine: A Diary of the Red River Expedition, 1864.* Washington, D.C., 1975.

Lockett, Samuel H. "The Defense of Vicksburg." Johnson and Buel, eds., *Battles and Leaders of the Civil War,* III, 482–92.

Marshall, Jesse A., ed. *Public and Private Correspondence of Gen. Benjamin F. Butler During the Period of the Civil War.* 5 vols. Norwood, Mass., 1917.

Milligan, John D., ed. *From the Fresh Water Navy, 1861–64: The Letters of Acting Master's Mate Henry R. Browne and Acting Ensign Symmes Browne.* Annapolis, 1970.

Moore, Frank, ed. *The Rebellion Record: A Diary of American Events.* 12 vols. New York, 1862–71.

Nicolay, John G., and John Hay. *Abraham Lincoln: A History.* 10 vols. New York, 1909.

Osbon, B. S., ed. "The Cruise of the U.S. Flag-Ship *Hartford,* 1862–1863, from the Private Journal of William C. Holton." *Magazine of American History,* XXII, no. 3, Extra no. 87 (1922), 17–28.

Porter, David Dixon. *Incidents and Anecdotes of the Civil War.* New York, 1885.

———. *The Naval History of the Civil War.* New York and San Francisco, 1886.

Read, Charles W. "Reminiscences of the Confederate States Navy." *Southern Historical Society Papers,* I (May 1876), 331–62.

Scharf, J. Thomas. *History of the Confederate Navy.* New York, 1887.

Scott, William Forse. *The Story of a Cavalry Regiment: The Career of the Fourth Iowa Veteran Volunteers from Kansas to Georgia, 1861–1865.* New York, 1893.

Selfridge, Thomas O., Jr. *Memoirs of Thomas O. Selfridge, Jr., Rear Admiral, U.S.N.* New York and London, 1924.

Sherman, William T. *Memoirs of General W. T Sherman.* 2 vols. New York, 1875.

Soley, James R., "Naval Operations in the Vicksburg Campaign." Johnson and Buel, eds., *Battles and Leaders of the Civil War,* III, 551–70.

———. "The Union and Confederate Navies." Johnson and Buel, eds., *Battles and Leaders of the Civil War,* I, 611–31.

Thompson, Robert Means, and Richard Wainwright, eds. *The Confidential*

Correspondence of Gustavus Vasa Fox, Asst. Secretary of the Navy, 1861–1865. 2 vols. Freeport, 1972.

Walke, Henry. *Naval Scenes and Reminiscences of the Civil War in the United States.* New York, 1877.

Welles, Gideon. *The Diary of Gideon Welles, Secretary of the Navy Under Lincoln and Johnson.* 3 vols. Boston and New York, 1909–11.

Williams, Thomas. "Letters of General Thomas Williams, 1862." *American Historical Review,* XIV (January 1909), 304–28.

SECONDARY SOURCES

Abbott, John S. C. *The History of the Civil War in America.* 2 vols. Springfield, Mass., 1864.

Bearss, Edwin Cole. *Hardluck Ironclad: The Sinking and Salvage of the "Cairo."* Baton Rouge, 1980.

———. *The Vicksburg Campaign.* 3 vols. Dayton, Ohio, 1985.

Bennett, Frank M. *The Steam Navy of the United States.* Pittsburgh, 1896.

Boatner, Mark M., III. *The Civil War Dictionary.* New York, 1959.

Boynton, Charles B. *The History of the Navy During the Rebellion.* 2 vols. New York, 1867.

Bruce, Robert V. *Lincoln and the Tools of War.* New York, 1956.

Canfield, Eugene B. *Civil War Ordnance.* Washington, D.C., 1969.

Carter, Samuel, III. *The Final Fortress: The Campaign for Vicksburg, 1862–1863.* New York, 1980.

Coletta, Paolo E. *American Secretaries of the Navy.* 2 vols. Annapolis, 1980.

Edwards, John N. *Noted Guerrillas, Or the Warfare on the Border.* St. Louis, 1880.

Faust, Patricia L., ed. *Historical Times Illustrated: Encyclopedia of the Civil War.* New York, 1986.

Fiske, John. *The Mississippi Valley in the Civil War.* Boston, 1900.

Fox, William F. *Regimental Losses in the American Civil War, 1861–1865.* Dayton, Ohio, 1885.

Gambrell, Herbert P. "Rams versus Gunboats . . . A Landsman's Naval Exploits." *Southwest Review,* XXIII (October 1937), 46–78.

Gorham, George C. *Life and Public Services of Edwin M. Stanton.* 2 vols. New York, 1899.

Gosnell, H. Allen. *Guns on the Western Waters: The Story of River Gunboats in the Civil War.* Baton Rouge, 1949.

Green, Francis Vinton. *The Mississippi.* Vol. III of *Campaigns of the Civil War.* New York, 1885.

Hearn, Chester G. *Admiral David Dixon Porter: The Civil War Years.* Annapolis, 1996.

————. *Admiral David Glasgow Farragut: The Civil War Years.* Annapolis, 1997.

Johnson, Ludwell H. *Red River Campaign: Politics and Cotton in the Civil War.* Gaithersburg, Md., 1986.

Jones, Virgil Carrington. *The Civil War at Sea.* 3 vols. New York and Chicago, 1960–62.

Knox, Dudley W. *A History of the United States Navy.* New York, 1948.

Lewis, Charles Lee. *David Glasgow Farragut: Our First Admiral.* Annapolis, 1943.

Lewis, Gene Dale. *Charles Ellet, Jr.: The Engineer as Individualist, 1810–1862.* Urbana, Ill., 1968.

Lewis, Lloyd. *Sherman: Fighting Prophet.* New York, 1932.

Macartney, Clarence E. *Mr. Lincoln's Admirals.* New York, 1956.

Mahan, Alfred T. *Admiral Farragut.* New York, 1892.

————. *The Gulf and Inland Waters.* New York, 1901.

Malone, Dumas, ed. *Dictionary of American Biography.* 20 vols. New York, 1928–37.

McFeely, William S. *Grant.* New York, 1981.

Melton, Maurice, "From Vicksburg to Port Hudson." *Civil War Times Illustrated,* XII, no. 10, pp. 26–36.

Merrill, James M. *Battle Flags South: The Story of the Civil War Navies on the Western Waters.* Rutherford, N.J., 1970.

Miers, Earl Schenck. *The Web of Victory.* New York, 1955.

Milligan, John D. "Charles Ellet and His Naval Steam Ram." *Civil War History,* IX (June 1963), 121–32.

————. *Gunboats down the Mississippi.* Annapolis, 1965.

Newcomer, Lee Nathaniel, "The Battle of the Rams." *American Neptune,* XXV (April 1965), 128–39.

Niven, John. *Gideon Welles: Lincoln's Secretary of the Navy.* New York, 1973.

Parker, Theodore H. *The Federal Gunboat Flotilla on the Western Rivers During Its Administration by the War Department to October 1, 1862.* Pittsburgh, 1939.

Pratt, Fletcher. *Civil War on the Western Waters.* New York, 1956.

Quick, Herbert, and Edward Quick. *Mississippi Steamboatin': A History of Steamboating on the Mississippi and Its Tributaries.* New York, 1926.

Reed, Rowena. *Combined Operations in the Civil War.* Lincoln, Nebr., 1993.

Silver, James W., ed. *Mississippi in the Confederacy.* Baton Rouge, 1961.

Soley, James R. *Admiral Porter.* New York, 1903.

Starr, Stephen Z. *The Union Cavalry in the Civil War.* 3 vols. Baton Rouge, 1979–83.

Still, William N., Jr. *Iron Afloat: The Story of the Confederate Ironclads.* Columbia, S.C., 1985.

Stivers, Reuben Elmore. *Privateers and Volunteers: The Men and Women of Our Reserve Naval Forces, 1766–1866.* Annapolis, 1975.

Thomas, Benjamin P., and Harold M. Hyman. *Stanton: The Life and Times of Lincoln's Secretary of War.* New York, 1962.

Walker, Peter F. *Vicksburg: A People at War, 1860–1865.* Chapel Hill, 1960.

Wegner, Dana M. "Commodore William D. 'Dirty Bill' Porter." U.S. Naval Institute *Proceedings,* 103, no. 888 (February 1977), 40–49.

West, Richard S., Jr. *Gideon Welles: Lincoln's Navy Department.* Indianapolis, 1943.

———. *Mr. Lincoln's Navy.* New York, 1957.

———. *The Second Admiral: A Life of David Dixon Porter.* New York, 1937.

Winters, John D. *The Civil War in Louisiana.* Baton Rouge, 1963.

Wythe, John A. *Life of Nathan Bedford Forrest.* New York, 1899.

INDEX